Behind the Kitchen Door

Behind the Kitchen Door

Saru Jayaraman
With a Foreword by Eric Schlosser

ILR Press
an imprint of
Cornell University Press
Ithaca and London

First published 2013 by Cornell University Press
Printed in the United States of America

Library of Congress Cataloging-in-Publication Data

Jayaraman, Sarumathi, 1975–
    Behind the kitchen door / Saru Jayaraman.
        p. cm.
    Includes bibliographical references.
    ISBN 978-0-8014-5172-0 (cloth : alk. paper)
    1. Food service employees—United States.   2. Restaurants—United
States—Employees.   I. Title.
    HD8039.F72U563 2013
    331.7′61647950973—dc23   2012030668

Cornell University Press strives to use environmentally responsible
suppliers and materials to the fullest extent possible in the publishing of
its books. Such materials include vegetable-based, low-VOC inks and
acid-free papers that are recycled, totally chlorine-free, or partly composed
of nonwood fibers. For further information, visit our website at www.
cornellpress.cornell.edu.

Cloth printing   10   9   8   7   6   5   4

To the more than 10 million restaurant workers nationwide,
who struggle daily to feed us

Contents

FOREWORD

A powerful social movement has recently arisen in the United States, challenging industrial agriculture, questioning the American diet, and calling for fundamental changes in how we grow, process, and think about our food. Organic production has soared, and the need for "sustainability" has become so widely accepted that even companies like McDonald's and Coca-Cola now pay lip service to that worthy goal. The mistreatment of livestock at factory farms has gained enormous attention as consumers express revulsion at the cruelties routinely inflicted to obtain cheap meat. Free-range poultry, cage-free hens, grass-fed cattle, hogs allowed to wander outdoors and wallow in the mud, have all been championed as crucial elements of a healthier, more humane food system. But the food movement thus far has shown a much greater interest in assuring animal welfare than in protecting human rights. You would think that, at the very least, the people who feed us deserve as much attention and compassion as what we're being fed.

The abuses endured by American farmworkers, meatpacking workers, and restaurant employees violate even the most watered-down, corporate-flavored definition of "sustainability." Our food system now treats millions of workers like disposable commodities, paying them poverty wages, denying them medical benefits and sick pay, and tolerating racism and sexism on the job. The hardships of farmworkers and meatpacking workers have been well documented. This book eloquently reveals what is happening behind the kitchen door not only at chain restaurants, but at some of the most expensive restaurants in the United States.

Today it's not uncommon for celebrity chefs to earn millions of dollars a year, while the dishwashers and bussers in their kitchens get a wage of $2.13 an hour, plus a meager share of the tips. The typical restaurant worker makes about $15,000 a year, roughly one-third the annual income of the average American worker. And for decades the restaurant industry has led the battle against increasing the federal minimum wage. Since the late 1960s, the value of the minimum wage, adjusted for inflation, has declined by about 20 percent. For the poorest workers in the United States, that has meant an hourly pay cut of about $1.50.

When people ask what are the most important changes that we could make to our food system right away, I reply: Enforce the nation's labor laws and increase the minimum wage.

For more than a decade, Saru Jayaraman has been defending the rights of those who work hard but nevertheless find themselves at the bottom of the food chain. The organization that she helped found, Restaurant Opportunities Centers United, doesn't just represent workers. It seeks to empower them, gain them respect, and give them a voice in the workplace. *Behind the Kitchen Door* describes how Jayaraman got involved in this struggle, places it in a larger social context, and tells stories about individual workers that convey, more powerfully than any statistics, why we must not tolerate these injustices. Too many of our meals are now brought to the table by the misery of others. The problem can easily be solved, once people become aware of it—and that's why this book needs to be read.

Eric Schlosser, June 2012

ACKNOWLEDGMENTS

There are so many people to thank.

First, of course, I'd like to recognize all the staff, restaurant worker members, board members, allies in the food justice and other movements, and other supporters of the Restaurant Opportunities Centers United, who have coauthored this book through their hands, hearts, and minds. Without their hard work and contributions, the movement for change in the restaurant industry would never have come as far as it has. Many thanks especially to the members and staff profiled in this book and to ROC member, leader, and friend Sekou Luke for producing the extraordinary video trailer; ROC's research staff, Jonathan Hogstad and Teofilo Reyes, for data assistance; other national staff, including Meghana Reddy, Cathy Dang, Rekha Eanni, Juan Carlos Romero, and Christine Saunders, for support and promotion; executive team members Jose Oliva, Bonnie Kwon, Jennifer Dillon, and Sekou Siby for leadership; board members Rinku Sen and Abel Valenzuela for guidance; our film industry partner Joselyn Barnes for videography; our food justice partners at Slow Food; all of our funders, including Laine Romero-Alston and her colleagues at the Ford Foundation for supporting ROC's work and the book's promotion, Swanee Hunt and the Prime Movers Fellowship for providing me with the time to write, and our friends at the Ms. Foundation for providing space to write; our dear friend and comrade Bruce Herman, who dedicated so much of his life's energy to our movement; and my cofounder, codirector, and best friend, Fekkak Mamdouh. There are so many others unnamed but just as valuable to this movement to whom I am grateful.

Second, I'd like to thank the "book doctor," Esther Cohen, who spent countless hours helping me shape our data and stories into a book at the beginning, and my editor, Adrienne Davich, who spent an equal amount of time helping to finesse the book at the end. Thanks to Zachary Norris, Alex Kellogg, LaNysha Adams, my dad, and my sister Niru for taking the time to read the book and offer comments. Thanks also to Frances Benson and Cornell University Press for believing in us.

Finally, I'd like to thank my family for their unconditional love and support: my partner, Zachary Norris; daughters, Akeela Lalitha and Lina Abiani Norris-Raman; and my parents and sisters.

Behind the Kitchen Door

1

The Hands on Your Plate

When you work in restaurants you think the industry is everything. It's being outside, talking to people, serving people. You feel like you're part of something good. People mostly go to eat out for good stuff—proposals, weddings, birthdays—not to fight. You're part of someone's proposal—you bring the ring in an ice cream cake, you watch her reaction. You feel like you're part of their experience, their special moment, even if the people don't care who you are—you're just the server. Everywhere I go, I find restaurant workers are the same. They may move from restaurant to restaurant—maybe they don't earn enough money, or they don't like the way they're being treated. But they always come back. They have a hospitality mentality in their DNA. All over the world, they have it in them.

—Server, Man, 17 Years in the Industry, New York City

The events that forever changed me as a diner—and ultimately led to the writing of this book—happened shortly after 9/11. I had never given much thought to the inner workings of restaurants or the lives of restaurant workers, but a few weeks after the Twin Towers fell I received a call from a union leader representing workers from Windows on the World, the luxurious multilevel restaurant that had been at the top of the World Trade Center. Windows on the World had earned acclaim for its international cuisine and for its staff from almost every nation in the world. The caller wanted me to help build an organization to support the displaced Windows workers and some 13,000 other restaurant workers in New York City who had lost their jobs after the 9/11 tragedy. She knew I had experience organizing immigrant workers, including restaurant workers, on

Long Island and that I'd helped start Women and Youth Supporting Each Other, a national organization serving young women of color. But I had never actually worked in a restaurant.

I was also young. I'd always loved eating out, but I had no idea that, in accepting the union leader's offer and becoming at 27 the leader of a new restaurant workers' organization, I'd spend the next 11 years of my life meeting low-wage restaurant workers—servers, bussers, runners, dish-washers, cooks, and others—who are struggling to support themselves and their families under the shockingly exploitative conditions that exist behind most restaurant kitchen doors.

It took me a while to understand what I was getting into—helping to improve the lives of men and women who belong to one of the largest private-sector workforces in the United States. And these workers per-form important jobs—it's the people behind the kitchen door who make a restaurant. We interact with them daily, but few Americans know that the majority of these workers suffer under discriminatory labor practices and earn poverty-level wages. In fact, although the restaurant industry employs more than 10 million people and continues to grow, even during recent economic crises, it includes 7 of the 11 lowest-paying occupations in America—an unenviable distinction.[1] Plus, most employers in the indus-try refuse to offer paid sick days or health benefits.

So how do restaurant workers live on some of the lowest wages in America? And how do they feel about their work? What are their future prospects? And what impact does their mistreatment and poor compensa-tion have on our experience as diners? These are questions I asked myself in the months after 9/11 as I met some 250 displaced workers from Win-dows on the World. They described to me in heartbreaking detail how 73 of their coworkers, mostly immigrants, had lost their lives on 9/11. Since the tragedy occurred early in the morning, the majority who died were low-wage kitchen workers who were preparing meals and setting tables for a large breakfast party that was scheduled for that morning. Many of them were incinerated. Several jumped to their death from the 106th and 107th floors of the building. Not a single one survived.

The owner of Windows attended a memorial service for the fallen workers and promised all of his former employees that he would hire them when he opened a new restaurant. However, when he opened a new res-taurant in Times Square just a few months later, he refused to hire most of his former workers. He told the press that they were "not experienced enough" to work in his new restaurant.

The Windows workers were outraged. It would be almost impossible for them to find jobs comparable to what they had at Windows—with a union in that restaurant, they had higher wages than similar workers elsewhere, and benefits. Only 20 percent of restaurant jobs pay a livable wage, and women, people of color, and immigrants face significant barriers in obtaining those livable-wage jobs.[2] As I listened to the workers' stories, I felt their frustration and outrage—first, as men and women who wanted to be treated with dignity and respect in the workplace, and then as people of color who'd discovered that race affected their ability to hold a job and move up the ladder. I met a woman chef from Thailand who'd moved from restaurant to restaurant in the weeks after the tragedy; she couldn't find a new position that would pay a living wage. I met an African American man who had been bartending for two decades; he couldn't find a position that offered wages and benefits comparable to those he'd received at the Windows bar, "The Greatest Bar on Earth." I also met several undocumented immigrants from Asia, Africa, Latin America, and eastern Europe, all of whom had found themselves at the mercy of unscrupulous employers who relied almost entirely on immigrant workers (approximately 40 percent of New York City restaurant workers are undocumented immigrants); these employers threatened to contact immigration authorities when their workers complained about exploitation and abuse on the job.

The union hired Fekkak Mamdouh, one of the headwaiters from Windows on the World, to work with me. Mamdouh, a Moroccan immigrant, had been a leader among his coworkers when the restaurant was still open. Medium-built, with cocoa skin, dark brown eyes, and black curly hair, he has a strong Moroccan accent and a mischievous sense of humor. He walks and moves fast and talks and laughs loudly. He's the quintessential Gemini—the happiest guy to be around or, when his temper blows, the foulest in the world.

When I met Mamdouh, he had more than 17 years of experience working in restaurants. He'd started as a delivery person, worked his way up to server, and recently served as an elected union leader fighting on behalf of his fellow workers on a range of issues. Still, I was predisposed not to like him—people had told me he had an aggressive personality—but he completely disarmed me at our first meeting. He cracked jokes and made fun of my seriousness while also listening to me and respecting what I had to say. I found him sensitive, despite his bravado, always trying to make people feel welcome and comfortable. I also admired how he cared for his large extended family in the United States and Morocco—his wife and three children, his mother, and his eight brothers and sisters and their children.

Mamdouh and I cofounded the Restaurant Opportunities Center (ROC) in April 2002. We agreed that our mission would be to organize workers to improve wages and working conditions throughout the restaurant industry. Our first priority, however, was to advocate for the displaced workers from Windows on the World.

After one month on the job at ROC, Mamdouh and I called a meeting of all the surviving Windows workers, many of whom had applied to work at their former boss's new restaurant. Since we didn't have an office yet, we borrowed meeting space from the union. The workers packed the room. All of them wanted to do something. They felt desperate and humiliated, especially since their former boss had told the media that his former employees—many of whom had lost family and friends in the restaurant—were not qualified to work in his new place. After hours of heated discussion, the workers decided to hold a protest.

We protested loudly in front of the Windows owner's new restaurant on its opening night. The workers showed up with their families in tow and picketed as celebrities entered the restaurant on a red carpet. A headline in the *New York Times* declared the next day, "Windows on the World Workers Say Their Boss Didn't Do Enough."

The coverage prompted the owner to ask Mamdouh and me to meet with him. A few days later we met the owner on the cold, dimly lit ground floor of his multistory restaurant. It was still early in the day, the restaurant not yet open. Before we could say much, the owner told us he was setting up a new banquet department for which he would agree to hire almost all of the workers who'd wanted to work in the restaurant. I couldn't believe it. I thought it was a trick, or that perhaps it would be less than what the workers wanted, but Mamdouh assured me it was truly a victory. When we conferred in an empty banquet room of the restaurant, Mamdouh gave me a hug. "We did it!" he said.

The victory was covered in the *New York Times*. Best of all, the workers seemed happy. The next day I was interviewed on New York's Channel 1. I explained that ROC was a new organization established to serve restaurant workers, and then the floodgates really opened: workers started calling

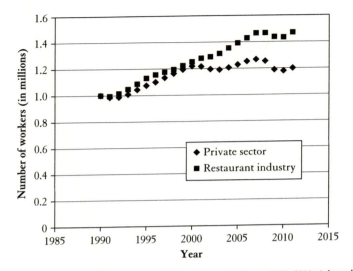

Figure 1. Job growth in the private sector and the restaurant industry, 1990–2011. Adapted from Restaurant Opportunities Centers United, *Behind the Kitchen Door: A Multisite Study of the Restaurant Industry*, technical report (New York: Restaurant Opportunities Centers United, 2011), fig. 1; http://rocunited.org/blog/2011-behind-the-kitchen-door-multi-site-study/.
Source: U.S. Bureau of Labor Statistics, Current Employment Statistics.

us from all over the city, seeking our help. I realized that problems in the restaurant industry were pervasive, often insidious, affecting workers from every background.

I didn't know it then, but the restaurant industry is one of the largest and fastest-growing sectors of the U.S. economy (see fig. 1). Restaurant workers are not just young people saving money for college or earning a few extra dollars while attending high school (a common misconception among American diners). They are workers of all ages and include many parents and single mothers. Many stay in the industry for 20, 30, or 40 years and take great pride in hospitality.

Unfortunately, although the industry continues to grow, restaurant workers' wages have been stagnant over the last 20 years, in part because for the last two decades the federal minimum wage for tipped workers has been frozen at $2.13 an hour.[3] Millions of workers regularly experience wage theft (not being paid the wages and tips they are owed) as well as discrimination on the basis of race, gender, and other factors, such as socioeconomic background, accent, and educational attainment.

Thus, as soon as the existence of ROC became news, Mamdouh and I were flooded with calls for help from restaurant workers all over New York City—and eventually all over the United States.

Our victory with the owner of Windows on the World made anything seem possible. If we could push him to do the right thing and hire his former employees, then we could get any restaurant to pay higher wages and treat its workers with dignity and respect. As more and more workers called us, I began to feel in my heart that we could radically change the restaurant industry for the better.

ROC grew quickly. We found our own office space and were able to get some funding to hire a small staff. We hired four new people—all former Windows on the World workers. Among our staff of six, I was the only one who had never worked in a restaurant, the only nonimmigrant, and the only person who was not a 9/11 survivor. I was also the only one who had professional organizing experience. I spent many long days training our new staff. I talked about the theory and history of organizing, sharing stories of successful movements from all over the world. I conducted political education sessions on the restaurant industry, labor history, and globalization. I also trained my new colleagues to conduct similar sessions for other restaurant workers so that they could inspire their peers to join us in changing the industry. I remember Mamdouh saying in one of our sessions that he had never thought about workplace discrimination before, but after discussing it with us he could see how all of the restaurants he had worked in maintained racial segregation, with lighter-skinned workers in the front, serving customers, and darker-skinned workers in the back, hidden in the kitchen. He also realized that in his 17 years in the industry he had never seen a white dishwasher in New York City. Dishwashers, who earn minimum wage or less, are almost always the darkest-skinned immigrants or people of color in a restaurant. In fact, of the 4,323 restaurant workers we surveyed around the country, we found that only 6.1 percent of all dishwashers were white.

I learned as much, if not more, from Mamdouh and his former coworkers about the issues workers confront daily in restaurants. During our long days of training we would eat lunch together in different local restaurants. Throughout our meal, Mamdouh would point out things I didn't know about the service, food, or ambience. He would say, "That's good service" or "That isn't." He would comment if the restaurant was understaffed or if the workers were carrying too much. He would talk about poor management and the problems that arise when workers are expected to live off their tips. He would always say, "If you don't pay your bill at the end of a meal, the manager will come running after you. But if workers don't get their tips, they can't say anything, or they'll be fired." I began looking at restaurants differently every time I ate out.

Of course, we weren't training all the time. We were also busy meeting with the workers who showed up at our door seeking help on the job. Many of them came because they hadn't been paid. Others had been injured while working. We helped some of them recover their wages and address their problems, but we knew that in order to really begin changing the industry, we needed to engage in high-profile campaigns that would send a signal to other restaurants that poverty-level wages, wage theft, discrimination, and lack of benefits were not sustainable for anyone.

A watershed moment for ROC came about when one of our new staff members, Utjok, visited his brother at a fancy steakhouse in Midtown Manhattan. Utjok met a kitchen worker there who told him that the restaurant had been stealing wages from its employees. He immediately brought the cook to see me. His name was Floriberto Hernandez.

Floriberto was a rotund, jovial Mexican immigrant. He had light brown skin and a baby face that dimpled when he smiled. He always wore a baseball cap. His coworkers, who were also Mexican or Central American, thought he was quite naive, and later told me stories about how they would play mean practical jokes on him. One of the woman workers told me that some of the guys in the kitchen also made inappropriate sexist jokes. For example, they made fun of her for being a little overweight. One day they told Floriberto that she was pregnant. He believed them and congratulated her on the happy occasion. The woman told me that she felt personally humiliated. She was angry with Floriberto's coworkers and with management for not doing anything about it, but she knew that Floriberto himself was not trying to be mean; he had congratulated her because he was genuinely, though mistakenly, happy for her.

Floriberto wasn't dumb, just overly trusting perhaps, which is why it hurt him so much when he realized that the company would never pay him and his coworkers their overtime wages without a fight. In fact, Floriberto was probably the most intelligent and courageous of the bunch. When his coworkers shrugged off the wage theft, Floriberto insisted that they do something about it. After coming to ROC and meeting with Mamdouh and me, Floriberto almost immediately brought 17 of his coworkers to our office and started a campaign. He was a true leader.

Floriberto Hernandez with other ROC-NY members on Human Rights Day.
Courtesy of Restaurant Opportunities Center of New York.

Over the next two years we launched a public campaign against the restaurant where Floriberto worked, demanding that it pay its workers properly and comply with the law. After all, we argued, a fine-dining steakhouse in Midtown Manhattan should be able to pay basic minimum and overtime wages. After giving the company a chance to respond to our requests for a meeting (and being ignored for several weeks), we organized weekly protests in front of the restaurant. Floriberto and his coworkers joined us. We circled the restaurant, ringing cowbells, beating drums, and of course raising our voices to demand that the company stop the illegal practice of not paying its employees. We handed out leaflets describing the restaurant's health-code violations to potential customers, and we chanted, "It's illegal! It's a crime! Pay your workers overtime!" As the weeks passed, Floriberto convinced more of his coworkers to join the campaign, and a young Latino busser—the only nonwhite waiter in the restaurant—filed charges against the company for giving him the lowest-paying shifts and tables, and for hurling racial epithets at him, even in front of customers.

At one point, we decided to let the restaurant's customers know what was going on behind the kitchen door. We found out that the restaurant had numerous health-code violations, including insects in the kitchen, food kept out too long, and meat not stored at the right temperature. As the customers entered the restaurant, we passed out handbills that described the nasty things going on in the kitchen. Our latest research shows that in every city across the United States in which we conducted surveys with restaurant workers, the restaurants that mistreated their workers were more likely to engage in unsafe food-handling practices that sicken customers. It made sense—if a restaurant was not a responsible employer, how could we expect that restaurant to be responsible with our health and safety?

The restaurant initially counterattacked, telling the press that our protest was a "shake-down." I was personally vilified. One columnist wrote an editorial in the *Nation's Restaurant News* arguing that we were exploiting 9/11 to change the restaurant industry. In a way, we were. We were using the attention that the Windows workers got to highlight deep problems in the industry that had existed long before the towers fell. The Windows workers had banded together, determined to make the industry better, in the name of their fallen coworkers. The editorial in the *Nation's Restaurant News* only strengthened my resolve to stick with the Windows workers and change the industry with them.

Floriberto stood strong, encouraging his coworkers to stay united and not allow the company to intimidate them at work or threaten them with retaliation. His leadership led us to victory. Unfortunately, just as we heard news that the restaurant was going to settle, tragedy struck. I had gone on vacation, accompanying Mamdouh and his family on their annual trip to Morocco. We were in Fez, an ancient city with narrow, winding alleys between old limestone buildings. Late one evening when Mamdouh's family had already fallen asleep I decided to check my e-mail. I asked a young boy to tell me where I could find an Internet café. He guided me through a dark maze of alleys to a brightly lit room full of computers. Almost the first e-mail I saw was news from home—Floriberto had passed away suddenly. Sobbing, I stumbled through the dark alleys back to the hotel where Mamdouh and his family were sleeping. Mamdouh and I had been fighting that day, but when I told him the sad news, all of our frustrations were washed away in the terrible pain of loss. We found our way to an international phone booth and called the ROC office. Our staff confirmed that we had suffered an incredible loss.

Just a week before, at a protest in front of his restaurant, Floriberto had complained that he was thirsty and tired. He'd brought a huge bottle of Coca-Cola with him to the protest; in fact, over a period of several days he had been buying 20-ounce bottles of Coca-Cola and downing a single bottle in less than a minute. Within a day or two his roommate, a single mother, had found him facedown on the floor of their tiny Bronx apartment. He was a large man, too large for her to move. She called 911. It took four paramedics to lift him onto the gurney and rush him to the hospital. He was in a diabetic coma, apparently having suffered from a sudden adult onset of diabetes. By the time he reached the hospital, it was too late. He had killed himself drinking Coca-Cola.

I immediately threw myself into crisis mode. Floriberto had no real family in the United States, and so I ended up dealing with the coroner, doctors, and his coworkers—who believed the restaurant had poisoned him—as well as with his family in Mexico. We discovered that Floriberto had lost touch with his family after crossing the border into the United States more than 10 years before, but we found his family in Mexico and sent them his body for burial, with $1,000 collected from ROC staff and members.

A few months after Floriberto's death we finally won the campaign against the restaurant company. We won not only $164,000 in unpaid wages but also real changes in the company, such as paid sick days and vacation days, a grievance procedure, and much more. The company's lawyer later said that the campaign had really forced the company to create policies that it should have created a long time before.

Floriberto led his coworkers to this victory, but he never had the chance to enjoy the fruits of his labor. His portion of the damages—the amount of unpaid overtime wages he was owed—totaled close to $15,000. I thought it would be easy to send this money to Floriberto's family in Mexico, but it was ridiculously complicated. I had to become an administrator of Floriberto's estate through the Bronx County Surrogate's Court—a process that is still ongoing. I remember Floriberto's family calling me from Mexico to say that they did not have enough money for a funeral and that they could really use the money that Floriberto had won. I could do nothing. The money still sits in a legal escrow account in New York.

This experience shook me to my core. I had never experienced the death of someone so close to me and with whom I'd worked so intensively. It blew my eyes wide open to the people who work behind the kitchen door, their lives, and their struggles. I knew these workers were poor, many immigrants, many struggling to survive. But I had never known this—that as jovial and innocent as Floriberto was, he lived a hard life, separated from his family, alone. Although he had told me that he loved working in the restaurant and hoped to move up one day to a position as sous chef or even chef, he had been living paycheck to paycheck for over 10 years. Fighting for the $15,000 of his hard-earned wages that had been kept from him was not just about justice. It was also about survival. He had no insurance to cover his medical bills or help his family when he passed away. Worst of all, he had had no one to care for him when he was alive. He had had no one but me—a then 28-year-old who had gone to law school but never really practiced law, and who was totally ignorant about nutrition and medicine. I barely took the time to see a doctor myself. We organized a memorial event for Floriberto at ROC, the only one that he had.

After that, every time I ate out I would look in the kitchen. For the first time, I saw every kitchen worker, every restaurant worker, as a human being, with a unique story, family, dreams, and desires. I would see these workers every time I ate out, and then I would talk to them at ROC. Many would express their desire to move up the ladder, maybe even open their own restaurant one day, but so few had the opportunity.

That was my *Matrix* moment. Suddenly I could see a whole world I had never seen over a lifetime of eating in restaurants.

Millions of Dreams Deferred

I am a daughter of immigrants from India. When I was young, my mother and father didn't take me and my sisters out to eat very often, maybe because my parents grew up eating delicious, home-cooked meals in Tamilnadu. They never seemed especially excited about dining out, but even in my earliest memories I loved eating in restaurants. Those rare family outings—my parents and three little girls in braids—to Denny's or McDonald's or a local Mexican or Indian restaurant were extraordinarily exciting and made "eating out" sacred to me.

After I moved out of my parents' house, I ate out every time I had the opportunity. Eating out became part of my lifestyle. I grew so accustomed to eating in restaurants that when I went on a trip to Italy with my parents as a young adult I assumed we'd eat out in ristorantes or trattorias for every meal. But my parents had other plans. When we got to our hotel room, they started unpacking their unusually large suitcase, and out came the family rice cooker, followed by jars of curry and chutney. I was horrified.

That trip made me realize that Americans have a unique relationship to eating out, and that I am an American. It isn't just my parents who prefer not to eat out. I've noticed people's resistance to eating out in countries around the world, from Latin America to Africa to Europe. It isn't that there aren't restaurants in other parts of the world; there are world-famous chefs and restaurants, new and old, busy and slow, all kinds, all over the world. It's the frequency with which Americans eat out, and the way we choose to mark so many of our major life events—birthdays, anniversaries, marriage proposals—in restaurants. Restaurants are a space in which families gather, friends meet, and new connections are made. Restaurants are where American culture happens.

I can remember one very special meal in a Chinese restaurant, a lunch with a guy I had briefly dated in my early twenties. It had been eight years since we'd seen each other, and we hadn't stayed in touch. A month before our lunch he'd called to say that he thought we should get back together. I was very skeptical.

It was a beautiful spring day in New York City, but I don't think either of us noticed. We sat at the back table in a dark, narrow storefront restaurant, which was almost empty. We were nervous about seeing each other after so long, and so our date was awkward. I asked him a thousand questions about why he wanted to get back together. His gentle, sincere responses to my questions reminded me why I had liked him so much when I was younger. Finally, the bill came, with the standard fortune cookies. He opened his, and I could see from his expression that it said something striking. I insisted that he show it to me. "Look no further," it said. "Happiness is right next to you." We got married a year later. We didn't get married because of the fortune cookie, but that moment certainly helped.

What I can't remember about that lunch is who served our food. I can't remember who brought our plates, or the fortune cookies, to the table. That, however, just makes me like most Americans. Every one of us can tell a story about a life-changing moment in a restaurant. We remember the way it looked, who was there, where we sat, what we ate, and how it smelled. However, we tend not to notice who is handling our food.

It's strange that most of us spend so much of our time and income in restaurants and yet think so little about restaurant workers. They perform the most intimate acts for us—cooking and serving our food, typically an act reserved for a parent or a partner.

When Mamdouh and I started ROC, I made the decision to dedicate my life to improving the wages and working conditions of the people who prepare, cook, and serve our food daily. Over the last 11 years ROC has led 11 campaigns against exploitation in high-profile restaurants like Floriberto's, winning more than $6 million in stolen tips and wages and helping to bring about policy changes to improve the lives of thousands of workers. We've educated and organized responsible employers to promote sustainable business practices. We've fought to change policies that have an impact on restaurant workers, such as increasing the federal tipped minimum wage from $2.13 an hour. We've also opened several COLORS restaurants, worker-owned restaurants in which we train workers to advance to living-wage jobs. We struggled for three years to open COLORS in New York, and we struggled another five years to make it successful, but now the restaurant has a sustainable business model in two cities. The programs we created at COLORS now train about 1,000 low-wage workers across the country every year.

In addition, ROC has conducted a massive amount of research, much of which confirms that Floriberto's experience was not unique. In surveys and interviews, restaurant workers continue to report that they simply can't survive on the industry's abysmal wages; their woes are compounded by lack of benefits, wage theft, and other challenges. Most restaurant workers can't see a pathway to a better position or a better life. Many say they don't want to leave the industry because they take pride in their work. However, almost one-third report that they have been passed over for a promotion because of their race. Others report that they've never even tried to seek a promotion because they've never seen anyone in a higher position who "looked like them." These workers tend to move from restaurant to restaurant, constantly seeking better wages and opportunities to advance, but usually never making it to the best-paying jobs.[4]

In the words of Langston Hughes, that's millions of "dreams deferred."

Voting with Our Forks

I realized early on what I could do as an organizer to change the industry, but I didn't immediately recognize my power as a consumer—and the power of all consumers nationwide—to take action to change the industry.

It took another special moment in a restaurant for me to realize that power. Not long after my first daughter was born, my husband, Zach, and I decided to take a springtime trip to Santa Cruz, California. It was our first family vacation with the baby, and perhaps the first time we took her to a restaurant. We took a lot of pictures and laughed at the funny faces she made.

As I sat there, I couldn't help noticing that all of the people who greeted and served us were white and all of the bussers were Latina women. I watched these Latina women work their tails off throughout our meal. They moved chairs, collected an impossible number of dirty glasses in one hand and dirty plates in the other, ran about the restaurant putting bread on the tables and refilling water glasses, and generally engaged in the most physical labor of anyone in the front of the restaurant. I knew that they weren't paid much; our research shows that bussers across the country generally receive the minimum wage for tipped workers (again, in most states, that's $2.13 an hour!), and the vast majority of them don't receive paid sick days or health insurance.[5]

After we ate and paid our bill, I decided to say something to the manager and asked about the restaurant's training and promotion opportunities. I praised the hard work of the bussers and asked if they were ever given the opportunity to advance to a server position. The manager was caught off guard, but he answered amicably. He said they didn't really have a program, but if an employee were interested, he'd be open to providing them with training. He said none of the bussers wanted to move up, or at least none of them had ever said so. I told him that as a customer it was important to me to eat in restaurants where I knew that there were genuine opportunities for everyone to advance, training programs that would encourage people to move up, and a transparent promotions policy. I told him that I wanted my daughter grow up in a world where everyone could have opportunities in the workplace and be able to eat in restaurants where the staff was diverse at every level. He said that he had never really thought about whether any of the bussers wanted to be waiters, but that he would ask them about it. He thanked me for my point of view and comments, and I left.

The experience really gave me hope. It wasn't that I imagined my comments had prompted the manager to implement a new training and promotions system. But I saw a very easy avenue for consumers to act and change the industry: if multiple diners told that manager that they appreciated seeing diversity and responsible labor practices in the restaurant—and if there were accessible resources to explain to owners and managers how other employers have successfully created these opportunities for their workers—it would certainly encourage him to consider training and promoting more of his bussers. Plus, I'd seen change happen this way in ROC campaigns. Just a handful of consumers could push a restaurant to comply with the law and improve how it treated and compensated its employees. In 2005, for example, ROC won a campaign against exploitation at a fine-dining restaurant company when consumers from all over the country wrote to say they wouldn't frequent the restaurant when they visited New York if the abuses continued. We've also seen that consumers can do more than speak up to individual restaurants. That same year, ROC was part of a campaign in which the people of New York told their legislators that tipped workers needed a raise. The people won. The tipped minimum wage was raised to $4.65 an hour.

I can imagine a day when millions of consumers across the United States advocate for restaurant workers in small ways every time they eat out. We may begin by speaking up to let managers know that we want our dining experience to reflect our values. We can also support the restaurants that are really trying hard to pay decent wages, provide benefits, and create pathways for advancement for all employees.

A bevy of books has been published about food, encouraging consumers to think about farmers, the land, animals, and our health. Americans are increasingly concerned about what they eat—where their food comes from, how it's grown and harvested, and how it's prepared. Still, despite the surge of interest in organic, locally sourced, sustainable, healthy food—and despite the TV shows and tell-all books by celebrity chefs, and the muck-raking of Eric Schlosser and Michael Pollan—most Americans are totally unaware of the horribly exploitative working conditions in restaurants, which affect the quality of our food and, ultimately, our health.

I want you, the consumer, to know that if you care about your health, thinking about whether your food is organic, sustainable, or locally sourced—or anything else related to how it's grown or raised—is simply not enough. Consumers also have to consider the health and well-being of the people who actually touch their food before they put it in their mouths.

The restaurant industry has grown meteorically over the last 40 years, and it continues to grow because Americans eat out more every year. Fifty percent of Americans eat out at least once a week.[6] The share of daily caloric intake from food Americans purchased or consumed away from home increased from 18 percent to 32 percent between the late 1970s and the mid-1990s, and the away-from-home market now accounts for more than half of total U.S. food expenditures.[7] That means our health—along with our pocketbooks—is very regularly in the hands of the restaurant industry.

So, what if consumers demanded that restaurants provide sustainable wages (definitely more than $2.13 an hour) for employees as well as sustainable food for customers? What if we based our dining choices on which restaurants promote diversity and good working conditions along with grass-fed beef and organic strawberries? What if we insisted that a clean kitchen include workers who can afford to take a day off when sick?

The people I write about in this book demonstrate not only how we can significantly improve the lives of workers in the restaurant industry, but also how the quality of our food depends on the conditions behind the kitchen door. Their stories may seem dramatic or depressing, but they are true and, in my experience, representative. Over the last decade I've heard stories similar to those related in this book dozens of times. In chapter 2 ("*Real* Sustainability, Please!"), I show how employment practices of many establishments in the restaurant industry are completely out of sync with the core values of the Slow Food or sustainable food movement.

To most foodies, sustainable food means food grown locally without the use of harmful pesticides, livestock raised more humanely without hormones, and other farming practices that support the health and diversity of our food system. However, sustainable food has to mean more than that, because food isn't really healthy if it's served in restaurants where abuse, exploitation, and discriminatory labor practices are commonplace. The stories of Daniel, a former dishwasher at celebrity chef Mario Batali's restaurant Del Posto, and Diep, the owner of Good Girl Dinette in Highland Park, Los Angeles, expose how unsustainable labor practices seriously affect our so-called sustainable food. Diep, a remarkable leader in the restaurant industry, shows us how a truly sustainable restaurant can operate and make a profit.

In chapter 3 ("Serving While Sick"), I write about workers like Nikki, who was forced to continue serving food in a Washington, D.C., restaurant after coming down with conjunctivitis, and Woong, a Korean American who served food in an upscale French bistro even after contracting H1N1, better known as "swine flu." The experiences of both Nikki and Woong attest to how the quality of the food that arrives at your table is not just a product of raw ingredients: it's a product of the hands that chop, cook, and plate it, and of the people to whom those hands belong. Restaurants that force employees to work while sick are also usually careless when it comes to food safety and customers' health.

Chapter 4 ("$2.13—The Tipping Point") looks at how millions of workers are struggling to survive—and often ending up homeless—on the $2.13 minimum wage for tipped workers. Both Claudia, an immigrant worker from Mexico, and Mike, a white worker from Detroit, earned $2.13 an hour and were lucky if they made $200 a week. Their experiences in the restaurant industry are particularly shocking, but in fact millions of restaurant workers make only $2.13 an hour before tips and can't afford to pay their rent or feed their families. Progressive restaurant owners—like Jason and Ben of Russell Street Deli in Detroit—demonstrate how restaurants can pay workers a livable wage and still be profitable. Their food is better, too.

In chapter 5 ("Race in the Kitchen"), I introduce workers like Oscar, a charismatic busser who couldn't get a promotion in a fine-dining restaurant in Miami because he "didn't have the right look." He'd previously been called names like "niggeraguan" on the job. Maya, who was raised in a Trinidadian neighborhood in Washington, D.C., repeatedly trained

white men to hold management positions in a fine-dining restaurant while
unable to advance from a hostess position herself. Racial discrimination
continues to prevent workers of color from obtaining living-wage jobs that
would allow them to support their families. In a survey of more than 4,000
restaurant workers nationwide, ROC found a $4 wage gap between white
workers and workers of color.[8]

Expanding on issues of discrimination, chapter 6 ("Women Waiting on
Equality") looks at the wage gap between men and women and at sexual
harassment in the restaurant industry. Women like Alicia, who threw her
heart and soul into culinary school and graduated with flying colors, are
regularly relegated to to jobs behind bakery counters in grocery stores and
to salad and pastry chef positions, which pay significantly less than chef
positions. Yelena, a young college graduate from Russia, worked in a bar
where the general manager kissed, touched, and taunted woman employees; Yelena's experiences with sexual harassment mirror those reported
by thousands of women surveyed across the industry. Finally, you'll meet
Shardha, a mother of four who struggled for years to pay for child care
while working in restaurants. Shardha ultimately joined a group of 9/11
survivors and helped open a "cooperative restaurant"; today she is the
restaurant's manager.

Let me be clear: I don't want the stories in this book to stop us from
eating out. On the contrary, I hope this book will enrich your experience
as a diner and empower you as a consumer. As diners, we have the power
to make life better for the millions of restaurant workers who touch our
plates daily. In chapter 7 ("Recipes for Change") I describe exactly how we
can support their struggle—in both big and small ways—to create a more
equitable, sustainable restaurant industry.

In the end, it is my hope that this book will enlarge your understanding of what it means to be a responsible diner. If we truly care about sustainable food and good health, we need to care about the workers in our
nation's restaurants—how they work, live, and struggle. This book is a
celebration of their lives as well as a call to action. There is a worker's story
for every plate on our table.

2

REAL SUSTAINABILITY, PLEASE!

Organic has become about one issue: protecting yourself from harm.
Sustainability is about contributing to a society that everybody benefits from,
not just going organic because you don't want to die from cancer or have a
difficult pregnancy. What's a sustainable restaurant? It's one in which as the
restaurant grows, the people grow with it.

—DIEP, OWNER, GOOD GIRL DINETTE

In 2007, Mamdouh and I visited several organic and sustainable farmers
on the east coast of Italy. We'd been invited by regional officials who were
interested in promoting "slow food" internationally. We were thrilled.
Neither of us had ever been to this region of Italy. Truth be told, I wasn't
even sure what "slow food" meant, though I'd been hearing for several
years that restaurants were increasingly trying to capitalize on organic,
sustainable, and even "slow food" menu options.

The Slow Food movement in Italy began as a reaction to the growth of
fast-food restaurants in the United States; the movement promotes "ethical consumption," a commitment to organic, sustainable, locally sourced
food.[1] Slow Food USA's former president, Josh Viertel, put it this way:
"Slow food is good, clean, and fair food—good for the planet, and good
for everyone in between—from the worker who picks it, to the cook who
cooks it, to the dishwasher who cleans it up."[2]

Viertel's description sounds wonderful. However, when Mamdouh and
I set out to visit the farms in Italy, we had no idea how "slow food," as Viertel

describes it, actually got to the restaurant table. I had a lot of questions: How could "slow food" values be practiced in restaurants in the United States? What would that look like? Why exactly should restaurant owners embrace "slow food" concepts? What was at stake for restaurant workers?

During our weeklong trip, Mamdouh and I visited various family farms, many of which also had little stores or stands at which the farmers sold their produce. These farms were surrounded by rolling green hills and castles. I distinctly remember one farm that had about 30 hogs. The farmers told us they named each of their hogs "affectionately" and watched them grow until they could be slaughtered for pork. This seemed like a strange practice to me, especially since I'm a vegetarian, but the hogs certainly looked happy rolling around in the mud; they had plenty of space and open air and looked well fed. After saying good-bye to the farmers, Mamdouh and I stopped in a little store at the entrance to the farm; the farmers sold all of their produce and meat there. The store gave people in the community the opportunity to buy their food locally and even build personal relationships with the people growing their food. The farmers, for their part, didn't need to load large trucks and pay for the fuel and labor required to transport their food to grocery stores in distant cities.

Another farm we visited had beautiful olive groves. We walked among hundreds of trees, and I noticed little red devices hanging from the branches. The farmer explained that these devices contained smells that drove insects away—making pesticides unnecessary. He showed us how he harvested the olives and put them into a large presser in his shed to make olive oil. We took home plenty of olive oil that day.

Near the end of our trip we visited the largest farm in the region. A driver brought us to a structure that looked like a barn but turned out to be the farm owners' inn and restaurant. The owners were wealthy entrepreneurs who'd decided to change careers and open a completely sustainable, green, solar-powered, farm-to-table restaurant and hotel. The food was great. The owners took us on a tour of the farm and showed us how they harvested the produce, milked cows, tended pigs and chickens, and made fresh bread and pastries.

Since Mamdouh and I had spent our adult lives advocating for workers' rights, we asked a lot of questions about the farm employees. We wanted to know how they were paid and treated. Our conversations were conducted through a translator, and so we had a number of miscommunications and misunderstandings. In some instances, the farmers couldn't understand our questions. Other times we couldn't understand their responses, but eventually we managed to get one answer, in particular, from every farmer: the farm "employees" were their brothers, sons, sisters, mothers, neighbors, and friends, who helped out during busy harvesttimes. Most important, their relationships were reciprocal: every farmer in the area helped his or her neighbors and friends when harvesttime came. These small farms were really family farms, and they took care of each other. They didn't use pesticides, not because it was trendy not to use them, but because they didn't want chemicals in the vegetables for their own meals. They treated the animals well, not because they wanted to be able to slap the "organic" label on the pork or poultry, but because they purchased and cared for each animal as part of the farm family. They sold everything at their farm stand or restaurant.

The trip felt a little like coming home for Mamdouh and me, since we both have immigrant backgrounds. It became very clear to us that food is essential, universally important to everyone, because every culture, no matter its beliefs and traditions, cares about food. These farm communities presented such a striking contrast to our lives in in the United States— and especially our lives in New York—where we are removed from the growing and cultivation of pretty much any kind of food. For us, pigs are parts in a package in a supermarket. When we saw real pigs rolling around in the mud, named, and cared for, we were surprised and touched—as if we'd forgotten or didn't know where they came from! We have become so removed from this cycle of life and from the values associated with it.

It might sound like I'm romanticizing these small Italian farms, which have their own share of difficulties, but one thing that struck me during our trip is that there is nothing romantic or revolutionary about this kind of "local sourcing," or organic and sustainable farming. It is what farmers have done for millennia around the world, including in Mamdouh's and my home countries. Although it seemed completely new and radical to us that a farm could be so small that no outside hiring was necessary—and that the pigs could be "affectionately" named, and the people could eat the food right from the farm—there was nothing new or radical about this at all.

So this is how I learned about sustainability. It's actually kind of funny to think about the American craze for locally sourced, organic, and sustainable food—which is generally perceived to be expensive, and exclusively the domain of the upper class. In some cases, we're just complicating our meals and then paying a lot of money to make them simple again. We typically pay much more to have our produce grown without pesticides and our animals treated humanely and raised without hormones on farms within 100 miles of where we eat—but this is food that people around the world have always enjoyed at no extra price.

America's obsession with organic, sustainable food began about 40 years ago. The craze started with the rise of environmental concerns in the 1970s and the success of the United Farm Workers movement in California led by Cesar Chavez, which championed "organic" food grown without the use of pesticides. In 1971, Alice Waters's Chez Panisse became one of the first restaurants in the United States to specialize in locally sourced, organic food.[3] However, the "food movement," as it's now known, really took off around the year 2000, as concerns about an "obesity epidemic" in the United States led to local policies and programs to reduce trans fat and other unhealthy ingredients in restaurant food. Eric Schlosser's *Fast Food Nation,* Morgan Spurlock's *Super Size Me,* and Michael Pollan's *The Omnivore's Dilemma* called the whole American food system into question, shining light on everything from the deleterious effects of industrial farming on the land to the extremely unhealthy and oversized meals sold to young and old in fast-food restaurants nationwide.

What struck me most in Italy, however, was that "slow food" not only included a focus on local sourcing and everything else the American sustainable food movement represents; it also embraced sustainable labor practices. The farms we visited took care of the people who handled the food—not just because it's the right thing to do, but because if you don't treat your family, friends, and neighbors with dignity and respect, they certainly won't help you season after season.

Escape from the Family Farm

Mario Batali was one of the first restaurateurs to promote "slow food" in the United States. A celebrity chef and television star, Batali is an icon, and his restaurants in New York, Las Vegas, and Los Angeles have been developed with the support of the Italian founders of the Slow Food movement.[4] Captains and waiters in Batali's restaurants are trained to speak with customers about the Slow Food movement and its origins in Italy; they can also describe every menu item's organic and sustainable ingredients, as well as provide information about the farms from which the ingredients come.

Batali's employment practices, on the other hand, have not always lived up to the values of the Slow Food movement. The restaurant company instituted major policy changes after a group of workers at Del Posto, Batali's signature restaurant in New York City, launched a very public campaign with ROC to end workplace discrimination and abuse.

Daniel, an Ecuadorean immigrant, was a leader in the Del Posto campaign. A former model, Daniel has a muscular build. He is soft-spoken and mild-mannered, but he can talk a lot once he gets started. His life as a waiter serving penne puttanesca and primavera de la terra in a four-star New York City restaurant stands in sharp contrast to his life growing up in rural Ecuador.

Daniel was born in Cuenca, Ecuador, a highland city in the Andes nine hours from Quito. He was the third of six children. His family lived on a farm that raised cows and pigs and grew corn, fava beans, sweet peas, cabbage, and potatoes—a lot of different things. Daniel and his brothers helped take care of the animals and harvest the vegetables and fruit. Their family didn't sell the food; they shared it. "We always had a big family," says Daniel. "We would share things with our extended family. When we grew potatoes, we would get them and share them with family and friends. Everybody had a farm, and everybody would share with each other. The only time we'd go buy cheese was when the cows were not lactating. We had about eight cows and pigs. Sometimes when we were celebrating family events, we'd get together 50 or more people and slaughter a pig. Most people who come from Cuenca have big families."

No one thought of using pesticides. Daniel and his father sometimes went to the city to buy little white balls (similar to mothballs), which they placed around the plants to keep the insects away. Daniel lived in an organic, farm-to-table household before the concept existed.

Daniel went to school until the age of 12, and then, like his father and brothers, left school to work in construction. He worked full-time, Monday through Friday, and spent much of the rest of his time tending the family farm. Although his family survived on the income from the farm and construction jobs, they always felt the "call of the North." Friends and family returned from the United States talking about being able to have their own houses and cars and simply being able to support their families with less of a struggle. When an opportunity arose, Daniel's father left for the United States, but only to pave the way for Daniel's eldest brother, Joseph, to go. As soon as Joseph got to New York City, Daniel's father returned to his family and farm in Ecuador.

Joseph was determined to stay in New York City and earn enough money to support his family. He immediately began working as a cook in a restaurant and sending money home. He saved as much as he could and periodically returned to Cuenca. "When Joseph used to come back to Ecuador dressed all fancy, I was jealous," says Daniel. "I wanted to have my own house, my own car." Daniel decided he wanted to go to the United States as well. His second-eldest brother had experienced terrible trauma and difficulties crossing the border; he'd even been kidnapped and jailed at different points. But this didn't deter Daniel from planning his journey.

Daniel had to pass through several countries to join his brothers in the United States. First, he took a bus to Panama, then a short plane ride to Guatemala, then a train to Mexico City. He traveled north from Mexico City with "a coyote"—a guide for undocumented immigrants. This was the difficult part of his journey: he had to cross through the desert and mountains at night with a group of about 25 people. His group blindly moved forward in the dark by holding hands in a long line, making sure not to lose the coyote. At one point they stopped at a small house in the mountains. To avoid being seen by American immigration authorities, they spent the night in the attic of the house—all 25 of them crammed together in the small space like sardines. Immigration authorities ended up coming to the house and looking around that night, but because the group was in the attic, they went undetected. When the sun rose the next day, Daniel and his fellow travelers realized they were in terrible danger of not making it across the border. "We were in the mountains in the desert, up super high," says Daniel. "We had to go on small pathways. If we took one wrong step, we'd roll down all the way. They told us not even to pray, just close our mouths."

Daniel finally made it to California, where he boarded a plane to New York City. When he landed, his brothers helped him settle in and find a restaurant job, a typical first job for any newly arrived undocumented immigrant. Daniel started as a dishwasher in a small Italian restaurant in Manhattan. The owner and chef treated him amazingly well, ensuring that he was comfortable in his new surroundings and encouraging him to learn English. His Latino coworkers in the kitchen told him about English classes in Queens, and so Daniel began taking classes at night while working full-time in the restaurant during the day. He slept just three or four hours a night, but he was enjoying his new life and learning.

Daniel continued to work as a dishwasher in the Italian restaurant for more than five years because his boss treated him well. He worked there while finishing English courses, passing an advanced English exam, and then moving on to enroll in Jamaica High School in Queens. He dreamed about becoming a pilot and planned to enlist in the U.S. Army as soon as he obtained his GED. "I went to apply for the army," he says, "but they told me, 'Without a Social Security number, you're not an American.' But that was the only reason I finished school! It made me so mad. It was what I had wanted to do. I loved being with airplanes. I had wanted to go far away from family so I could show them who I am." Daniel was crestfallen. He was stymied in his effort to serve his new country by his new country's immigration policies.

When Daniel finally made peace with the fact that he couldn't join the U.S. Army, he decided that he wanted to move up the ladder in the restaurant industry. He spoke English fluently now, so his new dream didn't seem unreasonable. The owners of the Italian restaurant encouraged him to seek a promotion, and soon he was hired as a busser in a fancy French restaurant in Midtown Manhattan. The money he earned allowed him to start college; he enrolled in a local private college to study computer science. "They asked me to play soccer for the college, so I joined the team and got really focused on soccer," says Daniel. "But then my grades went down. The college told me I couldn't play until I fixed my grades. It took me a month to fix them, but then 9/11 happened." The French restaurant lost a lot of business as tourism declined, and Daniel was laid off. "I had to stop going to school because I had no way to pay tuition."

At this point, Daniel decided to devote himself to restaurant work full-time to support himself and his family. He also needed to pay off his school loans. He took a job as a busser in a fancy Italian restaurant, and then became a food runner—a step up—in another white tablecloth restaurant. A short stint there led management to recommend him for a runner position in Mario Batali's newly opening restaurant, Del Posto. They knew it would be a great opportunity for Daniel, and he agreed.

Four-Star Double Standards

Daniel had worked in many fine-dining restaurants, but Del Posto was a whole new ball game. The luxurious decor, the opulent dining room, the elegant guests—all this implied a new level of service for Daniel. Del Posto was trying, from the beginning, to become a four-star restaurant, with the highest-quality food, ambience, and service. "The opening of the restaurant was smooth," says Daniel, "but there was so much pressure. Everything had to be sharp and done just their way."

From Daniel's perspective, this also seemed to mean that management wanted the people in the restaurant to look a certain way. The general manager was European, and he brought European waitstaff from another Batali restaurant to work as waiters and captains. None of the bussers and runners, all of whom were Latino, were considered for positions on the waitstaff. "I told the general manager that I'd like to move up, because I have the knowledge," says Daniel. "He told me he'd think about it. About 100 times I asked him. He'd say, 'I don't think you're capable of handling that kind of responsibility.' I even told him to give me a test, that I was ready. He told me, 'You don't know how to communicate with our clients. You'll always be a runner.'"

In fact, the general manager repeatedly made comments about the Latinos' inability to communicate, even though workers like Daniel spoke English fluently, and several of the European waiters and captains had very heavy, sometimes incomprehensible accents. At one point, when one of the European waiters quit, another manager asked Daniel to serve as a waiter two days a week. Daniel was ecstatic. Since he excelled at providing service, he asked the manager to allow him to serve full-time. "I'm working on it," the manager replied. "But let me ask you a question. Why doesn't the general manager want to make you a waiter? You've been here a long time, and you're doing an excellent job. I don't understand why he doesn't want to promote you." The manager kept talking about how surprised he was that the general manager kept talented people of color in the kitchen and hired white waiters, several inexperienced, who did not know the menu or the restaurant, couldn't handle the pressure, and left after only a few weeks. The waitstaff experienced a lot of turnover; meanwhile, plenty of highly skilled runners and bussers were waiting to be promoted.

Daniel knew the answer, but he couldn't say it aloud. It was clear that the Latinos were treated differently than the white workers; every small mistake a Latino person made resulted in insults and yelling, while similar mistakes made by the European waiters were ignored. The general manager yelled when a Latino busser dropped something, "If you don't know how to do your job, I'll have to fire you." He said nothing when a European waiter dropped an item. The general manager was also often found in the back of the kitchen chatting with the chef, who was openly racist. They would commiserate loudly about the runners and bussers. "Those fucking Mexicans don't know how to work," the chef would say. "They don't know what they're doing. They should go back to their country." The chef was known for calling everybody "fucking Mexicans," regardless of where they were from, as if it were the universal insult.

The chef was particularly hard on the Latino workers, including Daniel. "There was a dishwasher who caught the chef doing drugs downstairs a lot of times, so the chef couldn't fire him," says Daniel. "But the chef would fight with him all the time. He finally fired the dishwasher." Daniel was forced to work closely with the chef after the general manager asked him to take on the extra responsibility of expediting or communicating orders to the kitchen from the waitstaff. Expediters were typically paid more than runners. The restaurant promised Daniel a raise but never followed through, and when Daniel complained, the chef became even more aggressive. He yelled and cursed, "You stupid Mexican! You don't know how to work. You don't know how to do your fucking job."

One time Daniel dropped one of the two hot plates he was carrying because another runner bumped into him. He set the plate he'd saved back on the counter, apologized to the chef, and turned around to pick up the dropped plate. As he kneeled down, the chef grabbed the saved plate on the counter and threw it at Daniel's back. The plate missed him by less than an inch. "If I had turned around," says Daniel, "the chips from the broken plate would have flown in my eye. Whatever happened in the kitchen, it was always my fault. He hated me. He didn't want me there anymore, but even though I wanted to leave the kitchen and get promoted, he didn't want me to leave the kitchen either. So he would insult me." One time, for no apparent reason, the chef started screaming at Daniel, "Get the fuck out of my kitchen!" Then he called the manager to the kitchen and said, "I want you to take this fucking stupid asshole out of the kitchen right now. I want you to fire him." The manager didn't say anything, knowing full well that Daniel hadn't done anything wrong. He just took Daniel aside and told him to take the night off with pay and come back the next day.

The worst for Daniel was Captain Jack. Captain Jack was the Hungarian captain, whom the general manager and chef had deputized to terrorize the staff on the dining floor to make sure that service was up to four-star standards. Captain Jack towered over the runners and bussers as they brought food to tables and explained different dishes to the customers. Afterward, he yelled at them for doing it wrong. "All the time he was chasing you down to punish you for mistakes," says Daniel. "He'd grab your arm and shake you like a baby. He'd say, 'What the fuck is wrong with you? You're fucking stupid. Fucking Mexican. You fucking Ecuadorean.' All the time. In front of the customers. Management didn't get upset with him. The managers needed him there to punish everyone, to keep everyone in line. It was like that all the time."

When one soft-spoken Brazilian busser was promoted to a runner position—and, for the first time, in the position to explain a dish to a customer—Captain Jack stood over his shoulder, glowering. The worker was terrified but did the best he could. When he was done, Captain Jack screamed at him for not explaining the dish properly. The worker was demoted back to busser two days later. "He used to treat with disrespect anyone who let him," says Daniel. "If you talked back to him with a strong voice, he wouldn't do it again. But most of us were quiet because we thought, 'We're just here to work.' So we let him take advantage of us."

The irony was that these captains, who abused workers on the dining floor, proudly explained the concept of "slow food" to customers who walked in the door. In fact, Del Posto took tremendous pride in its "slow food." The management hired a "director of sustainability" and made a great show of the restaurant's connections to the Slow Food founders, the great number of organic and sustainable items on the menu, the local farms from which they sourced, and the restaurant's environmentally friendly practices. However, there was nothing "slow" about immigrant workers getting screamed at in the kitchen, where the "slow food" was prepared in unsustainable ways; and there was nothing "slow" about captains screaming at bussers on the dining floor, where these same captains regaled customers with descriptions of the menu's organic ingredients.

Then there was the funny business with the tips. "Every time we worked a banquet, the tips were going somewhere," says Daniel. "They used to do some tricks to make us believe that we had to pay a part of our tips to someone else, but we weren't being told the truth. They told us we had to share tips with the guy who works in the kitchen prepping the cheese and chocolates for sample on the table, but at the end of the shift we would do the math and ask those workers if they ever got the tips, and they would say no. The money was going to the restaurant—they were keeping it." The customers—who chose Del Posto because of its promotion of the "slow food" concept—thought they were paying gratuity to workers, but in reality their money was going to management.

In Daniel's view, the restaurant was promoting "slow food" without actually embracing the principles of the Slow Food movement. He remembers, for example, being told in staff training that the restaurant's strawberries were organic. When a persistent customer asked him to make sure the strawberries in an expensive dessert were organic, Daniel went to the kitchen to double-check, whereupon the chef told him that Del Posto had never had organic strawberries. Daniel had to apologize to the guest.

Daniel took note. It turned out that only about 10 percent of the items on Del Posto's menu were organic. The restaurant seemed to be buying organic ingredients when debuting a new dish—a way to showcase the restaurant's commitment to organic food—and then buying nonorganic ingredients a few weeks later. After all, organic ingredients were much more expensive. Customers at Del Posto also frequently asked where menu items came from, and although the restaurant prided itself on its local sourcing, less than 50 percent of the restaurant's ingredients appeared to come from local farms. "The abalone we sell—customers would ask where it came from," says Daniel. "We'd say it came from Monterey, California. The ostrich comes from New Jersey. We're not sure it's organic. The pork comes from New Mountain Farm in Missouri. The ribeye steak comes from Las Vegas. Half of the things came from outside of New York."

Getting "Fair Food"

In part, Daniel's observation that Del Posto sourced fewer items locally than diners might have thought reflects the reality of the restaurant industry. It's almost impossible for any restaurant to source a majority of its menu items from local, organic farms. The American food system is enormous, and most of our food is now grown or raised on large industrial farms across the United States.[5]

However, it's also true that the Slow Food movement was never supposed to become a consumer trend for the wealthy—the people who can regularly afford a $28 plate of spaghetti, for example. Slow Food began as a social justice movement against globalization—the unregulated spread of multinational corporations—for fair treatment of the world's peoples.[6]

And how is the restaurant industry treating the world's peoples? Although restaurants continue to provide job opportunities for millions of women, immigrants, and people of color, the industry fails to provide equal opportunities for these people to advance to jobs that allow them to support themselves and their families.

In 2010, Daniel and his coworkers had had enough of the double standards at Del Posto. Daniel had experienced good treatment at other restaurants, and so he knew things could be different at Del Posto. Since he'd heard about ROC-NY from other workers in the industry, he decided to contact our office. He met with Jeff Mansfield, a priest and former restaurant worker who had become an organizer at ROC-NY after many years of conducting prayer vigils in front of restaurants that regularly exploited workers. Daniel and Jeff gathered about 30 workers from Del Posto and held a meeting at ROC-NY. The group brainstormed a list of demands to present to Del Posto's management and planned to launch a public campaign for workplace justice, starting with a demonstration outside Del Posto during a dinner service. Daniel, his coworkers, and about 100 other restaurant workers and allies marched to the restaurant. The managers came out to speak with the workers on the sidewalk, at which point Daniel handed them a letter.

Over a one-year period the Del Posto workers and ROC-NY held several more demonstrations in front of the restaurant, courted media attention, found community support, and filed a federal lawsuit. ROC-NY also organized a "Fair Food Potluck," cleverly demonstrating to customers that the "fair food" was to be found outside, not inside, the restaurant. There were also some cold nights when we gathered outside the restaurant with a preacher who led prayer vigils for the workers.

Del Posto workers also began speaking out inside the restaurant against inhumane treatment. A few weeks after the campaign began, the chef yelled at Daniel, but at this point Daniel felt empowered to yell back. "If you need help," he told the chef, "you need to know how to talk to

ROC-NY member and Windows on the World survivor Shailesh Shrestha at
a fair food protest in front of Del Posto restaurant, where Daniel works.
Courtesy of Restaurant Opportunities Center of New York.

a person. You know my name. You don't need to yell. I'm warning you.
This is the last time you will yell at me." The chef didn't say anything. He
looked at Daniel very seriously, and Daniel left the kitchen. "All the guys
at ROC-NY said, 'You did it!'" says Daniel. "I said, 'It's time to step up.
I can't let this guy pick on me anymore.'"

It took protests, litigation, and some great press, but in the end ROC-NY
won over $1 million in stolen tips and wages, promotions for several of the
Latino bussers, and a new, transparent promotions policy at Del Posto.

The general manager fired the chef who'd intimidated and insulted employees, instituted procedures for workers to report grievances, and much more. Daniel was overjoyed. He could see and feel the power of change that occurred when workers got together to demand what was fair and just. "The next time I'm abused anywhere," Daniel says, "I will know what to do. Before, we waited too long. We were afraid of getting fired. No one wanted to stand up. Next time I'll know what to do."

For its part, Mario Batali's company responded with admirable willingness to change its practices and expand its definition of "slow food." It agreed to join ROC's Restaurant Industry Roundtable, a regular meeting of responsible restaurateurs who learn best practices from one another and generally work together to promote the "high road" to profitability in the industry. In making these changes, Batali set the model for the "high road"—which is not about being the perfect employer, since no one can ever be perfect, but about consistently striving to do better.

The Batali campaign helped ROC—and even allies in the sustainable food movement—define "sustainable food." To most foodies, "sustainable food" refers to food that is grown without the use of pesticides or other harmful chemical agents, and livestock that is raised humanely and without hormones. When we hear the words "sustainable food," we also tend to think of food that is produced locally to reduce the amount of environmental damage caused by transporting food thousands of miles to cities across the country. Most foodies care about how we define "sustainable food" because they are concerned about their health and the environment. However, "sustainable food" also needs to embody fair and equitable labor practices. Food can't really be healthy, ethically consumed, or sustainable if it's prepared and served in an environment that permits abuse, exploitation, and discrimination. It's definitely not sustainable to eat food served by workers who cannot afford to feed their families and face the added burden of having their wages and tips stolen. Sustainable food, by definition, must include sustainable labor practices.

Sustainable Food, Sustainable Restaurant—Defined

So what must a truly sustainable restaurant do to live up to the core values of the Slow Food movement?

Over the last 12 years I've learned that a truly sustainable restaurant should look something like the Good Girl Dinette in Highland Park, Los Angeles. Of course, dozens of restaurateurs around the country are trying to embrace "slow food" values, but one of those who, I believe, is embracing a more holistic concept of "slow food" is Diep, the owner of the Good Girl Dinette. She is doing everything in her power to embrace sustainable food and labor practices, not because it's trendy or because she thinks it may attract more customers, but because she truly believes that she serves better food when it's made sustainably.

Diep was a child refugee during the Vietnam War. "As a child, nothing was strange—every experience was new," she says. "So it didn't feel unusual to me to be in a refugee camp. I remember food was dropped from helicopters. Cans of peaches came from the sky. No one explained it. It just was. It felt normal to live with 20 other people in a house."

Diep and her family were "boat people." They fled Vietnam and moved to Los Angeles when Diep was six. Diep's father, however, remained in a Vietnamese concentration camp, and her mother died at sea. Diep and her brother and sister were raised by their grandparents, aunts, and uncles—all refugees. "I come from a family of people who owned several restaurants in Orange County in L.A.," says Diep. "I came in 1978. All my aunts and uncles had degrees. They were doctors and professors in Vietnam, but when they came to the States, their degrees didn't transfer. Only two of my uncles were young enough to consider starting school again. So my family opened up restaurants."

Diep was the youngest in a long line of women entrepreneurs. "My grandmother grew up working in her great-grandmother's mercantile shop, trading in rice futures at a very young age," she says. "She hustled all her life. At the age of 13 she would go to the port and negotiate deals with Algerian fabric merchants. She was so tiny, so she took her big, brawny man cousin with her as a bodyguard to negotiate the prices of things."

Diep's grandmother was married at the age of 16, but after marrying she was unwilling to give up on her entrepreneurial dreams. She sold her wedding jewelry, without her husband knowing, to start her first business. She became very successful, so successful that she eventually earned enough money to replace all of her wedding jewelry; her husband didn't notice the difference or just ignored it. "My grandfather was a very enlightened man," says Diep. "He saw her work hard. He didn't have an ego about it.

It was awesome. She was tough. He was gentle. Even though they had an arranged marriage, the matchmaker did a great job. If she had been with someone more macho it wouldn't have worked."

Diep's grandparents lived in North Vietnam, so when the country became fractured by political turmoil, they had to leave everything behind—the business, the estate—and reestablish themselves in the south. Twenty years later, when South Vietnam was about to fall to the North Vietnamese Army, they had to move again. They left everything behind to seek refuge in the United States. "My grandma was a tenacious woman," says Diep. Her grandmother already knew she could make sure they survived anywhere.

When they arrived in Los Angeles, Diep and her brother and sister lived with their grandparents. It was time for the next daughter in line to become an entrepreneur. Diep's aunt was the first in the family to open a restaurant. All of the relatives chipped in to make it a success. "In the backyard we had a Jacuzzi and a beautiful lawn, and my grandparents tore it up," says Diep. "On every kind of arable land we had we began growing something for the restaurant. As kids we were like, 'Can we just have a lawn?' They composted everything. My grandparents were frugal businesspeople. They didn't waste anything. Every Vietnamese household did that. You grew for yourself or your restaurant. It was a vibrant underground economy."

Diep's grandparents grew herbs, providing the restaurant with hot mint and basil. "They grew Vietnamese mustards and chayote, and really anything they could pickle," says Diep. They composted because it was cheap and created great soil. "We were homesteading and local-sourcing before those terms even existed," she says. Her family was not being trendy or environmentally conscious; they were just thrifty and wanted to put the land to its best use.

Diep and her brother and sister helped out in the garden at home and in the restaurant from the time they were 11 years old. They watered the garden, hung up the seaweed, and prepared bouquet garnishes for pho, or Vietnamese noodle soup. They also watched their grandmother cook. "We never actually got to cook until we went to college," says Diep. "My grandma would never trust us to cook Vietnamese food. My sister and I loved to cook when we were kids, but it had to be non-Vietnamese food. Our grandmother would criticize the food if it was Vietnamese. She just had really high standards. She'd say, 'You call that a decent stew?' My sister would specialize in French desserts to cook something outside of Grandma's purview. I did more American cooking and Victorian English cooking. I was really into Victorian literature. I wanted to make pudding and roast beef. I had read *Anne of Green Gables,* and the era spoke to me. Plus, I knew Grandma wasn't an expert in it."

Diep and her siblings spent weekends and summers in the restaurant making sodas and bussing tables. Diep remembers spending hours pre-plating the table salads for pho. In this way, long before she knew what she wanted to do in life, she was immersed in a world in which women entrepreneurs prepared homegrown, homemade food and sold it successfully. When she went to college, she pursued other interests and passions, but she always had in the back of her mind the dream of opening her own Vietnamese restaurant. She spent her days reading and writing about Victorian literature, and in the evenings she finally had the freedom to cook Vietnamese food without the critical eye of her grandmother. "I needed to be able to make mistakes," says Diep. "It was hard to make mistakes with Grandma. Having my own kitchen was great. It was like Virginia Woolf's *Room of One's Own.*"

Diep experimented with all kinds of Vietnamese food. She also learned by going to restaurants and meeting South Vietnamese people. "I was slowly realizing what I gravitated toward," she says. "Northern food—it was rustic, simple. I gravitated toward simplicity. South Vietnamese food is exuberant, cosmopolitan, influenced by so many things. I do enjoy southern cooking, but what I like to cook, what's really compelling, intriguing, is northern cuisine. It can be deceptively simple. It can use just three ingredients and take your breath away."

In her junior year, Diep came out to the world as a lesbian. Her extended family didn't take it too well, but her father—who had just been released from the concentration camp—was much more open to it. He had met gay people in the camp and in prison.

As a queer Asian woman, Diep became more open to and interested in understanding inequity and injustice. She became active in the Asian Pacific Student Union and volunteered for local social justice organizations. "I heard somewhere randomly that nonprofit work has a shelf life of 10 years," she says. "I decided I'd give my youngest years to nonprofit work, before having kids and worrying about a pension plan. When I wouldn't care about a mortgage. Then, I'd open a restaurant." She became an outreach worker for an Asian American AIDS intervention organization, educating people all over Orange County about the disease. Then she transitioned into doing community organizing and cultural programming for young Cambodian women in Long Beach.

Seven years out of college, Diep made a promise to herself that she would open her own restaurant in her tenth year after graduation. She started attending evening classes to learn how to write a business plan, and she puzzled through how she could develop a restaurant that truly reflected her values. "If I didn't have 10 years of social justice work under my belt, I might not have created a restaurant that has social justice values," says Diep. "I wouldn't have been exposed to the myriad issues in the community. Working with and collaborating with organizations gave me a breadth of understanding of what it means to struggle. Advocating for social change for low-income Cambodian women made me believe that, as a business owner, I needed to be able to provide something comparable to what I had advocated for."

After so many years of doing community work, meeting all kinds of people, and learning about their struggles, Diep knew she had to develop a business that reflected her strong belief in social justice. She wondered how to do it. How could she pay people a living wage and make a profit? She began to read every article she could get on the restaurant business. She read voraciously about restaurateurs who were known for fair employment practices. She remembers reading about Traci Des Jardins, who offers benefits to her workers in San Francisco and supports them in every way possible. A "living wage campaign" was also under way in San Francisco, and Diep followed it with interest. "I was trying to figure out what I could afford," says Diep. "I thought, if I pay a living wage, do I need to have a white tablecloth restaurant? Not for my people. My people won't be able to afford going there. How can I make it an affordable restaurant and still have living wages and organic food?"

When Diep was still working in the nonprofit world, she'd gone with her girlfriend to the Hollywood farmers' market every weekend. Her girlfriend was Japanese and belonged to a family of Japanese farmers. "I learned about organic certification," says Diep, referring to how farmers obtain official recognition for growing food without the use of pesticides, "and I learned about the pleasurable act of eating. Going there every weekend was like going to church." Diep also found out about a sustainable agriculture center at the University of California at Santa Cruz. She took a weekend trip to the campus and visited the farmers associated with the center. The farms surrounded the campus. Diep got a tour of the farms and asked every grower she met, "How can I run a sustainable restaurant that still provides affordable food?" She was really puzzling through it; organic food was just more expensive! Diep didn't want to open a fine-dining restaurant; she wanted her family and community to be able to eat there. One of the master gardeners and instructors at the university farm said he understood her struggle: "Why don't you figure out which items can reasonably be organic on your budget, instead of having 100 percent of your menu items certified organic?" He suggested, for example, that maybe her onions wouldn't be organic. Restaurants use a lot of them, and no farmer wants to sell really cheap organic onions.

That helped Diep. "I broke out from my purist, 100 percent organic mind-set," she says. She realized that if she could do some items organic, and others not, she could perhaps work closely with one farmer to get as many organic items as she could, rather than spreading her resources among several different farms.

She picked one farm—Yang Farm—which was an organic farm run by a Hmong refugee family in Fresno. Diep had been their customer for years at two different farmers' markets in the Southern California area. She could see how hard the family worked. "I knew never to complain about working too hard in front of a farmer," says Diep. She knew she wanted to buy from Yang Farm, but when she told Farmer Chan about her plans to open a restaurant, he didn't want to take preorders from her. Diep understood: they didn't want to get stiffed.

Diep was patient. She finished her 10-year stint in the nonprofit world and finalized her business plan. She also started talking to family and friends about investing in her restaurant. When she found the perfect location in Highland Park, she had to raise $50,000 in 30 days or lose the location to another prospective tenant. It was do or die. She asked 200 people and ended up with 25 lenders. None of her lenders had much money, but they believed in Diep and what she was trying to do—to build a truly sustainable restaurant.

Diep opened the Good Girl Dinette in 2009, and then she went back to see the Yang Farm family. She started buying large amounts from them at the

Diep at the Good Girl Dinette. Courtesy of Restaurant Opportunities Centers United.

farmers' market for her restaurant. "I would buy lots of noncertified organic ong choy from them," says Diep. "It's like collard greens to southerners. It grounds you. It's the thing you crave. If they were harvesting it, I'd take it."

Her orders grew larger and larger until finally the family agreed to take preorders from her. Since they traveled from Fresno to Los Angeles each week for the farmers' markets, they asked Diep to meet them at their hotel to pick up larger orders of certain items. Soon Farmer Chan's daughter began calling Diep directly to see if she was interested in buying upcoming crops. Chan's daughter would say, "We're growing ong choy now. We'd love to sell it to you." Diep would buy the week's harvest and develop a new vegetarian recipe. She took vegetables that weren't selling well and developed new menu items with them. She also took items that she knew were grown organically, even if they weren't certified organic.

Diep figured out how to sell sustainable food at affordable prices by working with one farm's crops. In addition, she made reasonable portions and cooked big batches of certain items. She didn't want to stop there, however, because sustainability meant more to her than just buying organic food from a local farm. It also meant figuring out how to pay her workers enough so that they could survive.

When Diep started hiring workers for the restaurant, she listened to their stories of workplace abuse. New cooks told her how they'd left other restaurants because they were made to work double shifts and were paid in cash with no overtime. Other workers told her they were never able to move up. Diep assured them these things wouldn't happen in her restaurant. She was committed to figuring out how to pay her workers a living wage *and* keep her menu prices affordable.

Diep concluded that she could create an affordable menu without making meals so dirt cheap that she'd find herself cheating her workers. Some customers might complain that they could get a Vietnamese sandwich for $3.50 in Little Saigon, Orange County's Vietnamese neighborhood, but she didn't care. For just a few dollars more, customers could get delicious, fresh, mostly organic sandwiches that were not made by exploited kitchen workers. In turn, she found that her crew worked with her to be frugal and keep other costs down. "I taught my crew to make sure portions are not too much or too little and to stay on top of waste," says Diep. "You can use cilantro tops for something, use the stems for something else. Be more frugal. My prep cooks are all environmentalists." She taught them not to waste anything, to compost with the community garden, and to turn off the air-conditioning each night. She practiced sustainability through simplicity—like the farmers in Italy—and in this way she was able to save precious funds so that she could pay her workers well.

Diep also worked the line herself. She worked when her employees were sick, and she gave raises to make sure good people stayed and moved up in her restaurant. "I'm not the easiest boss," she says, "but my job isn't to make sure everyone's happy. It's to pay people ethically. I'm as fair as I can be. When I'm stressed out, the most important thing is to keep in communication. I tell the workers, 'These are the stakes—we do well, that means better tips for you.'"

It's a constant struggle, but Diep says she can sleep at night because she isn't taking advantage of people.

Today, the Good Girl Dinette is a vibrant restaurant that is almost always packed. Diep is proud of the food as well as the morale in her restaurant. Over the last four years she has continued to hear horror stories from her employees about their past experiences. She says, "They've told me that restaurants I really respected—and that I know make a lot of money—stiffed people."

On the other hand, Diep tells me that she really understands the struggle of small restaurant owners—how hard they have to work to make sure they pay everyone fairly. She's not a perfect employer—her starting wage is not much higher than the California state minimum wage of $8 an hour, and she doesn't offer health insurance. Nevertheless, she's working toward offering more benefits to her employees as her business grows. She believes that the growth of her business has to come with consumers choosing sustainable business practices. She says that the fine-dining restaurants don't need to raise their menu prices any higher to be able to pay people well. Small businesses, however, have less wiggle room—which is why Diep was upset when a *New York Times* writer raved about a $1.50 Vietnamese sandwich in Little Saigon. "I knew that reporter could afford more than that," she says. "My sandwiches cost $8.00, and my customers understand why."

Diep says she also feels conflicted because she knows the folks who own the Vietnamese restaurants in Little Saigon. They are her community. People demonize them for paying low wages and sometimes breaking the law, but they are operating on shoestring budgets. Diep says, "They're not evil. They're just not doing it right. They need encouragement. Especially with immigrant restaurants, we need to explain the viability of doing it right."

Nowadays Diep works closely with ROC because she feels strongly that uniform policy changes—like an increase in the minimum wage and a paid sick-day policy—would be important steps forward for the industry. She knows family restaurants might perceive it to be difficult to raise wages and provide paid sick days, but she believes they'd find a way if it was the law.

So what's Diep's definition of a "sustainable restaurant"? "It's one where as the business grows, the people grow with it," she says. "As we expand our offerings, I'd love it if the same staff stayed with us for a long time. I love the idea of staff being there for 10 years, and creating an environment where that can happen. Where the restaurant becomes something I don't even recognize, but the same faces are there. A sustainable restaurant is a successful business, where the people who helped create that success are able to benefit from that. I'm committed to everybody's excellence, here or elsewhere. I want you to come in to work—it's not free money—and feel a sense of fulfillment, appreciation. It's growing, dynamic, you're present."

Diep also worries that "organic food" has become too narrowly defined. "Organic has become about one issue: protecting yourself from harm," she

says. "Sustainability is about contributing to a society that everybody benefits from, not just going organic because you don't want to die from cancer
or have a difficult pregnancy." In a truly sustainable food system, everyone
would benefit—family farms like Yang Farm, small business owners like
Diep and her family, and workers like Diep's employees at the Good Girl
Dinette. Diep believes that conditions in the restaurant industry today are
reminiscent of scenes from Upton Sinclair's *The Jungle*. Sinclair's historic
novel documented the horrific working conditions of immigrant workers
in the meat- and poultry-processing plants at the beginning of the twentieth century. American readers were disgusted by the idea that they could
possibly eat a finger, but not by the fact that workers were losing their fingers and limbs in the first place. "It's not just because you don't want to eat
a finger," says Diep. "No one should be working under those conditions!"

When asked what would happen if we had a sustainable restaurant industry, Diep doesn't skip a beat. "You're going to eat better food!" she says.
"It will create better food. When you support food justice, you're going to
eat better. With just wages, there's not as much worker turnover, and so
the food is better. When you work at one place for a long time, it becomes
a craft. If you're moving from place to place, you're only going to learn so
much. When you stay in one place, you get better and better, working at it
every day." Working at a job they love, Diep and her team learn more and
more—and we, the diners, benefit.

Of course, Diep is not perfect, and Mario Batali is not a bad person—in
fact, he has proven himself to be admirably adaptable to change. I firmly
believe that every employer, every restaurant, every restaurant worker,
every human being, has room for improvement, and no employer wakes
up in the morning thinking, How can I exploit my workers today?

However, I also believe that the restaurant industry's structure allows
and even encourages abuse, inequality, low wages, and the misappropria-
tion of tips—basically, a culture of unsustainability. Compared to other
industries, there's a huge imbalance of power—and voice—between restaurant workers and their employers. The National Restaurant Association (NRA) represents less than one-third of all restaurants in the United
States, but since, like much of the food system, it is dominated by large
multinational restaurant corporations that have a lot of money to spend on
lobbyists, the organization wields tremendous power in Congress and in
most state legislatures. Restaurant workers did not have a national voice

comparable to the NRA until ROC was formed in 2002.[7] The NRA has spent millions of dollars to keep the federal minimum wage for tipped workers at $2.13 for the last 20 years.[8] It has also fought for less regulation of the industry. That is why restaurant workers find themselves in an industry culture that encourages yelling, the misappropriation of tips and wages, a preference for white workers who are men, and sexual harassment. Deviating from this norm isn't necessarily rewarded either. As Diep discovered, a *New York Times* reporter was all too willing to rave about the $1.50 Vietnamese sandwiches in a Little Saigon restaurant that doesn't pay its workers a living wage.

But consumers can change this. We can have an enormous impact by rewarding restaurants that have sustainable practices. In other words, we can picket with our pocketbooks. We can choose to eat only in restaurants that practice "ethical consumption," embracing the real core values of sustainable, slow food. Over the last 10 years consumers have successfully convinced many restaurants across the country to become more sustainable. Del Posto is just one high-profile example; when consumers refused to eat at Del Posto during ROC's campaign, Del Posto decided to do the right thing—pay its workers and change its labor practices. ROC has also produced a *National Diners' Guide* to help consumers identify which restaurants have sustainable labor practices. You can find it online at www.rocunited.org/dinersguide.

However, that alone won't be enough. Consumers actually need to talk to employers and workers and let them know what they value in a restaurant. Just as consumers asking for organic, locally sourced food pushed Del Posto to purchase more of those items, consumers talking to employers about their employment practices will help move restaurants in the right direction. ROC's *National Diners' Guide* comes with "tip cards" that consumers can hand to an employer to say, "I noticed that you don't pay a livable tipped minimum wage. As a consumer, that's unacceptable to me and part of the criteria I use when considering where to eat."

If consumers can compel hundreds of thousands of restaurants in the United States to serve more organic, locally sourced foods, then surely we can push restaurants to be honest about their "slow food" claims and labor practices. The quality of our food—and our health—depends on it.

3

SERVING WHILE SICK

I had a really bad cold. My nose was running, I was sneezing, and I had a bad
cough and a fever. I could not call in sick because no work meant no money
and I couldn't afford it at that time. My kids were very young, so I went to
work to see if I could make it through the day. Halfway through the day,
the sneezing, coughing, and runny nose got worse. I said to the manager,
"I am really sick and need to go because I could make others sick and I am
dealing with food." She laughed and told me, "Try not to cough then." So I
had to work that day sick, and who knows how many customers I got sick
because I couldn't go to the back and leave the counter to wash my hands
after every sneeze or nose wipe. Later on, all of us got sick, one by one,
and all this came from another worker who came to work sick, like me,
and was not allowed to leave work!

—FAST-FOOD WORKER, WOMAN, 10 YEARS IN THE INDUSTRY, DETROIT

It's common sense: the meal that arrives at your table when you eat out is
not just a product of its raw ingredients. It's a product of the hands that chop,
cook, and plate it, and the people to whom those hands belong. Still, how our
food is handled in a restaurant—and by whom—is something over which
we have almost no control. Most of us have experienced food poisoning at
least once, but we don't usually know what—or who—caused it. My own
experience was unforgettable to me, though a common experience of many.

Mamdouh and I were in the process of trying to open ROC's first worker-
owned restaurant. The restaurant was Mamdouh's idea. After losing his
job at Windows on the World, he'd dreamed of opening his own restaurant
with a group of his former coworkers. All of them—the survivors—were

jobless after 9/11. We finally did open it—a restaurant called COLORS, which reflected the workers' extraordinary diversity—but it took many years of struggle and conflict, help from a lot of different friends, and lots and lots of meetings. One of those meetings was with Brian Glick and Carmen Huertas, law professors from Fordham University and the City University of New York who'd agreed to work with us to draft the bylaws and governing documents for the restaurant. Early in the process, Brian invited Mamdouh and me to eat lunch at an Indian restaurant in Midtown near the law school. Brian was treating—and it really was a treat. The restaurant was beautiful—gold-plated silver dishware, ornate chairs and tables, fancy folded napkins, and delicious food. Customers here expected perfection, and it definitely appeared as though they got it. It was a joy to be talking about the thrilling prospect of opening a worker-owned restaurant over creamed spinach, eggplant curry, and chicken tikka masala.

When I got home several hours later, my stomach started to feel strange. It had been an incredibly busy day, and I tried to relax by watching television. By nine that night I was doubled over in pain. I hadn't yet made the connection between my stomach pain and eating out at the fancy Indian restaurant. All I could think about was my discomfort.

What happened after that is familiar to most of us, and not something I need to describe. At some point in the middle of my misery I thought about what I'd eaten in the last 24 hours. The only meal that had been unusual for me was the one I had eaten at the Indian restaurant.

I was up most of the night and barely able to get out of bed the next morning. At the time I was helping Floriberto and his coworkers fight for their stolen wages and end other abuses at the restaurant where they worked (see chapter 1), so I had no choice but to attend a major settlement conference with the restaurant's defense lawyers that afternoon. I hobbled into the fancy law firm clutching my Pepto-Bismol. The opposing counsel joked that the defense counsel had made me "that sick."

From Poverty Wages to Poor Sanitation

The Centers for Disease Control and Prevention (CDC) estimates that 1 in 6 Americans suffers from food poisoning each year, and 3,000 of us die from it.[1] This seems only natural, given that most of us eat out at least once a week. We're bound to get sick at least once or twice with a foodborne illness when many different hands are touching our food. Incidents of food poisoning are of course not unique to Indian restaurants. Most of us do wonder, though, after getting sick, How did this happen? Where did this come from? And what exactly happens behind the restaurant kitchen door is a complete mystery to most of us. Although we have become obsessed with healthy, local, sustainable, organic, grass-fed, wild, and generally "better" food, we usually have no idea how that food is prepared and under what conditions.

We should, however, know this: the health and safety and overall working conditions of restaurant workers in the United States directly affect the health and safety of consumers (see fig. 2). ROC has found in industry-wide surveys that the vast majority of restaurants across the country pressure their employees to work while sick or injured—giving us, the diners, an extra helping of germs with our meals and putting us at risk for foodborne illness. If this doesn't surprise you, consider another pattern: the "low road" restaurants that don't take great care of their employees, especially with regard to wages, tend to be the same restaurants that don't take great care of their customers, especially with regard to food safety.[2] ROC research shows that the employers who steal tips, don't pay overtime, force employees to work off the clock, and don't provide health benefits are the same employers who pressure their workers to engage in practices that threaten the health and safety of customers. In our experience, this is because employers who cut corners and steal from their workers are also likely to cut corners when it comes to customer health and safety. Isn't that common sense? If a restaurant isn't responsible enough to pay its workers properly, how can we expect it to be responsible enough to make sure that the food doesn't include an extra helping of germs?

Thomas, a restaurant worker from the South, told me in graphic detail about the low road restaurants in which he worked in post–Hurricane Katrina New Orleans. A slender man who talks fast and moves constantly, Thomas has a kind of frenetic energy, but he's incredibly steadfast when it comes to relationships. He became a leader at ROC–New Orleans several years ago, speaking up for himself and fellow restaurant workers whose rights had been violated on the job.

Thomas grew up in Tampa, Florida, and had a middle-class upbringing. His mother was a nurse and psychologist for troubled children, and his father worked as a manager in an auto shop. "I got a car at 16," he says. "I had a job—I'd work at Hoho Chinese Restaurant during the

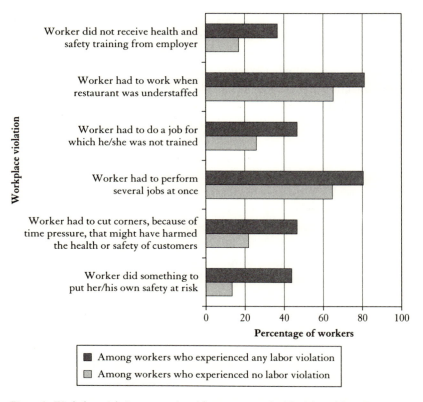

Figure 2. Workplace violations presenting risks to consumer health. Adapted from Restaurant Opportunities Centers United, *Serving While Sick: High Risks and Low Benefits for the Nation's Restaurant Workforce, and Their Impact on the Consumer,* technical report (New York: Restaurant Opportunities Centers United, 2010), fig.1; http://rocunited.org/blog/roc-serving-while-sick/.
Note: Data are drawn from analysis of 4,323 surveys of restaurant workers nationwide—the largest national survey sample of restaurant workers—as well as 240 employer interviews and 240 worker interviews on wages, working conditions, and access to benefits.

day, and then I worked in my dad's auto shop at night. I liked working in the restaurant because I liked Chinese food and I liked having money. It was neat working with my dad. I didn't have to ask people for money."

Thomas sped through high school, taking the GED test at 17 to earn his diploma early. After finishing school, he began working more hours at the auto shop and the restaurant, and he joined his dad every night at a local bar to drink. "My mom and dad got a divorce, and my dad looked like he was in his seventies," says Thomas. "We went to bars and started drinking a lot. My dad didn't care."

One evening Thomas met someone in the bar with whom he hit it off right away. It was a chance encounter that changed the direction of his life. He was 18. She was 35. Her name was Barbara, and she wanted him to join her in moving across the country to Las Vegas. Thomas considered it and ultimately decided to go. "I left because I didn't want to watch my father deteriorate," he says. "I figured if I left he would snap out of it."

In Las Vegas, Barbara arranged for Thomas to work with a friend of hers in a local casino. "Her friend managed a bar, and they needed a barback, so I learned how to bartend," says Thomas. "But then Barbara wanted to open a kitchen across town, across Spring Valley. I started cooking. Barbara was running food to tables. It was fun. My mom had taught me to cook when I was very young."

Unfortunately, the fun didn't last long. Barbara died of alcohol poisoning that same year, and Thomas was left in a city that he didn't really know. Then, his father came to visit him for his birthday and had a cerebral hemorrhage. "They had to put him on life support," says Thomas. "Life support was $975 per day, and the doctor said to me, 'You're the resident, you're responsible.' The doctor did an EEG, and it showed that my father had less than 10 percent brain activity, so I decided. My brother and sister fought me on it. They didn't want me to pull the plug. They felt that I had taken control of the situation, that I had killed our dad. I got really depressed after that."

Thomas decided to move in with his mother, who was now in Texas, but shortly after he arrived she was diagnosed with brain cancer. "I quit my job when my mother was dying so I could take care of her," says Thomas. "I was changing her IVs, cleaning her bedpan. I was her 24-hour caregiver because the hospice couldn't be there 24 hours a day." Nine months after Thomas moved to Texas, his mother passed away. His brother and sister came for the funeral. "They cleaned out her apartment of everything she owned," says Thomas. "They had me evicted from the apartment, and my sister told the landlord that I wasn't on the lease."

Thomas went back to what he knew—working multiple jobs. He combined restaurant work with other jobs—painting motor homes, for example. He moved all over Texas, first to Waco, then Austin, and Houston. In

Austin he worked for a restaurant catering company that served meals at professional golf tournaments. He found that, when he was treated well, he reciprocated because he loved the work. "The company took care of people," says Thomas. "I would show up on my days off to help out. It's part of my personality—I excel in the restaurant business. I enjoy the environment, the people, the food, the hours, the camaraderie with coworkers. It's like a family, your unit, your social circle. Restaurant workers are different than nine-to-five people. It's the mentality they have—they're easygoing, laid-back. When God created man, he said, 'Here are the restaurant workers. They have a different mentality.' After all, who are you going to have more fun hanging out with—an accountant or a restaurant worker?"

Restaurant workers are trained to sell hospitality and show people a good time. Serving became a rehearsed lifestyle for Thomas—so he was selling even when off the clock. "When you're a bartender or a waiter, you sell yourself eight hours a day," says Thomas, "and then you find yourself doing it to your mailman. You do it naturally. You enjoy it."

When a major golf tournament ended, Thomas decided to move to Houston. "A friend told me there were lots of restaurants in Houston," says Thomas. "It's the fourth largest city. I decided to go to the big city to make big money. I didn't have a place to live. I showed up and started looking for a job with only my backpack. I was living in a hotel for just a week before I found a job." In fact, Thomas found two jobs within one week—one waiting tables in an Italian restaurant, and one serving drinks in a trendy bar and nightclub. The bar owner was a Syrian Muslim who considered himself devout but still loved to drink. He took very good care of Thomas, paying and treating him with dignity and respect.

Then, Hurricane Katrina hit, and on an impulse Thomas decided to go to New Orleans. "I went from my job straight to the Greyhound station and took a bus," says Thomas. He felt certain there would still be restaurant jobs in the Crescent City.

Thomas found work in several different restaurants in the French Quarter. At one point he landed a job waiting tables in a famous fine-dining restaurant, Tony Moran's on Bourbon Street. "I was making good money, wearing a tuxedo. I liked it," says Thomas. "I wanted to have respect for waiting tables on Bourbon Street." He never saw his wages—they all went to taxes—but the tips were good.

When business was slow, however, he made almost nothing. He couldn't live on $2.13 an hour, the minimum wage for tipped workers, and to make matters worse, employees weren't being paid correctly. "There was a mystery deduction," says Thomas. "I wouldn't get all of my hours, and they'd screw us by making us clock off when we still had to stay and clean. The server report would show that we had clocked out, but we were still there cleaning the dining room." Thomas put up with it for two years, but finally he quit.

Thomas started moving from job to job in New Orleans, struggling financially, unable to pay rent. His situation improved slightly when he met the owner of a historic mansion on Bourbon Street. "The gate was open," says Thomas. "The guy inside waved me over—he was apparently the owner—and told me that he needed someone to live in the 'guest house' (the former slave quarters) and watch the main house while he was away." The owner had asked a number of other people to do the same, and so Thomas found himself living with several people in a strangely haunted house. It was a temporary situation, as many of his living arrangements had been. The owner ultimately sold the house to Paramount Pictures for use as a soundstage.

Thomas finally thought he'd found a stable living situation when Derek, a former coworker and friend, invited him to become his roommate. Derek also suggested that Thomas come work with him in another local restaurant that had just changed owners. The new owner, Mark, had asked Derek, who was the restaurant's lead waiter, to help him find new staff for the restaurant. Derek asked Thomas to apply.

Mark hired Thomas on the spot. "Derek had suggested I work a few shifts in the kitchen," says Thomas. "But when I got there, Mark said, 'We want you to run this kitchen.' He said he'd give me $500 a week. So we made that arrangement. I would be working full-time. I quit working at my other job."

After the first week of work, Mark told Thomas that money was really tight and that he'd pay him sometime soon. He argued that business was slow because they had just reopened under new ownership. Thomas agreed to wait. Mark told him to ride out the slow period; he'd make it up to him later.

A month later, Thomas and Derek still hadn't been paid, and so they received an eviction notice. It was incredibly disappointing. Thomas had given up his job and his home, but he still held out hope that the restaurant would turn around and he'd be paid for the time he'd worked. Thomas moved into a rooming house that cost $133 per month. "I made Mark promise that he would at least pay me the $133 I needed to keep my place," says Thomas. "Mark promised that he would." When it time came to pay, however, Mark made the same excuses. The restaurant was still slow, and they needed more time. When Thomas was kicked out of the rooming house, Mark made a new offer. "He said, 'You can stay here at the restaurant. There's a room in the attic that's open 24 hours,'" says Thomas. "It was a space where Mark would let some of his crack dealer friends spend the night or where he offered local call girls free drinks for a blow job. So I was living above the women's restroom. Every night I would climb up the water heater into my little cubbyhole. I had gone two and half months without any income, so I would eat at the restaurant and do my laundry in the back with the hose. I would go to the floor manager's hotel room to take showers every morning."

Thomas wasn't the only one being stiffed. Several other workers and many of the restaurant's vendors were not getting paid either. Worst of all, Mark asked Thomas to prepare spoiled food. "Sometimes I went into the kitchen, and there was almost nothing good to cook," says Thomas. "There'd be rotten chicken, rotten vegetables." The vendors would not want to provide fresh food because the restaurant was behind on its bills. "One time, all we had was a filet of salmon, and it was on the verge of turning," says Thomas. "I knew because it had this slimy coating. We had 2.5 pounds of it. They were going to serve it, so I did my best to rinse all the slime off."

The same dishonest practices were common at the bar. "Mark would run to Wal-Mart or Sam's Club to buy a bottle of liquor because there wasn't enough well vodka for vodka tonic," says Thomas. "Then they'd be marrying the bottles, watering down the bottles so the alcohol would last longer."

Besides that, Thomas couldn't convince the workers to care about the food they were serving. They weren't being paid, for the most part, and management didn't seem to care about the restaurant, so why should workers care about the food they served to customers? "People saw the place going downhill, so they didn't care about anything," says Thomas. "Why take any sort of pride in that place?" Thomas had never experienced such low morale at a restaurant.

Thomas went seven months without steady income, perhaps getting paid $1,000 over that period. He finally found a friend who let him stay at his place while he looked for another job. He found a server position and left Mark behind him. It had been the worst seven months of his life.

Behind the Veil of Hospitality—Working Conditions That Lead to Health Concerns

Thomas's story may seem extreme, but over the years I have heard an alarming number of stories about hellish working conditions in restaurants. Responsible restaurant owners like Diep (see chapter 2) know that workers are the front line of the restaurant, preparing the food and providing the service to customers. When employers cut corners with regard to their employees' health and safety, it affects the customers as well. I have repeatedly noted this link—just from listening to workers' stories—and even I have been shocked by the data confirming this pattern. Over 40 percent (42.5%) of workers surveyed by ROC reported that they've been forced, as a result of time pressure, to do something that might put the health and safety of customers at risk.[3]

This should be of concern to all of us.

Restaurant workers are forced to put the health and safety of customers at risk in many ways, for many reasons, but the primary reason is this: the industry puts workers at high risk of injury and illness without providing them with the income or health benefits to deal with either.[4]

In 2011, the U.S. Department of Labor ranked the restaurant industry as third highest in total number of nonfatal occupational injuries and illnesses. There are nearly 200,000 reported accidents in restaurants each year. Almost half of all workers surveyed by ROC (49%)—or almost 2,000 workers out of more than 4,000 surveyed—had suffered work-related cuts on the job; and 45.8 percent of all workers had been burned on the job.[5] In my 10 years of organizing restaurant workers, almost every kitchen worker I've asked about burns and cuts simply rolls up his or her sleeves and shows me the scars.

These injuries cost the restaurant industry quite a bit of money. The Occupational Safety and Health Administration (OSHA) estimated that just one serious cut can add up to $32,000, accounting for workers' compensation, the cost of time lost, and the cost of replacing the worker. The restaurant industry's trade press reports that on-the-job injuries cost the industry approximately $300 million in medical fees and lost labor every year.

A large part of the problem is that restaurants are fast-paced, pressure-filled environments. Just imagine the typical dinner service at a popular restaurant. To make sure that you get your meal within 20 to 30 minutes after ordering, every worker in the restaurant has to rush. Your server has to take your order, along with the orders of customers at about 6 to 10 other tables; input them into a computer; serve drinks; and then, after serving your meal, she must periodically check on you and the customers at the other tables to be sure that the food is satisfactory, sometimes taking special requests to the chef, and more. The busser has to refill water glasses, bring bread to the tables, clear dishes when guests are finished eating, and quickly sweep the floors and wipe down tables when guests are leaving so that the next customers can sit down right away. The food runner typically stands near the kitchen, receives on a little printer or on a computer screen the computer orders that had been inputted by your server, yells out these orders to the chef, and then, walking as fast as possible without actually running between the kitchen and the dining floor, carries hot plates to the tables. Back in the kitchen, the person in charge—most likely the chef or sous chef—hollers orders to the kitchen staff and ensures that the "line" of cooks is moving as fast as humanly possible. The "line" deals with "the heat of the chef" and the heat of the kitchen at the same time—frying, sautéing, and grilling vegetables, seafood, and maybe 100 pieces of meat during peak time—usually dinner service. The prep cooks, stationed next to the line cooks, frantically peel, chop, and slice the raw ingredients. At the bottom of the ladder, the dishwashers clean everything up. Slammed with hundreds of dishes, they operate hot, heavy dishwashing machinery at an extremely fast pace. This means that they typically spend their shifts soaked in dirty, soapy water, constantly at risk of slipping and falling on a wet floor.

It's not surprising, then, that more than three-quarters of the restaurant workers we surveyed say that they've often worked when their restaurant was understaffed, and that they've often had to do several jobs at once, like switching back and forth between working with a hot, steamy dishwashing machine and hauling items from an ice-cold freezer room. Or running back and forth between the host stand and the dining floor to take orders and clear tables. Or grabbing a knife while turning on a burner. In addition, almost half of all workers report that they have had to fill in in jobs for which they had not been trained.[6]

To top it all off, when most restaurant workers are burned or cut or injured, or even when they are deathly ill, they can't afford to take a day off from work. In ROC's survey of more than 4,000 restaurant workers, we found that 90 percent did not have access to paid sick days,[7] and, with a median wage nationally of $9.02,[8] most cannot afford to take a day off from work. The result? Two-thirds of all restaurant workers reported preparing, cooking, and serving our meals while sick.[9] *Two-thirds!*

Nikki, who is now an ROC organizer in Washington, D.C., is one of millions of workers in the United States who have stories about working while sick. More broadly, Nikki helped deepen my understanding of how poor working conditions in restaurants affect the health of workers as well as consumers. When I first met Nikki—a tall, lean, light-skinned African American woman in her mid-twenties—I thought she was a fashion model. We met at a national ROC meeting. She was serious about our work, but vivacious and rowdy during our after-hours activities. I later learned that she also has a temper. She can furrow her brow, raise her high-pitched voice, and wave her hands passionately when she is making an argument. She can curse you out like a sailor, but she also has a big smile, revealing a gap between her teeth that totally charms you.

Nikki is biracial. Her mother is white, and her father is black. After her parents divorced, Nikki and her mom moved several times—first to Virginia, then to North Carolina, and then to Pennsylvania. "In all these small redneck towns my mom was never able to find a good job," says Nikki. "I went to 24 different public schools. My mom worked in an office, a prison, a dollar store, even for Maryland social services."

Nikki remembers the first time she got really angry about racial discrimination. "My mother and I lived in Cumberland, Maryland, a small, old, town," she says. "It had been a railroad town, and it was a really depressed area. There were very few black people. My mom had showed me the movie *Roots* in the second grade, and I remember feeling so hurt by white people. We lived in the projects, and a poor little white boy once called out to me, 'You're nothing but a nigger.' I had always thought of myself as a nice little girl, so when I heard that, I cried. I yelled back at him, 'Oh yeah, well you're just white trash.' When I went home and told my mom, she said I should never call people that."

Nikki also dealt with taunts at school. "I went to Southton Elementary, and there were two other black kids in my grade," she says. "I felt so alone and isolated because people treated me differently. We had just moved from Jacksonville, North Carolina, where there were lots of mixed kids. At Southton, they didn't let you choose where to sit at lunch. We would file into the lunchroom in a line and sit down at whatever table was available. One time I was the only black girl at my lunch table. The other boys would not talk to me. They were whispering to each other, and I heard them say 'nigger.' I knew they were probably talking about me. Another little boy said, 'You're not allowed to say that word,' and called the teacher. The teacher came over and said, '*Nigger* is not the appropriate word to use. The word is *Negro*.' It was 1992. This experience was one of primary motivations for me wanting to educate myself about African American literature and history, and for me wanting to do racial justice work."

Many of the African American members of ROC-DC can tell a similar story.

Nikki managed to do well in school and eventually attended the University of Maryland at College Park, where she majored in English with a special concentration in African American civil rights literature. She was thrilled by the diversity of the student population and the university's close proximity to the nation's capital. She says, "I wanted to become a college professor or high school teacher to teach young people about the positive contributions black and brown people have made to the country."

She also wanted the things every other college student wants—independence, adventure, romance, sex, excitement. College allowed her to explore her interests and gain greater self-awareness, but as her graduation date neared she worried constantly about her debts. She had received many scholarships and grants but still had over $50,000 in student loans to pay off. She knew she wasn't ready to go straight to graduate school and needed to work right away. "At first I thought I'd find a job that could utilize my English degree," she says, "but I only found data-entry jobs."

Running out of money fast, Nikki turned to the restaurant industry. She had been working in various restaurants to support herself from the time she was 15 years old. (This is fairly common. Twenty-five percent of American teens obtain their first job in the restaurant industry.)[10] She began working as a server in an upscale Mexican restaurant in downtown

Nikki Lewis protesting against discrimination with other ROC members. Courtesy of Sekou Luke.

Washington. Politicians, bureaucrats, and popular journalists were regular customers. The restaurant *looked* like a desirable place to work. Nevertheless, it experienced a lot of manager turnover. "Over a six-month period we had two different general managers and all different floor managers," says Nikki. "There were four or five people who had been there since the beginning, and they'd always talk about how many different managers they'd seen." Nikki was promoted to manager within six months, and she felt for the first time that she had found a profession that she truly enjoyed, one that drew on her skills and talents. Her promotion came with higher wages, more responsibility, and the potential to have a positive impact on the workers she managed. She aspired to treat the workers fairly and offer them training that would help them move up the ladder too.

However, she knew the restaurant had serious problems. One day, Nikki overheard her coworkers talking about an incident that had happened earlier in the week on a day she was off. A Latino porter stood on the metal edge of a greasy deep fryer to clear one of the ventilation hoods in the grill. He slipped slightly, and one of his feet fell into the deep fryer. The frying oil completely melted off the bottom of his shoe and severely burned his foot. Management offered him a Tylenol and sent him home. They didn't tell him about workers' compensation insurance, take him to the hospital, or offer to pay his medical bills. The restaurant company didn't offer paid sick days to employees, and since the porter earned less than $10 an hour, he couldn't afford to take time off to heal. Nikki never even knew his name, but she later learned that he had found outside help to file a workers' compensation insurance claim against the restaurant.

Nikki herself struggled financially. She made very low wages, even as a manager. She moved into the cheapest studio apartment she could find, in the southwest area of the city. The neighborhood had a reputation as a heavy drug-trafficking area and was experiencing the first tensions brought on by encroaching gentrification and redevelopment. "On my first night in the new apartment I heard several rounds of gunshots and police sirens," says Nikki. "I was awake for hours. There were lots of other violent incidents there." Nikki biked home from work every night, passing the Capitol, which was only six blocks from her low-income neighborhood.

Since Nikki was the "new hire" in the restaurant and new to fine dining, she didn't feel comfortable confronting her manager about her pay or other experiences that made her uneasy. She was also the only black woman to hold a management position, and so she felt vulnerable. She found it impossible to help other workers of color move up the ladder in the restaurant because other managers controlled hiring decisions and promotions. She even found herself participating in the culture of discrimination. "I would give the two white servers who were men the best shifts and tables because I found them attractive and enjoyed working with them," she says. Customers would also buy more from the white servers, and that made a difference, since Nikki's performance as a manager was judged by the sales made under her supervision.

Nikki tried very hard to build camaraderie with her new coworkers. She wanted to make a good impression and learn the ropes. She supported her coworkers during the day, helping them with their customers, and hung out with them after work. However, everything changed when she attended a party at the apartment of one of her coworkers. After a few drinks she fell asleep on the couch, and when she woke up a few hours later, she found herself being raped by a coworker. She was shocked, paralyzed, and horrified.

"Someone else walked into the room, but it was too late," she says. "I couldn't even leave the apartment; it was way too late to get on my bicycle and ride home through the streets of D.C. I had to crash on that couch and wait until daylight. It was humiliating. While it didn't happen at the workplace, I feel very strongly that the culture of acceptance of rampant sexual harassment in the restaurant industry shaped my coworker's decision to rape me that night, because he probably had never seen serious consequences for that type of behavior…and neither had I. So I was silent."

She left her job at the restaurant to cope with the trauma.

Visible Signs of Illness and Poor Health

After a few weeks of searching, Nikki found a waitressing job at a popular late-night establishment. "I started serving martinis and other drinks on a tray," she says. "We worked long, long hours, like 10 or 12 hours per day. The very first Saturday night I worked there, I went into the bathroom because I started feeling nauseous. Around midnight, I threw up. I told the manager, who told me to rest in the restaurant's office and then go back to work."

Unfortunately, this happened several times. Most weekend nights Nikki ended up working so hard, without a break, in the heat, that she began feeling sick to her stomach. "I wouldn't have time to go to the bathroom," she says. On top of that, Nikki's coworkers started reporting that their paychecks were bouncing.

Nikki began looking for a better job, and she thought she'd finally found a better position when she was hired as a bartender at an upscale American restaurant. The chef there was committed to using organic and local ingredients. The servers were trained to talk to customers about the menu, emphasizing the organic and local items. "I didn't really know what organic meant," says Nikki, "but I knew it was a trendy way to sell."

However, there were all sorts of problems, even at this trendy, upscale restaurant. When she inquired about her first paycheck, management told her that she would not be receiving an hourly wage and would be expected to live off her tips. She put up with it for a while because she was able to make a decent amount in tips—enough to pay her rent, at least initially—but soon she discovered that the restaurant was not able to pay its vendors properly either. "At one point the vendor who provided paper goods and soap to the restaurant stopped delivering because their bill wasn't paid," says Nikki. "So there was no soap. There was no soap in the bathrooms or to wash dishes for a whole month. They'd just wash the dishes with hot water and reuse them for the next customer. Customers would complain about the lack of soap in the bathroom, and management would say, 'Oh my gosh, thanks so much for letting us know,' and then not do anything about it."

After a month on the job, Nikki contracted an allergy type of conjunctivitis, or "pink eye." She woke up with a bloodred, watering right eye. "It was disgusting—really, really nasty," she says. "I was freaking out about it. It was too nasty to be around customers and their food and drink." She called her manager, who told her to call around and find another worker to cover her shift, but when no one could take the shift, she had to work with pink eye because the restaurant was severely understaffed. "I had to go to work because I didn't want to risk losing my job or getting fired," she says. "Everyone said, 'Ewww, don't get near me! What's wrong with your eye?' I was pissed because the manager was standing behind the host stand the entire night, chatting. The restaurant was not that busy. The manager could have handled the bar. I didn't need to be there with something like that."

Nikki worked with pink eye for several days, without any insurance benefits that would have enabled her to see a doctor. "I needed to get better," she says, "so I started doing my own research. I started asking everyone where I could go to get help with this. I went to three different clinics, and they wanted $100 just to see me. One of my friends suggested I go to a CVS pharmacy. I went to three different CVS drugstores. Two said they couldn't help me without insurance. The third CVS told me they had some over-the-counter stuff. I found it and went online to learn more about conjunctivitis. I had an allergy-type infection. I had to learn about it all alone. It was so frustrating. It could have been easily solved with a doctor's help, but I had to deal with it all on my own."

Before long, Nikki couldn't survive on the tips she made. She stopped being able to pay her rent and received an eviction notice. She was forced to crash with her new boyfriend of only three months.

The restaurant eventually closed down. "It had been poorly managed," says Nikki. "It had gone through two or three chefs in the four years it was open. There was constant inconsistency on health and safety issues and the organization of the whole restaurant. Things were broken or poorly maintained in the back."

When Nikki found herself jobless again, she knew she needed to do something different.

Dangerous Dining

We don't just find workers serving while sick in a few "bad apple" restaurants. We find these workers everywhere, and most of them report feeling helpless about their situation. One reason for this is that the National Restaurant Association (NRA) has spent years lobbying to prevent restaurant workers from winning paid sick days. In Washington, D.C., the NRA struck a closed-door deal with the city council to exempt all tipped workers from a local paid sick-leave law. So, ironically, employers in the one industry in which we as customers would least like to see workers working while sick are the same ones leading the charge against any kind of paid sick-day legislation.

In 2011, the CDC reported that almost 12 percent (11.9%) of restaurant workers say that they'd continued to work while suffering from flu symptoms, vomiting, or diarrhea on two or more shifts in the last year. Imagine that—more than 1 in 10 times that you eat out, your server takers your order, goes to the bathroom to vomit like Nikki did, and then brings you your order. Not surprisingly, the CDC also found that workers were approximately half as likely to report working while vomiting or suffering from diarrhea if they had paid sick leave.

What message does this send to consumers? Well, for one thing, we're allowing ourselves to get sick. When workers feel compelled to serve food while sick, they are at higher risk of suffering prolonged illness on the job, and customers are at higher risk of contracting foodborne illnesses.

This is not news. The very first documented case of a "healthy carrier" of disease was a restaurant worker. Mary Mallon, an immigrant cook from eastern Europe better known as "Typhoid Mary," was the first person in the United States to be identified as a carrier of the pathogen associated with typhoid fever. She likely infected 53 people, 3 of whom died, between 1900 and 1907. Mary worked in seven different restaurant kitchens before authorities discovered that she was spreading typhoid to diners citywide.

Unfortunately, the easy transfer of illness in a restaurant is not a thing of the past. In fact, the CDC has cited restaurants as the third most frequent setting for outbreaks of foodborne illnesses—just behind cruise ships and long-term care facilities. In summer 2011, thousands of people were exposed to hepatitis in an Olive Garden restaurant in Fayetteville, North Carolina, because a server couldn't take a day off from work without losing his job. Nearly 3,000 people in the Fayetteville area had to be vaccinated by order of county health officials.

Forced to "Just Fight It Off"

In the summer of 2009, ROC's affiliate in Washington, D.C., opened its doors. Nikki found her way to ROC-DC, and so did several other workers, including a young man named Woong Chang. Woong had experienced one of the worst cases of serving while sick that I—or anyone at ROC—had ever heard of. His story opened my eyes to just how bleak life can become for workers who struggle with illness on the job.

Woong is in his early thirties, tall, lean, and handsome. He is a party animal, but also a serious thinker. You'd mistake him for a quiet guy if it weren't for the spike in his hair that gives away his wild side.

Woong was born and raised in Korea. Before he started school, his parents applied for and obtained a visa to come to the United States.

They wanted to give Woong and his sister the opportunity to get a better education than they'd been able to get in Korea. "After my dad graduated from dental school," says Woong, "he found that he was able to make enough money to support his family as a dentist. After several years of hard work building up his business, he received an envelope from the U.S. embassy with a letter saying that our visa was about to expire. So he called a family meeting. My parents had to decide whether they should risk the financial stability they had worked for over the last many years to move to America."

In the end, the answer was yes. Woong's parents felt that the most important thing was for Woong and his sister to have educational opportunities they'd never have in Korea. Woong's father decided to keep his dental practice; he'd return to Korea twice a year for three-month stints to work in his chosen profession. However, Woong's family gave up almost everything else they had. They moved to Los Angeles with a few suitcases, the clothes on their backs, and Woong's aunt and uncle following close behind them.

After going to UC Berkeley to fulfill his parents' dream of their children getting a better education, Woong became a carpenter for a few years before deciding to scrape together whatever money he could to travel. "I converted a diesel truck to vegetable oil and drove around the country for about six months," says Woong. "Then I decided to go see Latin America by bus. I lived in Buenos Aires for six months, and I managed a bar. I traveled through almost all of South America, and then drove on to Central America. I stopped in Costa Rica and worked as a food and beverage manager."

Nine years passed. When Woong finally returned to the United States, he was excited to take his career in the restaurant industry to the next level. He'd enjoyed serving food and drinks in many different countries and meeting all kinds of people. First, he returned to California, where he saw both the challenges and the opportunities of working in U.S. restaurants. While waiting tables at an upscale Berkeley restaurant, he saw a cook burn his hand so badly during a busy brunch shift that his entire palm was bubbly with blisters by the end of the shift. "It must have been so painful to work like that. But he never left the kitchen. He just worked through the pain. Later, when I asked him why he didn't go to the hospital, he simply said, 'You don't leave the kitchen. The guys on the line would've been in the shits.' No injury report or workers' compensation claim was ever

Woong Chang at work mixing drinks. Courtesy of Woong Chang.

filed." The restaurant, of course, did not encourage the worker to take any time off.

Nevertheless, Woong moved to Washington, D.C., full of optimism that he could make a living doing what he loved—serving food. Unfortunately, Woong arrived in the nation's capital just as a new pandemic—H1N1, or "swine flu"—started raising alarm bells.

Woong accepted a position in a brand-new, upscale French restaurant. He was only there one month before he contracted swine flu. "I worked for a few days while sick," he says. "The first day I had a sore throat. I just thought I was coming down with something. By the third day I really should not have been there. On the fourth day, I couldn't get out of bed. I called the restaurant to say, 'I'm really sick.' I didn't know how much longer I would be out. They didn't say I had to come, but there was no thought of paid sick time. I worked for as long as I could because I couldn't afford not to. They just said OK."

Woong had never been so sick. "Over two and a half weeks it just kept getting worse and worse," he says. "My throat was swollen shut, so I couldn't eat anything, no solids. Soups were the only thing I could eat. It was hard for me to breathe. I was running a fever. I had an unbelievable temperature. I was constantly drooling. My girlfriend was the one taking care of me. She had to come in the middle of night to check if I was still breathing. She was scared because I would pass in and out of sleep."

He ended up in bed for a month without pay. He piled on credit card debt to survive. When he was finally able to go back to work, he found out that he no longer had a job. He had been replaced. Demoralized and destitute, he wondered whom he had infected at the restaurant. Coworkers? Customers? The managers didn't let him return to work, so he never found out.

The days Woong spent in bed without a job, living off credit cards, were some of the worst he had ever known. He felt helpless without income or health insurance; he couldn't go back to work, and he couldn't get better. At one point he thought he'd seek help from the Korean community. "I went to Koreatown in Virginia to see if they'd treat me without insurance, cut me a discount," he says. "Since it was my own ethnic community, I thought I'd see if they could hook me up. I saw a doctor there, and he ran some tests." The doctor took pity on him and gave him a discount on a medical exam that confirmed he had indeed contracted H1N1. "Stay home," the doctor advised. "You'll just have to fight it off." The doctor prescribed some drugs and sent Woong away.

The experience made Woong very angry. Adding to his frustration was the fact that the minimum wage for tipped workers in Washington, D.C., was $2.77. "Coming from California, where tipped workers have the same minimum wage as everyone else, that wage for tipped workers was a huge shock," says Woong. "In California, I could expect to take home wages of at least $300 to $400 each week. In D.C., with a wage of $2.77, taxes would cancel out my wages, so that my take-home pay, without tips, would be $0."

There was never a guarantee of making enough to survive. If a worker got sick and missed just one shift, he risked not having enough money to pay rent and could easily end up homeless. Woong found this appalling, especially since he was a college graduate and was qualified to hold some of the higher-paying jobs in the industry. "I knew I wasn't like other immigrant workers I saw every day," he says. "I was fortunate because I spoke

English, because I was a college graduate, because I earned higher tips than other workers." He had privilege. If he could be wiped out because of illness, he shuddered to think how others made it, especially new immigrants working in the kitchen. "Those folks had the best work ethic of anyone I'd ever met in the restaurant industry," says Woong. "My friend José, one of the first real friends I had in a restaurant, was one of the kindest, hardworking souls I've ever met. He studied harder, worked harder, and deserved to be promoted more than anyone, yet he received terrible pay and endured discrimination simply because he was a more recent immigrant and didn't have the same privileges that I have been so fortunate to have." If he could be wiped out so severely by illness, Woong couldn't imagine how workers like Jose could possibly survive without paid sick days.

From the Kitchen to the Capitol

After recovering from swine flu, Woong started looking for a new restaurant job on Craigslist. He read advertisement after advertisement, until finally he happened on an announcement from ROC-DC. We needed instructors for our customer service and bartending classes. "I needed money fast," says Woong. "I needed any job that would bring in money. When I saw that ad, I thought, I can do that. I can teach classes."

Almost immediately upon arriving at the offices of ROC-DC, Woong knew he had found a community. He also met Nikki, who talked about how her love of the restaurant industry—combined with the challenges she'd faced as a worker—had made her incredibly eager to get involved with ROC. She had recently helped to conduct over 500 surveys of restaurant workers in the D.C. area. It had been grueling, tiring work, but she said she'd learned so much. Hundreds of women and men had shared their experiences with her—stories of exploitation, poverty, discrimination, and illness—and had energized her to work with ROC to change the industry.

Woong and Nikki hit it off right away. They joined the ROC-DC Policy Committee and began working to amend D.C.'s paid sick-leave law. They wanted to put an end to the conditions that left workers like them interacting with customers while suffering from pink eye and H1N1. ROC's national survey data showed that almost 90 percent of workers reported that they did not receive paid sick days or health insurance from their employer. One woman server joked, "Any benefits... well, a free sandwich here and there.... I have no health care right now so we all walk real lightly."[11] ROC's research also demonstrated that restaurant workers' lack of health care ended up costing taxpayers money. More than one in five workers reported that they or a family member had gone to the emergency room in the last year without being able to pay.[12] Restaurant workers without health benefits were three times as likely as those with health benefits to use the emergency room (they could not receive care elsewhere); these workers were also three times as likely as other emergency room visitors to go to the emergency room without being able to pay for it.[13] So the U.S. government must use taxpayer dollars to subsidize an industry that doesn't take care of its own employees.

Nikki and Woong decided to try a new, creative approach to confronting and raising awareness of the issue. They organized a local "Carrot Mob," an event intended to demonstrate consumer support for restaurants that are trying to be shining examples in the industry. The idea was for certain restaurants to be the "carrots" that get more restaurants to do the right thing. Nikki and the team at ROC-DC pulled together close to 100 restaurant workers and their allies to eat at Teaism, a local restaurant partner of ROC, to demonstrate the popularity of treating workers well. Woong spoke at the event about his experiences and presented the owner of Teaism with an oversized cardboard carrot. The owner was moved and decided to start offering paid sick leave to all of his workers in three D.C. restaurants. Another restaurant owner, who was the runner-up in the "Carrot Mob" competition, followed suit and provided sick days for all of his employees as well. As a result of the "Carrot Mob," 500 low-wage restaurant workers in D.C. won paid sick leave for the first time![14]

"Paid sick days seem like the most basic human right," says Woong. "Lots of other professionals receive them. People get trained and certified to work in the restaurant industry, but we aren't treated as professionals and just don't get these basic human rights. Why is that? It's not a good thing for the industry. It's bad enough when people go to work sick in an office setting, but we are talking about people who literally touch your food and beverages. I'm coughing up H1N1 in your face."

The "Carrot Mob" victory inspired Nikki to pursue a full-time leadership role at ROC. We hired her as an organizer, and a month later she attended ROC's Fourth Annual National Restaurant Workers' Convening in Detroit. She walked into a room full of other restaurant worker leaders, mostly immigrants and people of color, excited about the special role ROC-DC could play in bringing their voices to Capitol Hill.

In the spring of 2010, Nikki became a lobbyist for the first time. The National Restaurant Association (NRA), which represents large restaurant corporations, had been organizing lobbying days on Capitol Hill for many years. Of course, their priorities were clear: ensure that Congress did not increase the minimum wage for tipped workers, pass any kind of paid sick-leave law, or allow restaurant workers to unionize. The NRA held all-day meetings in the congressional buildings, and then they hosted fancy dinners and bar meetings, during which lobbyists and members of Congress could talk privately. Year after year the NRA had managed to be the only voice representing the restaurant industry in Washington, and it had succeeded in maintaining the status quo.

Nikki and some of her fellow ROC members had an idea. Why not organize a counter–lobby day with restaurant workers? They could gather members from ROC-DC and neighboring ROC-NY to visit with the same legislators targeted by the NRA—on the same day—to present a different perspective on the industry. "We had about two dozen restaurant workers and a few allies that we split into groups to meet with Congress members," says Nikki. "I talked to as many Congress members as I could, and I told them my story." She talked about her struggles in the industry, and why an increase in the tipped minimum wage, and paid sick leave, were critical for the health and well-being of workers *and* consumers. As a result of all the workers' efforts, more than two dozen new members of Congress signed on to the Healthy Families Act, which would provide seven paid sick days for all U.S. workers. In addition, Congresswoman Donna Edwards, a former restaurant worker herself, introduced a bill called the WAGES Act, the first bill in United States history to specifically address the needs of tipped workers. Sixty-three members of Congress signed on to the act, and it continues to move through Congress. The bill has a real chance of passing, but not without consumers across the United States voicing their outrage at being exposed to illness every time we eat out.

For Nikki and Woong and other ROC members nationwide, every time consumers speak up about the issue, every battle that is won to advance paid sick days, every opportunity that is seized to raise the issue with policymakers at the local, state, and federal levels, means a great deal. "Lots of ROC-DC members had lived in D.C. most of their lives but had never been on Capitol Hill or in the halls of these congressional buildings," says Nikki. "They had no idea that the people on Capitol Hill would listen—in fact, *had* to listen—to us."

Nikki and Woong's counter–lobby day in 2010 was the first time in U.S. history that a group of restaurant workers had lobbied on Capitol Hill against NRA interests. A reporter from the *Nation* later wrote a feature article on the visit, calling it "a battle of David and Goliath."[15] This was encouraging to Nikki and Woong and to all of us at ROC. In the Bible, David won.

Prioritizing Healthy Food, Workers, and Diners

I'm not arguing that no one will ever get food poisoning again if workers have paid sick days, access to health care, higher wages, and safer, healthier work environments. But I am arguing that these changes would make a significant, positive impact on the health and safety of both workers and consumers. Although more research is needed to prove a correlation, the number of foodborne illness outbreaks dropped from 18 to 4 in San Francisco after 2007, when a citywide ordinance compelled every restaurant to provide paid sick days to all employees.[16]

I'm also not trying to paint a picture of doom and gloom with nasty and disgusting tales of unsanitary kitchens. The industry has many shining examples of employers who take care of their workers'—and consequently, their customers'—health and well-being. I'm simply arguing that these shining examples need to become the norm rather than the exception—for everyone's sake.

One simple path to getting there is to win paid sick days for every restaurant worker in the United States. If every one of us who eats in restaurants demanded—through an e-mail, a letter, a phone call, or a visit—that our representatives in Congress vote for paid sick days, we could ensure that the people who prepare, cook, and serve our food are not forced to work while sick. In addition, we could ensure that the employers who are shining examples in the industry no longer have to stick their necks out, providing paid sick leave when others do not.

We as consumers should demand this for our own health, but we should also demand it because every time a restaurant worker serves while sick— every time a worker can't take a sick day because his or her wages are little more than $2 an hour and are completely eaten up by taxes—it eats away at the core belief we have in the restaurant industry and in America: that there is opportunity. It destroys the idea that you can start as a dishwasher and end up as a restaurant owner—because if you can never work your way out of medical debt and get a promotion, the "rags to riches" story is an impossible dream.

We should also care because the opposite is true as well. When workers are paid and treated well, they stay in one restaurant longer, and we eat better! The food is better, the service is certainly better, and we can feel better knowing our server doesn't have H1N1 or pink eye, isn't living in the attic, and has the chance to enjoy a healthy, prosperous life.

4

$2.13 — The Tipping Point

Right now, earning $2.13 per hour, I don't have enough for my
kids, I can't put them through college. I barely have enough to put
food on the table.

— Server, Man, New Orleans

I'm not even worth one cheeseburger an hour.

— Busser, Man, Six Years in the Industry, Chicago

We don't usually think of food service workers as poor, if we think of them at all.

I used to be a bad tipper. Even though I ate out frequently, I didn't understand what tipping really meant. Part of me resented the whole idea. Weren't servers being paid for their jobs? Why did I need to pay more than the price of my meal? Wasn't service part of the menu price? I worked hard for my money, and eating out was a guilty pleasure, so feeling compelled to leave something extra just didn't seem right. If I left $5 for a $40 meal, I felt good about myself.

It took me years to understand how tipping really works. First, I learned that my $5 is shared by many different people: the waiter who takes my order, the runner who brings out my food, and the bussers who clean my table and refill my bread basket and water. In some restaurants, the waiter has to ask a bartender to prepare the drinks, and a barback may assist. In the finest fine-dining restaurants, a captain greets customers and oversees the service they receive. All those workers get a piece of my $5.

Here's the worst part: the federal minimum wage for tipped workers is *$2.13 an hour.* That means the federal government permits restaurants nationwide to pay tipped workers an hourly wage of only $2.13, as long as the workers' tips make up the difference between $2.13 and the federal minimum hourly wage of $7.25. If the tips do not cover the difference, the employer is supposed to pay it. In 32 states, the tipped minimum wage is actually higher than the federal tipped minimum wage (e.g., $2.65 or $4.25 an hour), and in 7 states the minimum wage is the same for tipped and nontipped workers.[1] However, 13 states operate under the federal tipped minimum wage of $2.13, and another 8 states have a tipped minimum wage of less than $3.00 an hour. Thus, 21 states—almost half of the United States—allow restaurants to pay their employees less than $3.00 an hour. In several of those states, there is no state minimum wage at all. That means some restaurants in these states can get away with not paying their workers anything! As long as these restaurants bring in less than $500,000 in revenue annually (and therefore don't fall under the purview of federal law), they can force their workers to live entirely off their tips.[2]

The system is further complicated by the rules governing who gets a share of the tips. In a restaurant that complies with the law, the only workers taking a share of the tips are the nonmanagerial employees, who interact directly with customers. Ideally, a waiter collects tips from his or her tables and distributes them among the employees described above. In a "pooled house," the waiter puts all of his or her tips into a pool, and at the end of the night, all of the tips in the house are distributed among service employees using a point system—five points for captains, four points for waiters, and three points for runners, for example. In a "nonpooled house," the waiter collects his or her tips and then, using a percentage system, "tips out" the runner, bussers, bartender, and others at the end of the night.

However, many restaurants break the rules, allowing managers to take a share of the tips. Thirteen percent of workers nationwide report that managers regularly steal tips.[3] Some workers report that they've been forced to turn over all of their tips to management, and they've received a flat rate, or "shift pay" (also illegal!). Workers who work banquets or special functions in restaurants frequently complain that "service charges"—the "gratuity" charged to customers—disappear at the end of events; these workers end up receiving a flat rate for their work, without any knowledge of how much gratuity management collected.

When I began organizing restaurant workers, I knew that restaurant workers were poor, often living below the poverty line. I understood the basics: some workers don't receive the minimum wage, some don't get proper overtime payments, some don't receive pay for all the hours they've worked, and some get paid late or not at all. Some are even charged for things that aren't their fault, like a guest walking out of the restaurant without paying the check. Most of us have heard about the plight of fast-food workers in the United States, and it's not surprising when cheap chain restaurants pay their workers poverty-level wages.

I also knew, however, that the restaurant industry laid claim to some "shining examples," restaurant owners who wanted to abolish poverty-level wages and offer workers a decent standard of living. Jason Murphy and Ben Hall, an unlikely pair of longtime friends and former dishwashers, are shining examples of employers who not only pay their workers a living wage but also offer raises, IRAs, and health insurance and have a commitment to diversity. They own the Russell Street Deli, a bustling, profitable sandwich and soup restaurant in Detroit. Later in this chapter I'll tell the story of how Jason and Ben have shattered expectations, going from dishwashers to restaurant owners, and built a business using social justice principles.

Still, fair and equitable labor practices are extraordinarily rare in the restaurant industry. Restaurant workers hold 7 of the 10 lowest-paying occupations in the United States, earning less, on average, than farmworkers and all other domestic workers.[4] Although the industry has grown steadily over the last 20 years, restaurant workers continue to earn significantly less than workers in almost every other industry. In 2010, the median wage for restaurant workers nationwide was $9.02 an hour, including tips—a wage that leaves a family of four below the federal poverty line.[5] In 2009, restaurant workers made, on average, $15,092. Workers throughout the rest of the private sector made, on average, $45,155.[6]

All of this probably sounds confusing because it *is* confusing. The minimum wage system for tipped workers is totally dysfunctional. It's a system that permits and even encourages employers to underpay their employees, and forces us, the consumers, to try to make up the difference.

The American Dream at $2.13

Claudia, a former low-wage worker in a national pancake restaurant, is a slender, young Mexican immigrant with big brown eyes and long black hair. She laughs often and loves kids. She's also one of the smartest people I know. She reads voraciously and is an articulate, outspoken advocate for the needs of workers. Thus, I was really surprised when I learned that at one point she had not been able to speak up for herself or her coworkers. In fact, it worried me. If someone as brilliant and articulate as Claudia had not been able to speak up against exploitation, how could we expect anyone else to do so?

Claudia is from the foothills of Monterrey, Mexico. "I was the youngest of nine kids," she says. "My mom didn't finish second grade, and my dad only made it to third grade. But my parents always told me, 'You want to be something, you have to go school.' We weren't a poor family—I never went hungry or had to quit school to work—but we definitely struggled financially."

Before Claudia was born, her mother became friends with an American woman who was living in Mexico. The friend would often do her grocery shopping across the border in Texas, where groceries were actually cheaper in bulk. "My mom's friend told her there were people in Laredo giving out tourist visas for Mexicans to visit the United States," says Claudia. "She took my mom to the border."

A group of university students greeted Claudia's mom in Laredo and asked her why she wanted a tourist visa. "She said she had to buy groceries for her large family," says Claudia. "It wasn't an office, just a group of university students at a booth who gave my mom a pink visa that didn't have an expiration date. A month later the visa came in the mail." Claudia's mom got the whole family tourist visas this way. It was the 1970s. Immigration policies were more relaxed back then.

Claudia remembers a difficult, lonely childhood. "My dad was security guard for a newspaper," she says. "My mom had nine children. She was from a very, very poor background. She didn't even have shoes until she was in grade school. She was a devout Catholic, and she believed in having lots of children. She could sew very well, so she made dresses to sell and some for us. I remember my parents working, always working. There was a room in the house just for the sewing machines. I hated those machines because my mom was always with them. I had eight much older brothers and sisters, and they were all always working too."

Sometimes Claudia's mother would take her along on grocery shopping trips across the border. "I thought, Everybody's rich here. Wow. People have everything!" says Claudia. "I was always in awe of the United States. I remember when I was growing up, six or seven years old, Wal-Mart started coming to Mexico, and then Sam's Club, OfficeMax, all these American stores. I have very vivid memories of my brothers-in-law working for American companies. It felt like America was moving into Mexico."

Claudia struggled through elementary school. "The teachers were telling my mom that I was very smart, but I had a behavior problem," she says. Outside of school she got into trouble as well. She stole fruit from neighbors' trees out of boredom. "I would always be walking along the street, chewing stolen fruit," she says. "I didn't have any guidance. My brothers and sisters were two to three years apart in age, but I was eight years younger than everyone else. My mom was a great, loving mother and would make sure I ate, but she didn't have time for anything else. I was very lonely and angry. I remember loving school, but I didn't care about my homework, and that came from being angry."

Things changed somewhat when Claudia's school started a literacy program for parents and their children. Claudia's mother would go to school with her to read and write. "I was a little older, doing very well in school," says Claudia. "My mom and I became close. She wasn't working as much by the time I was 10, and my dad retired. When my mom started reading and writing, she spent more time with me."

Claudia finally got the time with her mom that she had craved. So it was especially hard for her when she found out a few years later that her mom had a brain aneurysm and would have to stay in the hospital. Claudia ended up at home alone again. Her eldest sister, whose infant daughter was born with heart issues, had left for the United States; she knew people in Austin, Texas, and so she moved there using the tourist visa her mother had acquired for her years before. Claudia's sister's husband had lost his job—but really, no job in Mexico would have paid for everything necessary to keep their baby girl alive. Another sister moved to Austin when her husband, an architect, lost his job; she and her husband started working in restaurants when they arrived in Texas, despite having degrees and professional experience.

Claudia began high school with her mother still in the hospital and many family members gone. She spent most of her time alone in the house in Monterrey. The neighborhood was changing, with drug-related crime on the rise, and soon she didn't even feel comfortable being there. One night someone broke into the house. Another night someone broke into her second-oldest sister Lupita's car. Claudia knew she had to do something. She would be graduating from high school in two years and didn't have money for college. When Lupita lost her job as a graphic designer, she suggested to Claudia that they leave Monterrey to join their older sisters and brothers-in-law in Austin. "My sister said, 'Let's go for three months, save money, and come back,'" says Claudia. "But we didn't. We stayed."

Claudia was 15. She and Lupita arrived in Austin and stayed with their fifth-oldest sister, Carolina, who lived in a studio apartment with her husband and three children. Carolina didn't work, but she cooked delicious Mexican meals—sopes, enchiladas, and more—for the household and took care of her three kids. After dinner, Claudia helped Carolina's kids with their homework before she started her own. Carolina knew she couldn't stay home for long with two additional mouths to feed. She was also exhausted from watching the kids and cooking for everyone. When Carolina found two jobs, Claudia had to start coming home right after school to watch the kids and everyone ate frozen food, Hot Pockets, and frozen pizza rolls.

The adults were not home much during the week, but on weekends the apartment overflowed with people. Carolina invited her other sisters and family to join them for weekend meals. "We wanted to re-create our life back in Mexico, where everyone would show up at our parents' house and eat the delicious meals our mom cooked," says Claudia. The kids played outside on a tiny lawn while the women cooked lunch and talked about life. The men watched soccer on television. "At some point we would all play Loteria, the Mexican version of Bingo," says Claudia. "Carolina's mixed tapes would be playing in the background." Carolina's tapes mixed Mexican and American music. "There'd be a ranchero song, then Madonna, then a salsa song, then Michael Jackson," says Claudia. The music reflected their hybrid life.

Of course, it was also a tough life in Austin. The studio apartment had a loft; Carolina, her husband, and her three children all slept there. Claudia and Lupita slept on couches on the lower level of the apartment. "We kept all of our stuff in a closet in the loft, which was hard because the kids would always play with our things, and we could never find anything," says Claudia. It was nice to be close to family, but seven people in one studio apartment naturally led to arguments and general discomfort.

Claudia also had a tough time in school. Americans were not as welcoming as she'd imagined. "For two months I would cry every single day," she says. "I didn't know English, and I was thrown into high school. I hated it. I wasn't welcomed like I thought I would be. It was a harsh reality: Americans didn't like me as much as I'd liked them in Mexico. People were mean. But my sister Lupita found a guy and fell in love one month after we got to Austin—a black guy she's still with. She told me, 'We have a real chance of remaking our lives.'" Claudia didn't feel that hopeful, but as a minor she had little choice but to stay.

Lupita worked multiple jobs to contribute to the household and enable Claudia to focus on school. Once Claudia realized that she wasn't going back home to Mexico, she decided to make the best of her life in Texas. "I just got used to the idea that I was going to have to live here," she says. "I started studying hard, made friends, didn't have much choice. My sisters were always at work. Everybody worked. There were times when I'd have to walk to school and back, really far. I decided I'd go to the library and stay until Lupita could pick me up from work. I started getting involved in extracurricular activities to kill time, because I was lonely. I didn't want to ruin my life."

Claudia wanted to fit in and have white American friends, maybe even be a white American. "I wanted to join the dance team, but it was very costly to do that," she says. "I knew I wouldn't be able to ride the bus, go on field trips. I knew I needed a job." A classmate told her that a national pancake chain was hiring, and so Claudia decided to apply.

When Claudia walked into the restaurant, she immediately noticed that all the servers were attractive women. Her friend introduced her to the manager, who quickly agreed to hire Claudia as a server. Claudia hesitated to accept the position because she couldn't speak English fluently.

"I said, 'Shouldn't I do something else?' He said, 'No, you can serve Latino customers.' But that didn't happen," says Claudia. "The customers would say very mean things, like, 'We don't want you as our waitress.' I would pretend like I didn't understand."

There was another problem: many customers wouldn't tip her. She was earning $2.13 an hour, the minimum wage for tipped workers, and working 30 to 40 hours a week. Her tips never made up the difference between the minimum wage for tipped workers and the full minimum wage of $7.25, and the restaurant manager chastised her for it. "We'll have to pay this difference," he told her, referring to the federal law mandating that employers pay the difference between the lower minimum wage for tipped workers and the regular minimum wage when workers' tips don't cover the difference. "The restaurant told us we had to make the money up in tips or get in trouble," says Claudia. "The manager said, 'If you don't make enough tips to make up the difference [between the tipped minimum wage and the regular minimum wage], you have to report that you made that money anyway.' He told me to report tips I wasn't making, so that the company didn't have to pay the difference." Since Claudia was a teenager and new immigrant, she accepted this. Besides, she wanted to join the dance team and couldn't afford to without her job.

Claudia's family continued to struggle financially. Both her brother-in-law and Lupita worked as cooks at a restaurant, and Lupita had a second job at a newspaper. Every day they drove 50 minutes to earn minimum wage in a restaurant. Although they worked 50 to 60 hours a week, they could barely afford the gas it took to get to their jobs. Claudia's brother-in-law, the architect, still works in that restaurant.

Getting through School as an Undocumented Immigrant

When Claudia was about to graduate from high school, she realized that she didn't even know whether undocumented people could go to college. She found a guardian angel, Alejandra, who helped her explore her options. Alejandra worked for the Austin Independent School District. "She was the immigrant person for the district," says Claudia, "and she was really open about that stuff. I started going to her office based on a flyer that said if you don't have papers, come talk to her." Alejandra encouraged

Claudia to get involved with local advocacy groups for immigrant students in Texas. She explained that many undocumented students in Texas end up having to pay out-of-state tuition for college even when they have spent their whole lives in Texas. Out-of-state tuition was often double or triple the cost of in-state tuition, making college impossible for thousands of immigrant students. Claudia got involved, participating in many lobbying events in the state capital.

Alejandra also told her about a special program at Prairie View A & M University, a historically black college about 20 miles from Houston. The university's president, Charles Hines, was sympathetic to the struggles of new immigrants and committed to making sure that undocumented students could receive a college education. The university offered a summer preparatory academic boot camp to any graduating senior interested in Prairie View. The top three students at the end of the summer received a full scholarship to the four-year college. Alejandra encouraged Claudia to attend.

Claudia, however, didn't want to go to an academic boot camp; she wanted to go on a trip to the beach with her high school friends. She also didn't want to go to a historically black college in the middle of Texas. "I talked to my family about it, like, 'What am I going to do in the middle of Texas, with all black people?'" she says. Claudia hadn't seen black people before coming to the United States. Lupita's partner was African American, but Claudia and her family still harbored a lot of anxiety about black people. Plus, after feeling the pain of being different as a new immigrant, Claudia had worked hard to become an "all-American girl," joining the dance team with her mostly white high school friends. Nevertheless, Alejandra pushed Claudia to go to Prairie View. She told her she could go on a beach trip anytime and said the Austin school district would cover her $300 tuition. Claudia agreed to give the program a chance.

That summer happened to be the fiftieth anniversary of the *Brown v. Board of Education* Supreme Court decision. The Prairie View administrators decided to honor the occasion by taking students on a tour of historic sites of the civil rights movement. Claudia saw the bridge in Selma, Alabama, where protesters were attacked with fire hoses. She saw places in Mississippi and North Carolina where thousands marched for freedom and equality. "I got excited," she says. "I started learning about the history of oppression in this country. I had been experiencing it, but I didn't know.

In Mexico I didn't think of America as oppressive. I thought of it as a place of opportunity. But in Austin I became really aware of who I am and where I fit in this country. I remember learning that my school had been a plantation. There was a slave grave at school. In Selma, I got to meet the people who had walked on the bridge. After that trip, I started studying harder to be able to attend the school."

Something long dormant in Claudia was awakened during the trip to historic civil rights sites. Her immigration experience took on new meaning. She became a lot more interested in attending Prairie View and started studying to compete for a college scholarship. She knew she wouldn't be able to attend college otherwise. "I was talking to my family as I was learning about the civil rights movement," says Claudia. "And I told them, 'I have to understand their history. I really want to go to college.' My sister told me, 'I didn't have the chance to go to college, so I will keep my two jobs to support you.'"

Claudia's mom, now recovered from the brain aneurysm, decided to come to Texas on her tourist visa for Claudia's graduation from the summer academy. "I didn't know I had won the scholarship," says Claudia. "My mom came for my graduation, and when they announced that I'd won, my mom was crying."

Still, Claudia thought she'd have to turn down the scholarship when she found out that it didn't cover living expenses. She couldn't afford to live on her own. Once again, though, Alejandra came to the rescue. She spoke to a university administrator about Claudia's situation, and the administrator invited Claudia to live with her and her husband.

College was a dream for Claudia. She became a leader on campus, organizing her classmates in support of the DREAM Act, which would allow undocumented students nationwide to go to college, and other racial justice issues. After the hanging of nooses and other race-baiting actions led to physical violence at a high school in Jena, Louisiana, Claudia organized two busloads of students to rally in support of the "Jena Six." At one point someone contacted Claudia about an exciting community-organizing internship opportunity in Washington, D.C. "Alejandra had always wanted me to work with the community," says Claudia. "I was so excited when I heard I got the internship. Two days before I was to go—when I had already purchased my ticket—they called me to say that they had talked to their lawyers and couldn't hire me. It really struck me. I was heartbroken. I cried. In this country even when you want to do something good, sometimes you can't."

Claudia at her graduation from Prairie View A & M University, with her older sister Maria.
Courtesy of Sandra V. Reyna.

Nevertheless, Claudia managed to do a tremendous amount of community-organizing work during college. She even spent one of her summers interning with Interfaith Worker Justice in New Orleans, helping to support immigrant workers who had been recruited to work for minimal wages after Hurricane Katrina. She graduated from college with flying colors and had high hopes of attending law school and continuing to advocate for the rights of the oppressed. However, she quickly realized that her options were still very limited. She didn't know of a law school that would accept her as an undocumented immigrant, so she decided to stay at Prairie A & M to earn her master's degree. Since she no longer had a scholarship, she also needed to come up with money for her food, gas, rent, and other living expenses.

She decided to apply for a job at the national pancake chain once again—this time in Houston.

Flirting for Food

Claudia became the only Latina server at the Houston pancake house. There were four white and two black servers working with her, and business was slower in this restaurant than in the Austin establishment. White servers were almost always chosen over Claudia and the black servers to work banquet events—the rare parties that pulled in higher-than-average tips.

Once again managers also forced Claudia to report more tips than she actually earned. They didn't want to have to pay her the difference between $2.13 and the minimum wage of $7.25. In addition, they never paid her overtime. "I would have to work off the clock," says Claudia. "They told me to clock out before doing side work. I was always scheduled to work 5:00 p.m. to 12:00 a.m., and exactly at midnight, even if I hadn't finished clearing tables, I had to clock out. Sometimes I'd stay two more hours. Late at night they'd only keep one or two people, and we had to do all the side work: make silverware packets; clean coffee pots, orange juice pots, and the soda machine; refill the butter, syrup, and ketchup; make sure the syrups were in alphabetical order, all filled up. The tables had to be left spotless. I had to refill the sugar, salt, and pepper. I had to make sure the supply room was clean, organized, and everything labeled. I had to make sure the stockroom was refreshed, and cut lemons myself."

Worst of all, the managers forced Claudia to translate their nasty comments to the Latino bussers and dishwashers. "When the managers were mad, they'd take it out on bussers and dishwashers, and they'd make me translate all the horrible things they were saying," says Claudia. "The workers would cry when I told them they were being sent home. I would apologize and feel horrible. They would say, 'Please don't send me home. I need to make this salary.' I would say, 'I'm sorry, that's what they're making me tell you.' They saw me as a sellout. I knew that this was the only job I could get, and the only one they could get. The managers would take the most vulnerable people and take stuff out on them when things were going bad. It was inhumane, horrible, how they treated them." Although Claudia was a firebrand at school, she somehow could not bring herself to advocate for these workers on the job. She told herself she really needed the money, and tried hard to ignore the pleas of her Latino coworkers.

Claudia made about $30 to $40 a day in tips, working five to six days a week. The $2.13 she earned in wages amounted to a weekly paycheck of about $10.00 after taxes. So, in total, she earned about $150 to $200 per week. She used that money to pay for books, car payments, gas to drive the 20 miles to Prairie View, and other living expenses. She would have been homeless had it not been for the university administrator who gave her a place to stay. Sometimes Claudia had to choose between going to school or to work. "I remember having to make the choice, 'If I go to work today, I can afford to go to school tomorrow,'" she says. "Half of my income every week would go to gas. I definitely couldn't afford to get sick."

She was also hungry all the time. She couldn't afford food and tried to survive on pancakes she ate at the restaurant. "I had to eat less than $6.50 for the employee meal," says Claudia. "If I wanted an omelette, I went over $6.50. I could only afford pancakes. If you were on the schedule for only five hours, you couldn't get a meal. There were days when I wouldn't eat all day."

She was a food service worker who couldn't afford to eat.

At times Claudia and other waitresses would try to get food from the cooks. "When we were really hungry, we would flirt with the cooks to get food," she says. "Sometimes we wanted shrimp, but they wouldn't let us eat it even when it came out bad. The cooks were all Mexican, so I would put on makeup and make jokes that only Mexicans would know. I was really hungry! They would ask me for my number, and I'd say, 'Can I have three pieces of butterfly shrimp?' I'd give them a fake number, so later they'd ask me why I lied. I'd just tell them, 'I have to eat!'"

To make matters worse, the restaurant required servers to bring $20 each night as their "bank" so they could make change as necessary for guests. Claudia had to scrimp and save to bring the $20 every night; sometimes she asked her family to lend her the money. If she didn't have the $20 when she got to work, she had to ask the manager to change larger bills given to her by customers requesting change, and she'd get in serious trouble.

On the weekends the restaurant stayed open 24 hours. One extremely slow weekend night a manager asked Claudia to roll silverware in napkins for two hours. This meant that she got only one table to serve. She knew she wouldn't make any tips this way—she'd make little more than $2.13 an hour—and she'd still be asked to report that she made the minimum wage of $7.25 in tips. Meaning, with taxes, she'd have worked for free. After two hours, Claudia approached the manager and said, "I'm done with the silverware, and other servers are getting tables. Can I serve another table now?" The manager got upset with Claudia for asking this question and berated her on the dining floor. Customers watched. The manager then told her to punch out and go home, and to tell the customers at her one table that someone else would serve them. When Claudia relayed the message to the customers, they asked to speak to the manager. They were upset by the manager's treatment of Claudia. This only enraged the manager further. She then accused Claudia of telling the customers about their exchange.

The manager realized that having three servers on a weekend night didn't work, and so the next weekend she asked only Claudia to work— but it happened to be the night of a football party. "I was alone on the floor for four hours," says Claudia, "and some people walked out without paying their bill. That night I had to stay until 7:00 a.m., and then come in the next morning at 10:00 a.m. I told the manager someone had walked out, and she said, 'We'll take care of it at the end of your shift.' But at the end of my shift, new people started coming in. The manager told me to clock out and then do my side work. Then she talked to me about the people who walked out. They owed a bill of $98. 'Why did they walk out?' she asked me. I told her, 'Because we were busy. I was the only person on the floor.' She told me that it was my fault, and that I'd have to pay the bill. I had made $80 in tips that night. So after tipping out the busser and the dishwasher, the manager took all my tips and told me I still owed the restaurant $18. I had worked from 10:00 p.m. until 9:00 a.m.—though I had clocked out at 7:00 a.m.—and instead of paying me anything, they were telling me I had to pay them."

At that point, Claudia quit. "I felt like I was being robbed," she says. She walked out to her car in the parking lot and cried.

Stolen Wages

Not long after Claudia quit working in the pancake restaurant, she got a phone call from the supervisor of her college internship in New Orleans. The Restaurant Opportunities Center of New Orleans (ROC-NOLA) was looking for an organizer to fight for the rights of workers in New Orleans's growing restaurant industry. Claudia jumped at the opportunity to interview.

I remember interviewing Claudia over the phone from my house. At the time I was living in Oakland, California, and I had just had my first baby. I interviewed her with my infant daughter lying by my side. I could hear the excitement and passion in her voice, her commitment to fight for people like her family members still in the restaurant industry. I offered her the job almost immediately, and she accepted almost as quickly. That week she threw her stuff into her old, beat-up car and drove across the state border to start a new life as an organizer.

When Claudia joined ROC-NOLA, a new campaign was just getting started. Several workers, including Thomas from chapter 3, had come forward from Tony Moran's, a fine-dining restaurant in the heart of the French Quarter, right on Bourbon Street, to protest wage theft and discrimination. White workers at Tony Moran's were serving customers on the ground floor; black servers were being sent upstairs to serve the few customers who ventured to the upper floors to eat. Some of the black workers had also been asked to live in apartments owned by the company on the top floor of the restaurant; the apartments resembled "servants' quarters" of the old South. For years the workers had been terrorized by the owner, who carried a Taser and had a team of large bodyguards known for beating up workers who complained. A few of the workers had finally had enough, and although they'd previously told ROC organizers that they would never be able to fight the injustice at Tony Moran's, they found the courage to step forward. They were shocked to learn that wage theft affects over 50 percent of restaurant workers nationwide. In addition, almost half (45.5%) of all workers surveyed by ROC report that they have been denied proper overtime payment, and one-third report working "off the clock" without pay.[7] Managers regularly ask these workers to end their shift early and continue working, or, as one bartender who has been in the industry for eight years explained it, "clock out and have the company make money off us."[8]

As soon as Claudia came on board at ROC, she helped double the number of workers willing to speak out against Tony Moran's management publicly. She also helped organize a number of powerful, creative demonstrations in front of the restaurant, including prayer vigils and a "funeral march" through the French Quarter to draw attention to workers' rights. Workers from several other restaurants started coming to the ROC-NOLA office to seek justice in their workplaces as well. They buzzed about the protests, the first of their kind in the French Quarter.

At one point Claudia was invited to speak at a conference of the National Lawyers Guild. She found herself addressing several hundred lawyers from around the country. "At first I felt a little nervous, addressing a crowd of that kind and size," says Claudia. "But after I started to talk about the injustices the workers were facing, I really started to warm up. I talked about the struggles of Tony Moran's workers, and how we had come so far with our campaign. But I was also thinking about all those years of serving pancakes, and all those things my sisters and my brothers-in-law went through." The audience responded with rousing applause, and that evening 200 lawyers showed up at Tony Moran's to support the ROC campaign. Under Claudia's leadership, the lawyers held a spontaneous sit-in at the restaurant, demanding justice from the owner. Claudia later told me, "That was my proudest moment."

The sit-in was too much for the company. Tony Moran's management called Claudia and requested a meeting to resolve the campaign. In the months that followed, Tony Moran's management agreed not only to pay the workers but also to institute an employee handbook that ROC-NOLA created with the workers' input. The handbook guaranteed a new, transparent promotions policy, a grievance procedure, and much more.

Claudia, for her part, has gone on to advocate for restaurant workers and immigrants nationwide. Her family members, all of whom still work in restaurants, are counting on her. Her family never hoped or planned to stay in the United States. Claudia's sister and brother-in-law even made payments on a house in Mexico for several years, hoping to return at some point, but when the payments increased, they had to sell the house. They've stayed in the United States far longer than their tourist visas permitted and are now undocumented workers. New immigration laws have eliminated any chance they might have once had to obtain citizenship.

Claudia believes that her experiences in the Houston pancake restaurant forever changed her perspective on the plight of restaurant workers in the United States. "You know, I think my experiences in Austin hadn't shown me what working in the restaurant industry is like for many people," she says. "But working in Houston definitely showed me. In Houston there were a lot of older people—women in their fifties. They had children, families. Some were single mothers. It became more real. People were always really bitchy and feisty. For them, this was it. This was their job. For me, I was in college. I knew there'd be something else eventually. For them, this was everything they had. When a table was not assigned to them, they took it personally. They got in your face about it. They had families, and $2.13 plus tips was all they had for themselves and their families. It really opened my eyes. It was Latinos cooking, white women working graveyard shifts, men working days. I saw the racism, sexism, and low wages in the industry. Everything I remember from that place was horrible."

Living Hand to Mouth

Workers who are already living hand to mouth can't afford to deal with late or stolen wages. Some workers, like Thomas (see chapter 3), end up homeless because of wage theft. Other workers, like Claudia, barely survive. Those who are American citizens often qualify for food stamps. This, however, sheds light on a discomfiting irony: *Food service workers in the United States need food stamps!* In fact, servers in the restaurant industry use food stamps at almost double the rate of the rest of the U.S. workforce.[9]

Should taxpayers really be subsidizing the restaurant industry, which is growing so rapidly, to allow its employees to eat?

Claudia worked in a family-style or franchise restaurant, a step above fast food, and so it's not surprising that she didn't earn a living wage. In fact, more than 80 percent of all food service workers, even waiters in big cities, don't earn a living wage (taking into account basic needs such as rent, food, transportation, child care, and health care).[10] Most restaurant workers can't even afford to pay their rent. According to the National Low Income Housing Coalition (NLIHC), the fair market rent for a two-bedroom unit in the United States is $959. A full-time restaurant worker, working 40 hours per week, would have to earn $18.25 an hour to afford the two-bedroom unit.[11] ROC data show that 8 out of 10 restaurant workers nationwide earn less than this. The average restaurant worker, earning the national restaurant median wage of $8.90 an hour, would have to work approximately 107 hours per week to rent a two-bedroom unit at the fair market price.

Not surprisingly, some white men who are servers in fine-dining restaurants are the only restaurant workers in the United States who generally do earn a living wage; they hold the second-highest-paying position in the restaurant industry.[12] Still, being a white waiter in a fine-dining restaurant doesn't guarantee a living wage. In my early days as an organizer of restaurant workers, I had no idea that even white men who are servers in some of the fanciest restaurants in the United States end up on food stamps and suffer through periods of homelessness.

Mike Morganroth's story served as a reality check. Mike lives in Detroit and is among the many white servers in fine-dining restaurants who live in poverty.

I should note that I found Mike's story particularly compelling because it takes place in Detroit, a city that has almost developed a reputation as a lost cause, the bottom of the barrel among American cities. People don't usually think of Detroit as a happening place; they think of its poverty, segregated neighborhoods, and dying auto industry. Detroit is a tough city, and it's a poor city, with one of the largest income gaps between black and white households of any urban center in the United States.[13] However, I've been amazed and intrigued by what I've seen in Detroit. I've been introduced to people and restaurants there that shatter all stereotypes of the city. Some of ROC's most energetic, dynamic members come from Detroit. I also count a handful of Detroit restaurants among our nation's most vibrant, innovative, progressive establishments.

Mike is an athletic guy in his mid-thirties. He has dark brown hair styled in a military buzz cut. He has a serious look, but every so often he shows one of his tattoos or tells a joke that reveals a different side of his personality.

Mike Morganroth in front of his mother's Detroit home.
Courtesy of Restaurant Opportunities Center of Michigan.

He is also the primary caretaker for his mother, who struggles with mental illness. He wants nothing more than to have a family of his own, but the economics of having kids—and his mother's situation—discourages him. He lives with his mother, saddled by debt. "If I had a one-bedroom house, I'd let my kid sleep in the living room," he says. "But I can't even afford the gas to take a woman out for a date. I can't afford a cover charge at a bar, or even a $1 drink. Women don't want to walk up to my mom's door. I've been to every free dating site in the world, but I haven't been on a date in over three years....I don't have high standards. At this point, I'm just looking for someone without a penis."

Mike grew up during Detroit's golden age, when the car industry was booming. "My dad was a car guy," says Mike. "Cruising around town, he caught my mom's attention. He used to show me pictures of him driving a Corvette. He was a young guy, but he'd just gotten his first job, in a Ford dealership." Mike's parents bought a house in Warrenville, just outside of Detroit. "Warrenville was a nice place," he says. "Families would work nine to five and go to church on Sundays. It was a real community." It was also incredibly segregated. "I remember when the first black family moved in," says Mike. "People said, 'There goes the neighborhood.' There was the Mexican part of town, the black part of town, and still some white people left in town. Most people in the area had something to do with auto industry."

Unbeknownst to Mike, things weren't exactly right inside his own home. "When I was a kid, my mom was hospitalized a few different times," he says. "I didn't know she was trying to kill herself, although I always thought she had mental health problems." His mother suffered from depression and repeatedly attempted suicide.

Mike's parents finally divorced when he was nine years old. The good news, however, was that Mike's father had obtained his dream job, testing vehicles for General Motors. "He was testing new vehicles in water and ice," says Mike. "They sent him all over the world—Australia, Japan. He made $90K to $100K per year."

Mike's father bought a beautiful home in the suburbs and remarried, this time to his boss at GM. Mike moved in with his father and stepmother, both of whom worked almost all the time. He saw his father only every so often. "I was lonely growing up in a house in the country all by myself," says Mike. "I had to learn to cook for myself or I wouldn't be able to eat. I learned through trial and error, ate lots of burnt food. By the time I was 12, I could make a complete breakfast. At first I would burn everything I touched, but over time I got to really enjoy cooking." He dreamed of becoming an executive chef.

During high school, Mike took an interest in sports. He practiced all summer long and tried out for his school's football team in ninth grade. He made the team, but his low grades made him ineligible to play. Feeling lonely and defeated, he started smoking pot and doing acid. "I had a reputation as the guy who could sleep through a hurricane," he says. "I would sleep through school."

Mike dropped out of school his senior year. His father insisted that he pay rent, so he started looking for a job. Since he remained interested in becoming a chef, he decided to take a job in a chain pizza restaurant. The restaurant mostly filled takeout and delivery orders, but there were some tables where people could eat if they wanted to stay. Mike started as a line worker, earning $4.75 an hour—the minimum wage at the time—but management recognized his intelligence and entrepreneurial spirit and promoted him to the position of general manager when he turned 18.

Mike had the potential to do very well in the restaurant industry, but his entrepreneurial spirit got him into serious trouble pretty quickly, and he fell even further off course. As general manager, he earned $450 a week, which seemed like a lot of money at first. He decided to move in with a friend in Flint, where the pizza restaurant was located, but soon he found that he didn't have enough money to pay his bills. "The money I was making didn't enable me to live," says Mike.

At this point he figured out how to beat the system. The restaurant company's regional management counted the number of pizza boxes the restaurant used each day to determine how much money should be in the cash register. Mike located the factory that produced the pizza boxes and offered the factory workers free pizza in exchange for extra boxes. He then sold pizza to customers in the extra boxes and pocketed the sales. In less than a year, he made $80,000 this way, but he also continued to increase his credit card debt.

The restaurant company eventually caught on but couldn't figure out what exactly Mike had done. "The general manager called me in for a meeting," says Mike. "In exchange for no prosecution, they asked me how I did it, so they could correct the problem." Mike lost his job—carrying $20,000 in credit card debt—but he escaped criminal prosecution. The company ended up changing its accounting practices throughout the Midwest after learning about Mike's embezzlement scheme.

Mike decided to try to get his life together. He went back to school and stopped using hard drugs. He graduated and looked into culinary school more seriously. "I looked into being a chef," says Mike, "but it cost too much money. I felt like these schools were ripping me off." His father and stepmother wouldn't support him anymore, and no restaurant would pay him enough to cover culinary school fees.

At that point, Mike's mom, still in Detroit, also needed support. Her mental health had deteriorated to where she needed an in-home caregiver. Mike moved back to Detroit to take care of her. She needed him, and he couldn't afford to live anywhere else. "If I didn't live with her," says Mike, "she wouldn't have a place to live—and I wouldn't have a place to live either."

Detroit looked nothing like the city of Mike's childhood. "Big Auto" had left the region, leaving Detroit in ruins. Hundreds of thousands of people had left the city, and those who didn't want to leave or couldn't afford to leave lived mostly in poor, underserved neighborhoods. Mike saw many people who'd once held good jobs committing crimes and taking other desperate measures. "A family moved out down the street," says Mike, "and the next day the windows were busted, and the siding had been taken off. You'd see a 40-year-old with an education asking, 'Would you like fries with that?' And uneducated people, who used to have decent jobs in the auto industry, were breaking into cars. Detroit had 1.7 million people when I was nine years old. Now it has 800,000."

Given his skills, Mike was able to find a job in a popular family-style chain restaurant fairly easily. He started as a busser and was quickly promoted to server. Management treated him well. "Once they forgot to put the payroll in, so the district manager made a special trip to the restaurant to pay me," says Mike. "They treated the employees fine."

Mike began to truly enjoy restaurant work. He also enjoyed the camaraderie among the staff, who were white, black, Asian, and Latino. "We were a close staff, all poor, but we got along together," says Mike. "At two in the morning, you'd see 30 of us hanging out in the parking lot." As a server, Mike made $250 to $300 a week, and that was the most anybody in the restaurant made.

Mike worked for seven years in two family-style restaurants. He could barely afford gas and other bills, and he could never afford to leave his mother's home and live on his own, but he was happy. He had a girlfriend. Things seemed to be going well.

Mike even thought he'd get his big break. One night he took his girlfriend to one of the finest restaurants in town. He wanted to impress her. The restaurant belonged to a large, multirestaurant company that served fine Italian food. During dinner, Mike observed the service. He knew that he could serve as well as any of the waiters there. "I knew I had enough serving experience," says Mike, "so I tried to apply." He felt motivated by his desire to make enough money to live on his own and still help his mother.

After multiple tests and interviews, the restaurant hired Mike as a server. He thought his days of poverty were over. He spent a month in training, shadowing more experienced servers, and during that time he was paid the Michigan state minimum wage—$7.40 an hour—for 40 hours of work per week. That gave him $296 a week before taxes, which was all right.

As soon as training finished, however, the company paid him the Michigan state minimum wage for tipped workers—$2.65 an hour, slightly more than the federal minimum of $2.13—and expected him to make the re-mainder of his wages in tips. The problem was that all of the "reservation tables" were given to certain servers whom management favored, and Mike and several others were left with "walk-ins," the customers who happened to walk into the restaurant without a reservation. However, this fancy res-taurant wasn't in a heavily trafficked area, and it just wasn't the kind of restaurant people walked into without reservations. Mike was lucky if he made $30 to $40 in tips each night. That meant that he made a total of $150, or a maximum of $200, per week, every week. Although he worked 50 or 60 hours a week, he took home $8 paychecks or slips that said "THIS IS NOT A CHECK." His hourly wage of $2.65 was almost entirely eaten by taxes.

"I thought I would make more at this restaurant compared to others," says Mike, "but I made less than half of what I made previously. The place is gigantic, too big considering the small amount of business. It's a poor design. Management thought that if they filled the restaurant, we wouldn't be able to take care of guests well. So they'd rather have 10 servers—which is like 4 too many—who can't get enough work to make a living."

Mike knew that the bussers were in an even worse position. The serv-ers in the restaurant were mostly white; the bussers were mostly Latino. When the Latino bussers were hired, they received the full state minimum wage of $7.40 an hour, but then management announced that they could no longer afford the bussing staff and laid off all the bussers. "The restau-rant had a live singer," says Mike. "They were making all these new addi-tions to the restaurant, and then saying, 'We can't afford this, we have to cut back.'" Shortly after that, they rehired a select few of the bussers and forced them to sign a document in which they agreed to be paid the lower minimum wage for tipped workers—$2.65—plus tips. That meant they would start earning about $140 a week.

Mike didn't know how anyone could survive on less than $200 for 50 to 60 hours of work. These wages certainly weren't allowing him to make ends meet. He couldn't afford gas—then about $3.85 per gallon (1.5 times his hourly wage)—to get to work or to drive the 30 extra miles to a special wine training that the restaurant required all the servers to attend every other week. If he had been without the "luxury" of living with his mother, he would surely have been homeless; the cheapest rent he could find any-where was $700 per month, which was almost his entire monthly salary. He couldn't afford basic living expenses, even while living rent-free with his mother. "I had to ask a friend to move in with us," says Mike. "He helped pay the bills. After relying on tips for two months, I had to start selling my belongings. I sold my stereo equipment and my spare car with gas in it. I was left with a car that had bad brakes." Even then, it was hard to pay bills and have any money left for food, clothes, paying down his credit card debt, or having fun. He broke up with his girlfriend. And then another stroke of bad luck: Michigan had a bedbug epidemic, and his mother's apartment was infested. The bugs started eating his flesh, but he didn't have the money to get medical help, let alone buy a new bed. "I had to pay $85 for doctors to look at me and prescribe things I couldn't afford," says Mike. "I just took long, very hot showers to try to scrub the bugs out of my skin."

Things seemed to spiral downward from there. Mike moved from restaurant to restaurant looking for decent work. Nothing was beneath him. "I took a job making pizza with 16- and 17-year-olds," says Mike. "I earned the minimum wage, which barely covered gas to drive half an hour to the restaurant." When another restaurant hired him as a cook, he thought he could work his way up to chef, his original life goal. However, he soon noticed something was wrong. Having learned how to embezzle money from a restaurant at the tender age of 18, he quickly realized that the general manager was embezzling money from the restaurant. He told the owner, who fired the general manager and hired Mike as an interim general manager—but a few weeks later the owner hired a new general manager and fired Mike.

Mike continued to search for good work. "I was about to take a coffeepot to the bridge and start begging when my mom said she saw an ad for a restaurant job fair," says Mike. "So I went. IHOP was hiring 20 people, and 550 people showed up to apply. I actually got a server position in the restaurant, and they treated me well. I turned things around for myself pretty decently."

Despite all the difficulties, Mike says he takes great pride in restaurant work and feels sorry for his father who dedicated his life to General Motors only to be laid off about two years ago. "My dad was an engineer at GM, a big success story," says Mike. "GM threw his life away. You work 60 percent of your life. If you're miserable, the money you're making is not worth it. You're going to take out anger and pain on your family. I would rather be on my deathbed, have 18 to 20 people loving me, than to have a bunch of people go to a state funeral when I die." Nowadays, Mike describes restaurant work as a labor of love. "I like the satisfaction of making someone smile," he says. "I like helping people. In a factory you get no gratification from the machine. When you see some 16-year-old girl get surprised by 30 servers singing 'Happy Birthday' or a 90-year-old woman in tears on her anniversary, it feels great."

Raising Standards—Taking the High Road

Of course, some employers do pay more than $3 an hour. They manage not only to stay in business, but also to become wildly successful. Jason and Ben, mentioned at the beginning of this chapter, have certainly built up a profitable, popular business without sacrificing the rights of their workers—and they've done it in Detroit! The story of how they transformed Russell Street Deli illustrates that employers *can* take the high road and benefit just as much as their employees.

Jason and Ben are the owners of the same restaurant in which they started as dishwashers, and both come from working-class families.

Ben's father is African American; his family came from the South as part of the Great Migration. Ben's mother is white; her family is from upstate Michigan. Both of Ben's parents grew up in the city of Detroit. His mother worked as a server at the Playboy Club, where, on one of her shifts, she met Ben's father. "I was more or less a happy accident," says Ben. "I grew up mostly in the city of Detroit until the age of 12, and then we moved to California for a few years. I ended up coming back at the age of 19."

As a mixed-race child, Ben noticed racial patterns in Detroit at early age. "My dad was a bookie," says Ben. "He'd have me on weekends, so he'd pick me up on a Friday night, and we'd go to bars and collect money all night. We'd go to places that were all black, and we'd go to places that were all white. There was no thought of integration."

Ben attended four different high schools, and he learned to cope with constant change and financial challenges. The food industry, however, was a constant source of income for his family. "For a while my dad worked in the Eastern Market in Detroit, doing every kind of meatpacking job you can get fired from," says Ben. "My mom always had two to three jobs. When she reached her mid-thirties, and they thought she was too old to work at the Playboy Club, she ended up becoming a diner waitress. But my mom has epilepsy. She had a seizure while working at Cracker Barrel, and they fired her for it. She didn't sue them."

Ben worked in many different restaurants throughout his teenage and young adult years. At one point he worked as a cook in an Italian restaurant in an all-white suburb of Detroit. "I was working in the back of the house," says Ben. "It was always very clear—black people in the back, white people in the front. It's a carryover from the era of segregation." One day Ben noticed that a black prep cook was being instructed by his superior to cut off certain parts of a celery stem and throw them away. The owner walked in, noticed the celery stems in the garbage, and yelled at the worker, "You wouldn't throw away the heart of a watermelon, would you?" He was referencing the old white American belief that African Americans have a weakness for watermelon—a stereotype from slavery days. Ben didn't say anything. "It was beautiful how asinine it was, this overt type of racism," he says. "It was a Mel Brooks, *Blazing Saddles,* kind of racism."

Jason, who met Ben as a dishwasher at Russell Street, grew up in between Detroit and its suburbs. "I come from a very conservative Irish family," says Jason. "My mother was a cashier at Burger King, and my father was a Detroit police officer. My father was an extremely racist person, and an extremely violent person. I don't know why, but from a very young age I questioned all his beliefs. I thought he was so crazy. It was always, 'nigger this, nigger that.' I'd be thinking, You're crazy. I don't think you know what you're talking about. He'd be beating my mom, and in the back of my mind, I was always going, 'No.'"

Jason worked in 14 different restaurants while growing up. "My first job was at Big Boy at the age of 16," says Jason. "I was a dishwasher, and then they made me the Saturday line cook. From 7:00 a.m. until noon I was to cook bacon. And then lunch would start, and I'd basically cook hamburgers for five hours. I remember the craziness of trying to fill the orders in the afternoon. Those people were not nice to work for. I remember washing a bunch of dishes in the dish sink on my second day of work. When I finished, I was standing there looking around, like, 'What do I do now?' No one had told me what to do next, and no one had given me permission to find something else to do. Then the owner walked in and said, 'Why are you standing around? Because of your laziness, no one's going to be able to take a break today.' I was just 16. The owner would be completely nasty, and then an hour later he'd be a normal person again. Working in those restaurants you feel like you're an abused dog. Your owner hits you sometimes, and then an hour later he'll be petting you."

Jason's mom kicked him out of the house when he was 17 for doing drugs. He finished high school in the city of Detroit, but he moved from an all-white high school to an all-black one. "I thought, This is crazy," says Jason. "My father is white, and he was trying to kill me, but these black people are nice to me. I liked them better than white kids in Waterford. It was nothing like what people told me it was going to be. I was raised to believe that black people were violent, of a lesser intelligence, that they were lazy. All they ever cared about was drugs, alcohol, and welfare. I remember my grandma saying, 'Niggers will jump in the car and stab you. Keep the doors locked.' I was 12. I remember feeling like, I just can't imagine that happening. My father always referred to black people as 'porch monkeys.' I heard it quite often in the eighties, a term that meant black people were monkeys always sitting on their porches. It was insanity." After coming to his own conclusions about racial stereotypes, Jason started dating a black woman and eventually met Ben, his lifelong friend and business partner.

When Jason moved out of his parents' house, he moved in with his brother and sister-in-law, who demanded he find a job immediately or leave. "I ended up finding a job in another Big Boy restaurant as a dishwasher," says Jason. "I thought it was going to be easy because I'd worked for the company previously, but I was working with a lot of chefs who were sexually harassing me. I was 18. They'd say, 'We're going to take you in the cooler and fuck you in the ass.' I told my manager, who said, 'Why are you talking to me? Deal with it.' So I quit." Jason's sister-in-law was not sympathetic when she found out he had quit his job, and demanded that he find another one by the end of the week. "It was Detroit in 1995," says Jason. "I didn't know my way around the city, so I asked my brother what to do. He said, 'Go see my friend Bob at Russell Street Deli.' I walked across town to the restaurant, and Bob said, 'Go grab an apron. We'll make you a dishwasher.'" Jason spent the next 12 years working off and on in the restaurant. "Bob had always paid people a pretty decent wage," says Jason. "Some of the line cooks were making $10.00 an hour. It wasn't great, but it wasn't bad. It was better than Taco Bell, where I made $7.85."

Jason learned a lot working at Russell Street Deli, and he moved up the ranks fairly quickly. "It was the first time I'd worked in a restaurant that wasn't a franchise," says Jason. "The food didn't come out of boxes or bags. I moved up from a dishwasher to a salad prep cook. I saw green leaf lettuce really for the first time. I remember being like, 'This is what it looks like when it's fresh. And red leaf lettuce. What the hell is that?' I was really introduced to all these different things. I was cooking my own sirloin and corn beef from scratch. I didn't know what any of these things were. I started as a dishwasher. Over time I was sous chef. They trained me for a waitstaff position. And they brought me on the line as a prep cook, line cook, grill man, expediter, and cashier. Over time I had done everything."

In 2000, Ben started college. Jason started in 2004. They both went to Bennington College in Vermont to study painting and printmaking. Both came back to Detroit during the summers and worked in various restaurants, including Russell Street Deli. One summer Ben invited Jason to eat at the Russell Street Deli. Jason initially refused. "It's kind of an expensive restaurant for someone who's low-income," says Jason. "If you have an entrée and a cup of coffee, it could be up to $23 for two people. Ben said, 'Let's go,' but I said I couldn't afford to eat. He said he'd treat. There were times when he was in school and I would buy lunch for him, and vice versa. This time I didn't have enough money to pay for French toast. While we were eating there, we were offered the restaurant."

The owner, Bob Cerrito, was getting older and wanted to sell the restaurant to people he thought could actually make it successful. "Ben and I had worked there for a very long time," says Jason. "We were good employees, worked hard, no-nonsense. We come from hardworking, blue-collar families who thought they were middle class. We had both gone away and were doing other things. Ben was showing his art in galleries. It was impressive to Bob. The restaurant was very popular, and he wanted to keep it going. He had owned it for 13 years. He was a very nice man, but not the best business owner. It was wearing him out, and he wanted to give it to someone who could handle it."

Jason wasn't sure what to make of the offer. "He offered the restaurant to us, and we took it," he says. "But he was also a very melodramatic person. I remember I'd be working part-time, and he'd say, 'Are you coming in to work Saturday, or do I have to close the restaurant?' It was the typical passive-aggressive, asshole owner thing to do. So when he offered us the restaurant, my initial reaction was, 'He's not serious.' Another reaction was, 'I can't afford French toast. How can I buy a restaurant?'" Jason was scared. "It was like that scene from *Casino,* where these two guys get a casino, but they screw it all up," says Jason. "One of them says something like, 'It was the last time that street guys like us were ever given anything that

Jason and Ben, owners of Russell Street Deli, in Detroit's Eastern Market.
Courtesy of Russell Street Deli.

fuckin' valuable again.' Ben and I had degrees in painting, printmaking, and music. We were not setting the world on fire financially."

Ben, on the other hand, thought that buying the restaurant was perhaps a good idea. "We had a lot of different conversations when Bob offered us the restaurant," says Ben. "I actually owned a record store at the time, and I was doing well. I had already saved some money, and I was planning to go to grad school. Jason was unsure. It was a lot of money, and it would be hard if we failed. But it was an opportunity to radically change our lives. It was a big thing, and we didn't know how good we'd be at it. We both had qualms, but we were both excited. We encouraged each other to make that jump, and we're very grateful that it worked."

Ben set up a payment plan with Bob so that he and Jason could pay for the restaurant over time. The initial idea was that he and Jason could run the restaurant well, make some money, and sell it. They could then move on with their passions—art and music. "We can make a living with this was our initial thought," says Jason. "We weren't thinking about wages, high road practices, paying $5 or $6 per hour to the wait staff, health insurance, or anything like that. We were just thinking, Let's do this damn thing. Once we started, though, we remembered all the things we'd learned at Bennington in Vermont.

They decided to change the wage structure in the restaurant. Bob had always paid people well, but Ben and Jason agreed that no worker at the Russell Street Deli should be paid the abysmally low Michigan tipped minimum wage of $2.77. Servers in the front of the house began earning around $5 an hour, plus tips. Cooks made $12 or $17 an hour, depending on their experience.

Jason explains how they reached the decision to pay workers almost twice the wage required by law: "We figured that's what would work for us because we are both pretty independent guys. Neither of us liked punching a clock. Neither of us wanted to run a restaurant," says Jason. "When I'm not at the restaurant I spend 95 percent of my time alone doing watercolors. Ben has a record label. He's an underground musician. So neither of us wanted to be there all the time. Both of us initially said, 'Let's turn this place around, fix it, because it isn't profitable—it had never made money. Let's manage it well, sell it, and walk away with $100,000.' But once we started running it, implementing some of our ideas, we made the restaurant profitable, and we found that we were both taking home a good wage. So after the first year and a half we said, 'Let's not flip it. Let's make $700 a week from this restaurant for the rest of our lives, plus health insurance and IRAs.' Part of the plan was that each person would have six months off while the other was in school. So we'd be six months on, six months off." Ben is currently in graduate school at Columbia University. Jason runs the restaurant. When Ben graduates, Jason will take his turn and go back to school.

"So no matter what, you have six months off to work on your art career or whatever else," says Ben. "You don't want to be there 80 hours a week, six months on. You don't want to find yourself cutting pickles. So we thought, How do we get our employees to do the lion's share of the work? We've got to give them a strong sense of ownership. We've got to pay people better. If line cooks are making $13 or $14 per hour, we can say, 'This is how we want it. We don't want to hear about it. We're going to tell you if we don't like it, because we're paying you well. We understand you have dreams and aspirations outside of the restaurant, so instead of having to work 40 hours for $400, you get $600, you don't have to work a second job, and you have time to do what you want in your life.' We were creating a work environment that was conducive to happiness. We'd say to them, 'You guys have to get along. You have to communicate, treat each other respectfully. You are the tip of the iceberg. You see everything. We like your input. You decide whether or not something should be implemented. If you've changed something and I don't like it, I'll tell you. If you play a good game, we don't have to worry about it. You guys handle the restaurant, we'll grow the business.' So now I work 40 to 50 hours per week. I tell them, 'If I've got to slice pickles and clean the bathroom, I can't increase sales and give you a raise."

Jason and Ben also decided to find a way to provide health care and retirement plans for the workers. "We had the idea that we wanted to have a core group of employees," says Jason. "These are the people who got our back. They're down for the program. They want to work here for the rest of their lives. We also understand that so many people have given their lives to the restaurant industry, and at the end they have nothing to show for it. It's not like working at Chrysler. So we decided to create the IRA program. We said, 'We're not going to make you millionaires, but when you retire, you'll be able to live out the rest of life, own a house, afford your medication. Getting sick won't be so stressful."

Ben feels just as strongly about paying people well. "After all, we both worked there for a number of years, so we knew what it was like," says Ben. "It's impossible to live on $8.50 an hour. Even 10 years ago that was difficult to live on, especially if you want to save. Anything else you'd want to do would be out of the question. God forbid someone breaks into your car. You'd lose a whole day of pay. When every dollar counts, it's imperative to pay people well. It's the best way to build loyalty. If you work for someone for a while, and you feel like they're screwing you, you start building up resentment."

Ben also talks about how important it is to share financial information with employees so they know exactly where the restaurant stands. "This sharing component helps people see that we're all in this together," says Ben. "It's hard to remember when you have a hierarchy, when you have a boss. But if you're making $2 more than your friend down the street as a dishwasher, and your boss takes care of you, it's harder to maintain disinterest."

In Jason's and Ben's experience, when employees feel valued, they're more likely to take pride in their work. "We felt that if people were happy with the money they were making, it would be easy for them to buy into this business," says Jason. "We could say to them, 'You guys are running the place. This is the Starship Enterprise. We're the captains, but the ship is flying itself.' That comes from us having worked in restaurants ourselves. It sucks working in most restaurants. The boss is hungover, sometimes a raving lunatic. You think, Where did this bozo come from? Why are these people fighting? A lot of restaurant owners act crazy because they're at the restaurant all the time.... It's like that song by Utah Phillips—the problem with punching a clock is that you give your owner your brain at the beginning of a shift, and eight hours later you get it back, but nothing's in the same place. At Russell Street we want to give you your brain back in the same shape we found it. We don't want you to feel fucked with. In the meantime, we're going to do our best to make this as painless as possible."

Do Jason and Ben have to raise prices to pay for the higher wages, raises, IRAs, health insurance, and equitable employment practices? "We've owned the restaurant for four years," says Jason, "and there are certain prices we won't ever raise. We're never raising the price of soup, for example. We want there to be something in the restaurant anyone in Detroit can afford. We hope everyone will be able to eat in the restaurant. We also remember a time when we didn't have enough money to eat in restaurants. So part of what we have to do is raise prices on fancier sandwiches, like, from $8.95 to $9.25 after two years. Another big part of our business plan involves increasing our number of catered events. If you feed 100 people at a catered event, you don't have to wait on them or wash dishes. You can charge more for catering at a law firm. They can afford $15 per person. We've also started a wholesale business. We sell our soup to other restaurants. In the end, it works. We use local products. We buy organically grown black beans from a farmer 40 miles down the road. We get the highest-quality products we can get, and that makes people want to come in. We buy these products to help local people make money."

Besides paying people really well, Ben and Jason are committed to diversity. "When we took over the restaurant there was 1 full-time black employee," says Ben. "Now, out of 20 employees, we have 13 black employees, in both the front and the back. I don't feel comfortable myself eating at restaurants if I look in the kitchen and it has all white staff. I think, Where are the black employees? Why have you hired all white people? Detroit is 85 percent black. The restaurant should reflect the environment. If you just put out an ad for waiters, you're going to get mostly white applicants; they're already trained. We've had success because we'll hire dishwashers, train them to be prep cooks, then take them to the front. Then they have a better understanding of the menu, the way the business functions, on the ground level. They speak with confidence, as people who understand the food, how something is prepared. Our new rule is that every time we put out an ad, it's for a dishwasher."

Jason and Ben maintain decent hours and a healthy lifestyle. They are pursuing graduate degrees and careers in art and music, and they want the same kinds of opportunities for their employees. Paying people far above the minimum wage, Jason and Ben have managed to create a decent income for themselves, their employees, and even local vendors who rely on their business. Their employees do not rely on tips alone for a steady income, and as a result, they're much more invested in the success of the business than they would be in most restaurants.

Why wouldn't every restaurant owner want to do the same? Should Jason and Ben have to stick their necks out as the one of the few employers in Michigan paying tipped workers more than $3 an hour?

Equal Wages for Tipped and Nontipped Workers

Jason and Ben have been lucky. It's extremely rare for anyone to go from being a dishwasher to a restaurant owner, and it's also rare for a restaurant employer to pay servers more than the tipped minimum wage. The reality is that Russell Street Deli—a shining example in the restaurant industry—is surrounded by restaurants that rip off and exploit their employees every day.

It's hard to stomach, right? The United States lays claim to some of the world's most prosperous, celebrated restaurants, but the workers inside those restaurants are getting nickeled-and-dimed. They are some of the nation's poorest citizens and immigrants. In 2010, when the U.S. Department of Labor announced the 10 lowest-paid occupations in the United States, food service workers won the dubious distinction of holding 7 of these 10 occupations and 2 of the lowest-paid positions of all.[14] That's based on their reported income, before their wages are stolen.

It's possible that the whole tipped minimum wage structure is just as confusing to employers as it is to workers and customers. I certainly didn't understand how tips worked before I started organizing restaurant workers, and I feel for employers who are confused by how to calculate who's owed what. However, there's a very simple solution for everyone involved: let's give tipped and nontipped workers the same minimum wage! Seven states—Alaska, California, Minnesota, Montana, Nevada, Oregon, and Washington—have the same minimum wage for tipped and non-tipped workers, and all have thriving restaurant industries.

If all workers received the same minimum wage, then there'd be no need for Mike's and Claudia's employers to make up the difference between the tipped minimum wage and the federal minimum wage for nontipped workers. Jason and Ben wouldn't be sticking their necks out. Taxpayers wouldn't have to pay for food stamps for food service workers. We, the diners, wouldn't have to worry about tipping extra for fear that our food servers will starve to death.

5

RACE IN THE KITCHEN

They will not hire someone for waitstaff who is not white. They use the
excuse that they need to have 100 percent English. But there have been cases
where workers who are European are hired even if they have an accent.
But they are white European, and that's OK.

—Cook, Man, New York City

We get complaints or I've heard even my customers say, like, "Oh, he
only hires light-skinned girls." And I've heard a customer say in the
bathroom that she felt offended, because she was a darker-skinned
African American woman....I don't know, some people say that he has,
like, a color issue. I mean, honestly, I believe he does. I've heard stuff like,
"Everybody behind the bar has to pass the brown paper bag test." The
"brown paper bag test" goes back maybe to slavery days. A brown
paper bag is tan. If you're darker than the paper bag, basically, you
don't pass. You have to be lighter, or, you know...it's just crazy.
It's just ignorant, really, it's very ignorant.

—Cocktail Server, Man, Three Years in the Industry, Los Angeles

One of the things I love about "foodie culture" is its reverence for diversity, ethnic foods, and traditions. I'm the daughter of Indian immigrants,
and when I was young, I thought that the whole concept of "eating ethnic
food" was an experience unique to my family and a handful of other ad-
venturers. I was intrigued when foodies (and lots of Americans who don't
consider themselves foodies) began celebrating cuisines from around the
world. It suddenly seemed as though a much broader audience of Americans was incredibly passionate about and sensitive to other people's traditions. Indian food—especially Indian fusion—became haute cuisine, and

I saw many New Yorkers, who might not have previously dared to enter the world of spicy curries and chutneys, suddenly dive in. Of course, most of them didn't learn about Indian cooking and customs; they simply learned what they did and didn't like on the menu. I did the same as I fell in love with Asian fusion food, which combines culinary traditions from several Asian and other countries. I didn't think about the people creating my kimchi tacos. I just savored the new experience.

My experiences in both the United States and India have made me pay particular attention to race. Indians are notoriously obsessed with skin color and race. As a child, when my family took a trip to India, relatives and friends often commented that I was the "darkest child" among my sisters, and that I should stay out of the sun. This was not a compliment. Perhaps because British colonialism left its stamp on the South Asian psyche, lighter skin is almost always considered superior on the Indian subcontinent. During those long summer days of my childhood, I stayed out of the sun and in my grandmother's house, watching television commercials for facial bleach creams or other cosmetics that claimed to help women lighten their skin. Coming home to the United States was not a reprieve from thinking about skin color. I can remember teenagers yelling at my family to "go back home to Iraq," even though we aren't Iraqi, and seven different mechanics in Utah refused to fix our family's broken-down van because of our race.

Some people, like my ROC cofounder, Mamdouh, complain that I pay too much attention to race, but Mamdouh grew up as a man in a different part of the world—Morocco—with a different (though equally complex) perspective on race and skin color. He didn't have to deal with bleaching creams. Even so, I never thought about race relations and racial injustice in restaurants until I started organizing with ROC.

When I began doing outreach to restaurant workers, I felt as though I had been given "night goggles" in some *Matrix*-like sci-fi movie. I could suddenly see a world of color that had always existed around me but that I had never noticed before in restaurants. As I traveled around the country to help my ROC coworkers conduct surveys, I discovered that the people stuck in the restaurant industry's lowest-paying jobs were predominantly people of color. My coworkers and I saw these workers leaving restaurants after their late-night shifts in Manhattan, the French Quarter, downtown Los Angeles, and many other city centers.

If we headed out around 10:00 p.m. and walked the streets until around 2:00 a.m., we could approach a few hundred of them and ask them to take our survey. We became very good at spotting them. I had never before been able to pick restaurant workers out of a crowd, but now I saw them everywhere—white shirts, black pants, generally with their heads down, scurrying to get home as quickly as possible, exhausted. Sometimes they wore checkered pants, if they worked in the "back of the house," the kitchen; these workers looked particularly exhausted and sweaty in stained clothes. The "front of the house" workers, on the other hand, could hardly be distinguished from other people on the street; they typically wore plain black or tuxedo pants and a button-down white shirt. They could just as easily have been stepping out of a cocktail party. They, too, usually looked tired, but they often hung out with other coworkers in a bar or restaurant after work.

After a few years of doing outreach, another pattern became clear to me: servers and bartenders in urban areas, and particularly in fine-dining res-taurants, were mostly white; the bussers, runners, and exhausted, sweaty workers in the back of the house were usually a different color. There were exceptions, of course, but I started to see this pattern every time I ate out: white servers and bartenders in the industry's highest-paying, front of the house positions, and workers of color employed as bussers, runners, and dishwashers.

Before long I started making it a point to peek into every restaurant kitchen on my way to the bathroom. Again and again, I saw the pattern. Even when the front of the house was a little more diverse, the workers in the back were almost always darker than the workers in the front. The chefs and sous chefs were often white, but you'd certainly never find a white dishwasher in New York City, Chicago, or Los Angeles. The people doing physical labor—cleaning and carrying dishes and making everything in the kitchen run smoothly—were mostly nonwhite work-ers. I lost several potential boyfriends by interrupting a date to ask man-agement about their promotions policy. I relished every opportunity to encourage managers to promote their great bussing staff to waitstaff positions.

At the same time I noticed that restaurant workers tended to self-segregate. Whenever we had a meeting or function at ROC, members would find their social niche—the Latino bussers, the Bangladeshi runners, the

Arab servers, the white servers, the African American servers, the African cooks, the Haitian dishwashers and cleaners, the Asian sushi workers. I tried to force workers out of their comfort zone, making it an organizational priority to help workers unite across racial lines, but it was difficult. These workers saw each other daily in the restaurant but rarely interacted with one another, in part because they were often segregated by position and on different sides of "the house."

Today I believe that racial segregation is one of the restaurant industry's most pressing, deep-seated problems, and part and parcel of every other pattern of injustice in the industry. In fact, I remember when this became startlingly clear to me. One day in 2005 a Latino busser came to ROC from one of New York City's fanciest restaurants—one of the city's only four-star establishments—complaining about the fact that he was perpetually passed over for a promotion to waitstaff by less experienced white workers. He explained that he had to train these less experienced white workers from France and other parts of western Europe, and within one month they'd be promoted to server positions and earning five times what he earned. Literally. The servers in this restaurant earned about $150,000 per year, and the bussers earned less than $30,000.

ROC worked with the Latino busser and other bussers and runners to organize a large public campaign against discrimination in this restaurant—a campaign that included federal litigation. Our work was featured in a two-page article on the front page of the *New York Times* Dining section. The publicity prompted dozens of other workers to come to us for help. I remember hearing stories that baffled me throughout this campaign. Many of the workers' stories didn't make sense at all. Why wouldn't a manager want to promote a busser who everyone could see would be great at selling food and wine? Great servers make restaurants more money! As far as I could tell, the only reason managers preferred white servers and bartenders was that they believed white people were better salespeople and that customers preferred white waitstaff. I actually heard some employers openly state that the best servers have "the look" and "table talk" that appeal to customers—the assumption being that white people more often have the look and conversation style that make customers want to spend more money. So even when a white man applied for a lower-level position, such as a dishwasher or busser, restaurant managers would often quickly encourage him to move to a waitstaff position; these managers believed that their white employees' potential to sell was wasted in lower-level positions.

The Front and the Back of the House

Oscar is a former ROC organizer in Miami, and a former restaurant worker. He has dark brown skin, a mass of curly brown hair, and a slight, wispy moustache. He speaks softly with a slow drawl, and when he cracks a joke or laughs at someone else's comment, his smile overwhelms his round, dimpled face. When I was training Oscar to work as an ROC organizer, he actually irritated me. He stared intensely at me while I explained our model, didn't take notes, and rarely blinked. It drove me crazy. As an attorney, professor, and lifelong student, I am obsessed with taking notes when speaking with people, and since Oscar just stared at me when I spoke, I thought for sure he wasn't paying attention. He repeatedly proved my first impressions wrong, however, as he asked intelligent questions and made comments indicating that he had not only grasped what I said, but also carefully stored it somewhere under that mass of hair.

Oscar had held several labor-intensive jobs. He'd worked in construction, carpet installation, carpentry, and fast food. He had even performed manual labor, dredging on barges and tugboats on the Miami River. He was no stranger to challenge and struggle.

Oscar was born in Muelle de los Bueyes, a tiny town on the South Atlantic coast of Nicaragua, toward the end of the Nicaraguan civil war. His father had been a farmer, herdsman, tailor, and lumberjack. His mother was a schoolteacher, seamstress, and nurse. She'd raised four kids and graduated from seamstress school. The doctor who lived next door had trained her to be his nurse assistant.

When Oscar was born, his father was in prison. War had hit home. "We lived in a shack owned by the church," says Oscar. "I remember the tanks rolling up to our shack and soldiers asking for water to drink." Oscar's family had relatives on both sides of the war—among the Sandinistas, who had won power, and the Contras. Oscar's father was imprisoned after a cousin accused him of giving cigarettes and gum to the wrong side. Oscar spent the first four years of his life not really knowing his father. He rejoiced with the rest of his family when a date was set for his father's release;

but knowing that life would be difficult after leaving prison, Oscar's father planned an immediate escape to the United States and arranged for his family to follow him.

"I remember Christmas night, 1988, getting on a truck with our mom," says Oscar. "All of us kids were wearing 'Members Only' jackets. We were saying good-bye to all our aunties and our grandmother, and holding back the tears. We were kids—we had no idea what was going on. My oldest brother was only nine. We were four little boys. We were driving into darkness. You could hear the bombs and tanks. We rode in a truck, a bus, a car. We walked for several miles, then took more buses and trucks, all through Honduras, Guatemala, and Mexico. My mom wrote to my grandmother all along the way—like 25 to 30 pages of letters—so we have a full account of the journey. While we were in Mexico, we couldn't talk because people would be able to tell by our accent that we were Nicaraguan. We had to use sign language in Mexico. If we wanted to say, 'We're hungry,' we'd put fingers in our mouth. We had to do that to communicate to the Mexican 'coyote,' the guy who took us across the border, over the Rio Grande. I also remember being in a small motel in Texas with 10 to 15 people, waiting for a phone call or letter from my father. My dad was in Overtown, Miami, and he sent money for us to take a Greyhound bus to Miami."

Oscar arrived in Miami at the age of five. He grew up among other Latinos—folks from Honduras, El Salvador, and Cuba—and attended a predominantly African American high school. "I ended up knowing more about Malcolm X and Marcus Garvey at a young age than I knew about Cesar Chavez," says Oscar. When race fights broke out between the Latinos and blacks in Miami, Oscar worked hard to steer clear and remain neutral, the way his father had during the Nicaraguan civil war. He didn't graduate on time, but he did eventually finish school. "I had to go to night school, so I graduated at 20," says Oscar. "I was working at a company, subcontracting—installing carpets and going to school at night. I had to keep working to help my parents out with their house. I had to do side jobs."

Oscar's family was in dire need of financial support. Following a tip about a good way to make money, Oscar became a deckhand for a tugboat company dredging the Miami River. Oscar romanticized this job, thinking of himself as Mark Twain on the Mississippi River, but he dealt with extremely racist coworkers and supervisors. "They used to call me 'niggeraguan,'" says Oscar. "My parents said not to lose the job. My dad said, 'You're making more money than I am.' But I kept complaining about racism. Finally I told the people on the boat, 'My name is Oscar. Call me by my name or don't call me at all.' They thought, Wow, this guy is a troublemaker, so they doubled my workload and overscrutinized me. I was a backhand—I had to cook for the captains, clean for them, work the engine room. Every time they said something racist I wrote it down, so I almost had a book of the things they said. I talked back. They didn't like that, so they fired me. I got my job back three times, but the third time they threw all of my stuff out of my bunk, overboard. I got scuba-diving gear, jumped in, and found all my stuff near the side of boat, but I almost died doing that. When I got fired again, I filed a charge with the Equal Employment Opportunity office. I took my book of racist comments with me."

Oscar decided to go to college at the age of 23. His father couldn't read or write, and his mother hadn't made it past the second grade, but he was eager to learn and advance in the world. He took biology and political science courses at a community college in Miami and was hooked. "There was a hunger strike on campus to unionize the janitors," says Oscar. "I was talking to the striking janitors, and I saw my mother's face in the women. I was bit by the bug of social justice. I started educating myself about race relations."

Of course, he still needed to make money. He and his family were broke, and school had to be secondary to survival. So when his childhood friend Alan told him that he could get him a job as a busser in a fine-dining Spanish restaurant, Oscar didn't hesitate to apply. "I went to buy a white Oxford button-down dress shirt, khaki pants, and black dress shoes," says Oscar. "I combed my hair back with heavy gel. I went in, but the general manager was leaving just as I was coming. The restaurant was actually only 10 blocks away from my place, so I went back the next day, wearing the same thing because I didn't have any other dress clothes. I was interviewed by the assistant manager. Basically, he just asked me, 'Are you as good as Alan?' I told him, 'I can work better.' He said, 'I doubt that. Alan is amazing.' But he still offered me the job, because even though I had never worked in restaurants, I needed a job, and I love food!"

Oscar loved working in the restaurant. He loved skillfully balancing multiple plates in one hand, rapidly and efficiently clearing and setting tables, and, increasingly, attending to customers' needs. "I knew right away I was good at this," says Oscar. "I've always enjoyed labor-intensive work. I loved having the dexterity to carry so many plates. It was like second nature to me. I didn't yet have the finesse to be a waiter—I didn't know the wines or the different dishes. But I knew it would only be a matter of time before I got a promotion."

Customers soon started turning to Oscar instead of their server. "Once I got to know the food," says Oscar, "I was annoying to servers because customers wanted to order from me, the busser. I was a lot friendlier and more intuitive. The servers hated me because some customers would say, 'Where's the manager? I want to tell him the busser gave me better service than the waiter.'"

Oscar found his voice in hospitality, and the general manager took notice. "He saw that I was beginning to understand the culture of the business, and asked if I'd done it before," says Oscar. "I told him, 'I've worked in fast food but never in this kind of place.' He said, 'You're really good at it, seems as if you've been doing it for a long time.' I did love it, but I wanted to get a promotion. I had been working four or five months, and I was getting frustrated because the season was slow. I was working six days a week, and I was barely making the $650 per month I needed to pay rent."

Oscar knew that he was better than most of the waitstaff—after all, customers repeatedly told the management so—and deserved a promotion. He also needed the better wages that came with being a waiter. "Every time I asked to move up, though, they'd say no, and two or three new white servers were hired from the outside," says Oscar. "These white servers couldn't cut it—they didn't know the food, didn't know the restaurant, didn't know tapas. I knew the food, the language to describe it, the wines." Many of the newly hired white workers were actors, models, and students who didn't take their jobs as seriously as Oscar did; they also tended not to last in the restaurant for more than a few weeks. Oscar, Alan, and the other bussers—all workers of color—had families to support and, for the most part, had worked in the restaurant for many years, but they didn't have "the right look."

Not having "the right look" meant they had to do most of the hard physical labor in the restaurant, running food for the servers and setting and clearing tables. They earned about one-quarter of what their white counterparts earned. Oscar made $200 per week—simply not enough to survive.

Oscar continued working in the fine-dining restaurant for about six months and asked for a promotion several times. Finally, the manager,

Jim, called him in for a talk. "The manager had a talk with me sitting on milk crates in the storage area," says Oscar. "I had threatened to quit two weeks earlier, and he said there'd be changes. I told him I felt disrespected, and not paid for the work that I did. He said, 'All the servers say working with you is hell. You do your own thing, and you talk back to them.' I told him that the servers were very disrespectful of the bussers and weren't used to bussers talking back. So he said, 'I understand you're getting better. I understand your frustration is that you want to move up.' I told him, 'I don't want to be a busser for the rest of my life.' He told me, 'We don't have that kind of space for you.' People like me were in limbo. We could have been waiters, but we were stuck as bussers because we weren't white."

When Jim hired several new white servers just a few days after talking to Oscar in the storage room, Oscar decided he'd had enough. "I actually knew one of the servers from the neighborhood," says Oscar. "He was an irresponsible pothead and DJ with no discipline. Everything I'd learned in that restaurant meant nothing. Anyone could get a promotion over me based on skin color. I told Jim, 'I know this guy,' but Jim said the guy had passed the server tests."

Oscar quit.

A few days later he met Jean Souffrant, the coordinator of the Restaurant Opportunities Center in Miami (ROC-Miami). He told Jean about his experiences in the restaurant, and Jean encouraged him to apply to become an organizer for ROC-Miami. As an organizer, Oscar could reach out to his fellow workers and fight against the discriminatory practices they'd all encountered in restaurants. So he applied, became an organizer, and helped plan ROC-Miami's first big event—a party celebrating the release of a local industry report that analyzed more than 500 surveys of restaurant workers in Miami-Dade County. Oscar spoke at the event about his experiences in the industry. The event and report were covered in a front-page story in the local section of the *Miami Herald*.

Oscar also worked with Jean to build a local membership of low-wage restaurant workers. Oscar, in particular, worked hard to develop new leaders, some from the Spanish restaurant in which he'd experienced discrimination. Some of the workers that Oscar recruited worried that joining ROC might put them at risk of losing their jobs. Over time, however, Oscar was able to use his experiences with discrimination in the industry to relate to the workers and encourage them to stand up for themselves. "I felt vindicated," says Oscar, "like my time at the Spanish restaurant had produced something positive—a relationship, a connection, a campaign to confront discrimination in the industry as a whole."

A New Campaign against Discrimination

In the fall of 2011, Oscar and Jean started talking to workers at the Capital Grille Steakhouse, an extravagant fine-dining steakhouse in the Miami area. In fact, by this time African American and Latino workers from this same steakhouse had already approached ROC affiliates in the Washington, D.C., area, Chicago, Los Angeles, and New York. Capital Grille workers in those four cities had filed federal litigation complaining of wage theft and discrimination in hiring, firing, and promotions practices.

ROC viewed the Capital Grille campaign as a unique opportunity to make widespread change in the industry. The steakhouse is part of the Darden group, which claims to be the world's largest full-service restaurant company.[1] Besides the Capital Grille, Darden owns Olive Garden, Red Lobster, LongHorn Steakhouse, Bahama Breeze, Seasons 52, and other restaurant brands, employing almost 180,000 workers in 1,900 restaurants worldwide.[2] Restaurant corporations like Darden lead the National Restaurant Association (NRA) and actively lobby to keep the minimum wage as low as possible and to stop paid sick-day legislation from passing in any locality or at the federal level—with dire consequences for customers.[3] Although it raked in profits of over $7 billion in 2011 and has a CEO who earns $8.5 million annually and holds $22 million in company stock,[4] Darden pays its workers as little as $2.13 an hour (before tips) and does not provide paid sick days to any nonmanagement employee. In fact, just as workers from the Capital Grille in Miami were approaching ROC in the fall of 2011, Darden was found responsible for a major public health disaster. A server at an Olive Garden in Fayetteville, North Carolina, felt compelled to work with hepatitis A because she could not get paid sick days. While Darden was proudly announcing a new partnership between the Olive Garden and First Lady Michelle Obama to provide healthy food for kids at the Olive Garden, 3,000 people in Fayetteville had to get tested for hepatitis after eating at the restaurant.[5]

In late 2011, Oscar and Jean met Frantz, a young Haitian immigrant struggling to make ends meet while working as a dishwasher at the Capital Grille. At this restaurant, as at so many other restaurants we surveyed in Miami, the workers got darker—literally!—as you walked from the front door to the kitchen, and the darker the workers' skin, the less money they were likely to earn. Thus, whites and light-skinned Latinos were found serving and bartending, olive-skinned Latinos were found bussing and running food to tables, darker-skinned Latinos and African Americans were in the kitchen preparing and cooking food, and Haitians—the darkest-skinned, poorest, and most vulnerable population in Miami— were almost always dishwashers, the lowest-paid employees at restaurants.

Frantz was no exception, earning less than $10 an hour. Although he had been hired as a seafood prep cook, the restaurant quickly demoted him to dishwasher. What really upset him, however, was the way he and the other Haitian dishwashers were treated because of their position at the bottom of the restaurant hierarchy. Some workers made fun of Frantz and the other Haitians, mimicking their accents and calling them dumb and illiterate. Management witnessed the taunts and did nothing.

One time, on a particularly busy night, Frantz was paired with an older Haitian dishwasher, who was slower at rinsing and stacking the piles of dirty dishes. Frantz ended up doing his own work, plus most of the other dishwasher's work, moving dishes around so rapidly that one of the bussers made the offhand remark, "Frantz is working like a slave." Some of the kitchen workers laughed at the busser's remark, but the manager didn't say anything. This made Frantz particularly upset.

"Why would you say that?" he asked the busser, who replied that he was just joking. "I don't appreciate you calling me a slave."

During this time Frantz repeatedly asked Vladimir, one of the managers, for the opportunity to work as a busser. Frantz had previously worked as a busser at another restaurant in Miami Beach, so he knew he could do it. Vladimir said, "We'll see," but he continued hiring new bussers from outside the restaurant.

On top of the disrespect, Frantz often wasn't paid for all the hours he worked. He'd finish a long, exhausting shift at the hot dishwashing machine and clock out, only to find that the sous chef Fernando had already clocked him out, sometimes 15 minutes, sometimes half an hour before he had finished working. Frantz warned Fernando, "If you clock me out, I'm not going to finish the work," but it kept happening. The other Haitian dishwashers noticed this as well, and one went to management to complain, only to find his hours reduced shortly afterward. Frantz decided just to let it go—he couldn't afford to have his hours cut.

Eventually, however, Frantz decided enough was enough and met with Oscar, Jean, and ROC-Miami's newest organizer, Jaimie. "I wanted this to change," he says. "That's why I fought for it. People should respect the dishwashers, give them better pay." This conviction sustained Frantz even through difficult moments after the campaign launched. Frantz organized a group of workers and supporters to deliver a demand letter to the Capital Grille during dinner service. The letter notified Darden that workers at the Miami-area Capital Grille would be joining the federal lawsuit initiated by workers in other cities, and that it would be illegal for the company to retaliate against those workers.

A few of the workers who had made fun of Frantz before now tried to taunt him for demanding his rights. One stole his work shoes—$45 non-slip kitchen shoes that he had left in the restaurant locker room. Frantz told the sous chef Carlos that his shoes had been stolen and that he did not have enough money to buy another pair. Carlos was generous and understanding; at the end of the shift he walked Frantz to his car and gave him $40. According to federal law, the restaurant should actually pay for uniform or equipment needed to work in the kitchen, but neither Frantz nor Carlos knew that.

Although it was hard for Frantz and his coworkers to stand up to their restaurant's management, just delivering the demand letter brought about significant change at the Miami Capital Grille. The company, under new pressure to comply with the law, stopped clocking Frantz and the other dishwashers out before they finished their shifts.

Frantz's confidence also grew. At this time the Occupy Wall Street movement had been in full swing for more than a year, and Jon Ronson, author of the book *The Men Who Stare at Goats,* which became a Hollywood blockbuster, approached ROC about profiling a restaurant worker for *GQ* magazine (restaurant workers are, of course, among the 99 percent who serve the 1 percent). Frantz agreed to be the profiled worker: a Haitian dishwasher in a restaurant that served steak to Miami's elite. He told Ronson about his life, and how he struggled to make ends meet.

Frantz had grown up in Delmas, a suburb of Port-au-Prince, Haiti. He remembered playing soccer with his friends and being envied by most of them for the things his mother would buy him. She worked at the White

Frantz being photographed for his article in *GQ* magazine.
Courtesy of Restaurant Opportunies Center of Miami.

House, the president of Haiti's headquarters, but unfortunately lost her job after a time. When Frantz was 20, he had to drop out of college, where he was studying mechanical engineering, because his mother could no longer afford to pay his tuition. He began working for his uncle's T-shirt company until his father, who'd already immigrated to Miami, was finally able to pay for Frantz to immigrate as well. In 2008, at the age of 23, Frantz packed his bags and moved to Miami with his mother and brother to join his father, grandmother, and grandfather in a small house in Miami Beach, where they live today. Frantz's grandparents rent the house. He pays $200 a month for his room. His mother and brother share another room for which his father pays, and his father sleeps in a covered porch outside of the house. However, Frantz's wages at the Capital Grille do not always leave him with enough money to pay the $200, which makes it harder for his grandparents to pay the rent for the whole house. This really bothers Frantz. "Sometimes I worry about my life," he says. "I want to help my mother and my grandmother, but I can't always help them, and it gives me a headache. When she asks me for something, I can't give it to her. It's hard for me."

Frantz's worries extend beyond Miami and the United States. In 2010, just a year and a half after he left Port-au-Prince, Haiti was devastated by a massive earthquake. Frantz went to visit his aunt and uncle, who were safe and alive but had lost their house. "All the houses were broken up," says Frantz. "There were so many people on the street. The whole city was broken down. When I came back to Miami, I told my mom what I saw, and I was crying. I want to help my auntie and uncle, but I can't. I don't have the money to help them. It was terrible to see how they were living. Their house was cracked, leaning to the side. It was not safe to stay in that house—it had shifted. They ended up going to a field and sleeping in a tent with lots of other people."

In his interview with Ronson, Frantz explained that he joined ROC and helped launch the campaign against Capital Grille to stand up for himself, his family, and the rest of the 99 percent, who continue to endure outrageous working conditions, discriminatory labor practices, and poverty-level wages. At the time of this book's publication, the Capital Grille campaign has grown to include more than 70 workers in eight cities nationwide, and has already forced Darden to make company-wide changes. "I feel happy to have joined ROC and to be part of the campaign," Frantz says. "ROC has helped me stand up to make sure the restaurant respects everybody."

The Color of Fine-Dining, Casual, and Fast-Food Restaurants

People are segregated in the restaurant industry by position within the restaurant (server, busser, dishwasher), segment of the restaurant industry (fine-dining, family-style, or fast-food), and location (poor, middle-class, or upper-class neighborhood). In other words, workers are divided among "front of the house" and "back of the house" positions in fine-dining, casual, and fast-food restaurants. This segregation is due in part to outright racial discrimination when workers apply for these jobs. It also occurs because white workers are more likely to live in better neighborhoods, and as a result they are more likely to have easy access to fine-dining restaurants in which they hold higher-paying positions than people of color (see fig. 3). Workers of color are more likely to live in poorer neighborhoods, where they have easier access to lower-paying jobs in more casual, family-style restaurants and fast-food chains. The result? A race tax of over $4. In our national survey of over 4,300 restaurant workers, white workers reported a median wage of $14.00 an hour, while people of color reported a median wage of $9.88 an hour. Ninety-six percent of workers who reported that they earned less than the minimum wage were people of color.[6]

You can walk into almost any fine-dining restaurant in a big city in the United States and note the pattern: white workers in the front, serving and bartending; maybe a few workers of color in the front, bussing tables, running the hot food, and hosting; and mostly workers of color in the back, preparing and cooking food and washing dishes. Behind the kitchen door, you can almost find a replica of the segregated buses of the Jim Crow South. Restaurant managers reserve their highest-paying, most visible positions for white people, and workers of color are relegated to lower-paying, invisible positions in the back. Interviews with workers and employers reveal that this is a commonly accepted industry practice, thinly veiled by legalese and managers' self-righteous notions of "skills," "table manners," "language ability," and "professional appearance." In the Jim Crow South, workers of color would have been formally barred from even applying for front of the house positions; nowadays they are simply trapped in lower-level positions based on certain white employers' prejudiced views about what constitutes good service. As one Detroit manager with 20 years in the industry put it, "Well, diversity in Detroit usually means everyone in the back of the house is black, everybody in the front of the house is white. That's what you'd expect."[7]

In our national survey, three-quarters of all white workers held a position in the front of a restaurant, while less than half of all African American and about one-third of all Latino workers held a front of the house position.[8] Even when people of color made it to the front of the house, they

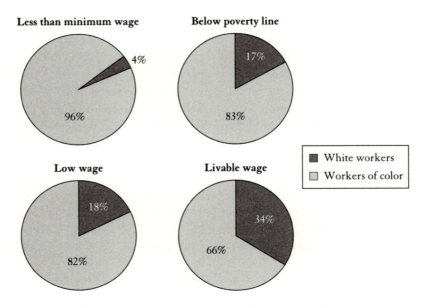

Figure 3. Racial makeup of wage categories. Adapted from Restaurant Opportunities Center of Washington, D.C., Restaurant Opportunities Centers United, and Washington, D.C., Restaurant Industry Coalition, *Behind the Kitchen Door: Inequality & Opportunity in Washington, D.C.'s Thriving Restaurant Industry,* technical report (New York: Restaurant Opportunities Center of Washington, D.C., 2011), p. 42, fig. 5; http://rocunited.org/blog/roc-dc-behind-the-kitchen-door/. *Source:* Washington, D.C., Restaurant Industry Coalition Survey Data.

usually earned less than white workers because they were more likely to be bussers than waiters, and waiters earn up to five times more than bussers. (Recall the Latino busser at the beginning of this chapter; he made around $30,000 a year as a busser, whereas servers in the restaurant earned up to $150,000.) One woman bartender with eleven years of experience reported, "The bussers at my restaurant are all black men. I think management definitely wouldn't let any of our busboys become servers. And it is somewhat racial."[9]

In Miami, where Oscar and Frantz live and work, the racial hierarchy at the Capital Grille is the norm, not the exception. As noted above, at the Capital Grille, as in too many Miami restaurants, restaurant workers get darker and earn less the farther back into the kitchen they work, with Haitian workers almost universally found as dishwashers in fine-dining restaurants throughout the Miami area. As Frantz exemplifies, this racial hierarchy has direct implications for these workers' ability to pay rent, support their families, and survive. In our survey of about 600 restaurant workers in Miami-Dade County, white workers reported a median wage of $11.29 per hour; Latinos, $10.00 per hour; non-Haitian blacks, $9.00 per hour; and Haitians, $8.21 per hour.[10]

Oscar was lucky because he worked in a fine-dining establishment, as wages and working conditions vary according to the type of restaurant. As can be expected, the more casual the restaurant the less a worker earns. There are some living-wage jobs in family-style and fast-food restaurants, but most such jobs are in the fine-dining segment of the industry; fine-dining workers report a median wage of $15.00 per hour, while workers in family-style establishments report a median wage of $12.13 per hour, and workers in fast food report a median wage of $8.50 per hour.[11] It's often the price of meals in fine-dining establishments, along with higher tips, that allows workers to earn higher wages than their counterparts in family-style and fast-food restaurants.[12]

Unfortunately, workers of color are overrepresented in fast-food restaurants. Nearly 60 percent (58%) of black workers surveyed by ROC reported working in fast-food jobs; only about one-quarter of white workers reported working in fast food.

Wanting a Tall White Man's Suit

Maya, an ROC leader and former restaurant worker living in Washington, D.C., jokes about what it feels like to be a person of color in the restaurant industry. "I wish I'd had a tall white man's suit to get ahead in the industry," she says. Maya left the restaurant industry a couple of years ago to work full-time as a fashion designer, but her original plan was to work her way up from hostess to restaurant manager.

Maya is anything but a tall white man. She is a curvy black woman with flawless brown skin. She wears her hair in many different ways—natural, in braids, straightened—but always neat and often pulled back with a cute headband. She wears trendy glasses and has a beautiful smile. She's upbeat, vivacious, and allergic to pretension. She's also book-smart and streetwise. She can talk to just about anyone, maybe because she grew up with a foot on either side of the tracks.

In fact, it's hard to put a "class label" on Maya. She's complicated. She was born and raised in the nation's capital, a third-generation D.C. resident. "I attended the same high school as my grandmother and was born in the same hospital as my mom," she says. "I've known my best friend since kindergarten. We grew up together in Trinidad." Trinidad is a close-knit Washington, D.C., neighborhood with a reputation for being rough. Maya stood out among her friends. "My parents were married," she says. "A lot of my friends didn't have that. The way I grew up reflected the fact that I had both parents in my life. I had been ice-skating and skiing when I was very young. My dad would bring cupcakes and flowers to school and take me to skating lessons. We had warm apple cider in the winter. My friends called me the Cosby kid."

Maya was sheltered from neighborhood violence, but as she grew older she began to notice how violence and poverty shaped the world around her. "It was a confusing time for me," says Maya. "I watched a lot of TV. I was watching an HBO documentary about prostitutes and pimps when I was in the fifth grade. I made some comment about it not being real, and my mom said, 'No, this is real.' She dropped everything and took me to Thomas Circle to see prostitutes in real life. I didn't know anything about that kind of life. I thought everyone lived the way I did."

As Maya entered her teen years, she began to understand the challenges confronted by other African American families in Trinidad. "My friends succumbed to the neighborhood," says Maya. "I went to a lot of funerals. My best friend from kindergarten had three kids before the age of 21, and that was the best form of contraception for me. I changed a lot of diapers and wiped a lot of asses from the time I was 16. So I stayed single with no kids. Most of my friends never went to college. They got involved with the criminal justice system or ended up being teen moms on welfare. Meanwhile, I was going to camp or skiing or learning at Archbishop Carroll. My friends from there got master's degrees. I always experienced both side of the tracks."

Maya's family also sheltered her from racial discrimination. She heard and read about it and watched *Roots* on television, but she never witnessed it until after she left for college in North Carolina. "I was with my friends who were getting food in Arby's—I don't eat fast food," says Maya. "I heard this group of people have an entire conversation next to us. They were a group of four white older people having a conversation about 'the nigger.' They weren't calling me one. They were just having the conversation." Maya was shocked that such overt racism still existed.

Since she had to support herself during college without her family's help, Maya decided to accept a friend's invitation to apply for a job at a local Applebee's restaurant. When she got a job as a hostess, she felt incredibly fortunate. After all, she didn't have any restaurant experience. She enjoyed greeting customers and taking them to their tables, and soon she fell in love with restaurant work. The chance to meet so many people, hear so many stories, and build community appealed to her outgoing personality. She moved on to work in other restaurants in North Carolina, and then moved to Miami, where she worked in restaurants while earning her degree at the Miami International University of Art & Design. After graduating, she returned to Washington, D.C., and looked for a position in a fine-dining restaurant. She loved the diversity in D.C., a city with immigrants from all over the world. "I had learned to speak Spanish in Miami, but in D.C. I learned to say 'hello,' 'good-bye,' 'thank you,' and to count to five in at least seven languages," says Maya. Of course, she'd noticed that her employers were not so diverse. They were typically white men—young and old, but all white.

Maya got a job as a hostess at a fine-dining steakhouse restaurant and started earning $10 an hour. Although her title was hostess, her job included sending out invoices, managing workers in the front and the back of the house, overseeing deliveries, and other management tasks. She took on more responsibilities and was hired as a weekend office manager. She practically ran the business—especially when the manager had to leave the office for heart surgery. She got to know the restaurant as if it were her own and felt fortunate to be working in such an elegant restaurant in the nation's capital, where so many of her friends from home couldn't get a job. She worked seven days a week.

"After six months I knew—this is what I want to do," says Maya. "I loved the combination of smells unique to all restaurants: the perfumes, cologne, ice-cold water in glasses, and the food." She loved the camaraderie among the staff and meeting the customers. One day she'd serve a large party of members of Congress, another day the White House press secretary. She met leaders from around the world. (D.C. restaurant workers often have the most exceptional stories about high-profile clientele.) On the other hand, she saw things that made her uncomfortable. "I saw congressmen get together with donors to smoke a pack of cigarettes," she says. "I saw congressmen and senators get together with the pharmaceutical companies. They'd have loud, raucous parties, rent out the private dining room. Congressmen would get all kinds of perks just for being there. They'd get thousands of dollars. One time a friend of mine caught a happily married congressman doing it with another woman in one of the restaurant's private dining rooms. Doing it there just because they could. These guys would smoke a pack of cigarettes and blow it in your face. We saw lots of adultery, lots of flirting. All kinds of people hanging out together—Republicans hanging out with Democrats, as if they were the best of friends. I'd watch C-SPAN, so I knew them all, and then I'd see them at the pharmaceutical companies' private parties. A lot of congressmen would show up. The pharmaceutical reps would pass out money, and then everyone would get some food. You'd actually see the envelope being passed."

One day Maya went on Craigslist to find out if any new restaurants were opening in the neighborhood and who was hiring, and she noticed an online advertisement for an assistant manager in the very same restaurant in which she worked. The managers had not informed Maya or any other workers in the restaurant that the position was open, denying them the opportunity to apply, but that didn't stop Maya. "I told the general manager I was interested, and he kind of laughed," says Maya. The restaurant ended up filling the position with a light-skinned man from the Middle East—the former manager of a Denny's restaurant. "The new guy had never worked in a fine-dining restaurant, didn't know the restaurant's online reservation system, didn't even know how to sell wine," says Maya. "He knew 'sunny-side up.'" Maya ended up training him in all of the restaurant's procedures.

The experience greatly disappointed her. She started making jokes about needing "a tall white man's suit." She thought that if she could buy the suit, she'd have a better chance of being promoted and everything would be better. White men seemed to hold the highest-paying positions in all of the fine-dining restaurants. Maya didn't have straight blonde hair and blue eyes. She didn't have the right look for management positions. She didn't fit the mold.

Where White People Live, Where People of Color Live

For all the Oscars and Mayas who can't move up the ladder in fine-dining restaurants, there are thousands of workers who never even make it to the neighborhoods that have fine-dining restaurants. Segregation in the industry is not just a matter of employers having discriminatory hiring practices; it's also about people of color not having access to more affluent neighborhoods, which are home to more affluent establishments.

Washington, D.C., is one of the most racially segregated cities in the United States, with more income inequality between blacks and whites than any other city in the nation.[13] Wards 7 and 8 are the lowest-income areas of the district, and the majority of people living in these wards are African American. The majority of workers ROC surveyed in Wards 7 and 8 worked in fast-food restaurants. Only *one* of those workers earned a livable wage, and more than half lived below the poverty line. On the other end of the spectrum is Ward 2, where Maya worked—a predominantly white, wealthy area with a higher concentration of restaurants in which there are more opportunities to earn higher wages.[14]

ROC's most striking finding was that even when residents of Wards 7 and 8 found work in more affluent neighborhoods, they couldn't earn higher wages. Residents of Wards 7 and 8 who commuted to other wards reported a median wage of $8.50 an hour—the same median wage earned by workers in Wards 7 and 8.[15] Why? The residents of Wards 7 and 8 lacked the social connections and training to access better-paying positions even when they traveled long distances to work.

I've observed this pattern in cities across the United States. In Detroit, a cook with nine years' experience explained, "With Detroit, for some reason...you see the black bussers and then you might have a white manager. Or in some situations everyone might be black, but that's usually in the city of Detroit. When you go past 8 Mile...anything above 8 Mile is considered white, and anything below 8 Mile, which is Detroit, is considered black.... there are different sections for different people...but ultimately it's all separated—like, the black people stick to the black people, and white people stick to the white people."[16]

Detroit has a surprisingly large and vibrant restaurant industry, with over 134,000 workers in the metro area. The city also has the highest level of residential segregation of any metro area with a population of over

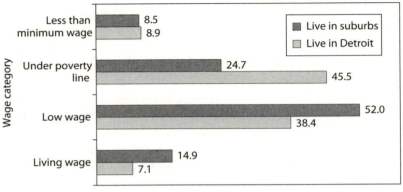

Percentage of workers

Figure 4. Restaurant workers' wages by geographical area, Detroit. Adapted from Restaurant Opportunities Center of Michigan, Restaurant Opportunities Centers United, and Southeast Michigan Restaurant Industry Coalition, *Behind the Kitchen Door: Inequality and Opportunity in Metro Detroit's Growing Restaurant Industry,* technical report (New York: Restaurant Opportunities Center of Michigan, 2010), p. 45, fig. 5; http://rocunited.org/blog/roc-michigan-behind-the-kitchen-door/. *Source:* Southeast Michigan Restaurant Industry Coalition Survey Data.

150,000 in the United States.[17] Where you live in the Detroit metropolitan area affects your wages (see fig. 4). White workers living in the suburbs are twice as likely to earn a living wage as black workers living in the city of Detroit. This is true even though the two populations are similar in terms of other demographic variables—gender, age, place of birth, and educational attainment.[18]

Low-wage workers of color who live in Detroit must commute long distances with little or no access to public transportation to reach the suburban living-wage jobs. In addition, they face tremendous discrimination outside city limits. One of ROC's leaders in Detroit told us that when she applied for a job in a fine-dining restaurant in Troy, a suburb of Detroit, she was first asked, "You're not planning on eating here, are you?" When she asked about employment, a manager told her that the restaurant had never hired an African American worker in its 10-year history.

Los Angeles is home to more restaurants than any other city in the United States, and it is one of the most sprawling metropolises in the world. The highest-paying restaurant jobs in Los Angeles are concentrated in white upper-class neighborhoods. This means every day thousands of workers commute long distances for better restaurant jobs, and many thousands more, the majority of whom are people of color living in poorer areas, simply don't have access to living-wage jobs. In addition, those who commute must contend with Los Angeles's woefully inadequate public transportation system. When public transportation fails or buses run more slowly than usual, these workers struggle to get to work on time and keep their jobs. They also endure difficult, sometime unsafe commutes home after late-night shifts. The commutes can be especially dangerous for women. Not surprisingly, women account for 63 percent (62.9%) of Los Angeles restaurant workers who turned down a job offer because of inadequate transportation.[19]

On top of all this, ROC has found that people of color win the prize for longest commute times. The average daily commute time reported by Los Angeles restaurant workers is 53 minutes, but people of color who work in fine dining must commute an additional 11 minutes every day.[20]

Why Discriminate?

Maya kept trying to move up in the restaurant business despite her setback at the D.C. steakhouse. She knew she had the skills to run a restaurant and hoped to find an opportunity to be promoted to management. She even sent in her résumé for a maître'd position in a very fancy steakhouse in D.C.'s city center. Her résumé was amazing by this point; she had worked practically every front of the house position except management. "I spoke with the steakhouse general manager on the phone for like five minutes and we hit it off, so I thought it was really promising," says Maya. "In my mind, I had the job. But when I got to the restaurant, the general manager said, 'You're Maya?' He was really taken aback when he saw me." He seemed surprised by her appearance, even though she was very well-dressed—impeccably dressed, actually. He told her, "You don't have the look to be a maître'd, but I can hire you as a hostess." The person he eventually hired for the maître'd position was a tall white man. Maya knew she had far more experience than he. She took the job as a hostess, but she was extremely disappointed. She no longer felt as though experience and skills mattered in the restaurant industry. She says, "I even saw some women having to do sexual favors to advance in the industry, but I had too much pride to do something like that."

ROC research shows that one of the main reasons discriminatory practices fly under the radar in restaurants is the lack of transparency with regard to job openings and what it takes to get a promotion.[21] Workers of color rarely know when there are opportunities to advance, enabling managers to hire white workers surreptitiously, from the outside. In the absence of any formalized promotion and hiring systems, employers are able to use whatever criteria they please when hiring and promoting workers. Many claim to consider "table talk"—the ability to converse with and easily relate to wealthy white clientele. Another criterion is appearance. (Women of color like Maya are often chastised by restaurant managers for their body type and hair.) A third criterion is language ability and accent, which is used against some workers and not against others.

When asked about diversity among their front of the house workers, many employers told ROC that they hired "those who applied." They were aware that front of the house workers were predominantly white and that back of the house workers were overwhelmingly people of color, but they maintained that this was because blacks and other people of color apply primarily for back of the house positions. One owner of a family-style restaurant said, "We have mostly white but also black and Latino employees. Mostly white in the front of the house, because white people apply for those positions. Back of the house is mixed."[22]

However, workers of color, even those who speak English fluently, have reported that they generally do not apply for front of the house positions because, in their experience, people of color are never hired for those positions. One woman of color from New Orleans with 13 years of restaurant experience told us, "In the front of the house I rarely see people like myself. I kind of know from both perspectives, being a patron and a worker, that there are some Hispanic people in front of house positions, but it depends on the place. At fine-dining establishments in the French Quarter, you can be as smart as this book right here, but they won't hire you for certain positions if you look like me."[23]

Asking Employers for Equality

When I started on this path to end segregation and discrimination in restaurants, I sometimes second-guessed myself. Part of me couldn't believe

that racial injustice could be so blatant in the twenty-first century and affect so many restaurant workers in the United States. My ROC coworkers and I decided that we needed a research study to back up our worker
surveys. We wanted something more concrete to support our antidiscrimi-
nation campaigns.

In 2006, we launched a study to examine how hiring practices affect segregation and discrimination in restaurants. We sent pairs of applicants—
one white person, one person of color, with the same qualifications—to
apply for waitstaff positions in fine-dining restaurants all over New York
City. Over a three-year period, we sent 200 pairs, or 400 people, to interviews. We found that, even holding accent constant, white workers were
twice as likely as workers of color to obtain living-wage positions in fine-
dining restaurants.[24] In addition, workers of color were questioned about
their qualifications at three times the rate of white workers. We also found
that a strong, even incomprehensible European accent is an advantage,
while a Third World accent is a serious detriment.[25]

This study certainly reflects what we saw in our campaign against the
four-star restaurant in New York City that refused to promote its Latino
bussers. Management in that restaurant constantly promoted less experienced French immigrants to waitstaff positions; these French workers
spoke with a very heavy accent and usually knew less about the menu than
their Latino coworkers. I remember one quote in particular from the *New
York Times* article about the workers' allegations. The restaurant's French
chef remarked that promotions in the restaurant "were a question of trust
and evolution." His comment really concerned me. What did he mean?
White workers were more trustworthy? Workers like Oscar and Maya
weren't as loyal? I'd seen how loyal workers of color could be, particularly
when they were offered an opportunity to advance. Workers of color often
didn't take promotions for granted. Many of them had families to support.

What surprised me most during our four-star restaurant campaign was
that I received a number of calls from angry affluent New Yorkers who
felt we'd gone too far in campaigning against discriminatory labor practices. Many said they enjoyed interacting with a diverse waitstaff in their
favorite fine-dining restaurants. A few wealthy customers yelled at me;
they said that the people on the dining floor were diverse and that they enjoyed speaking Spanish with them. However, around this time ROC also
received a visit from another waiter from the four-star restaurant. This

waiter looked white, but he was actually a very light-skinned Latino. Asking us to maintain confidentiality, he told us he'd been hired as a server in the restaurant because no one could tell he was person of color. His cousin, who had significantly darker skin, couldn't get a waitstaff position, even though he spoke perfect English and had several years of experience and exceptional skills as a runner. So while these wealthy customers might have indeed interacted with a diverse array of workers on the dining floor, the workers earning the highest wages—servers and bartenders—were predominantly white.

ROC eventually won the campaign against the four-star restaurant. The *New York Times* article seemed to help move the campaign, prompting the restaurant's management to promote several Latino and Bangladeshi bussers and runners and develop a new promotions policy monitored by the Equal Employment Opportunity Commission. Most important to ROC, the new promotions policy compelled management to inform all workers about new openings and provide training that would enable workers to advance to higher-paying positions.

For my part, I became even more aware of the chasm between American food values and business practices. Nowadays, though, I also see avenues toward closing that chasm. Many people, especially in urban centers like New York City, want a thriving, diverse food culture. My sense is that the majority of diners now see restaurants as windows on the world. After all, the term "foodie" is supposed to reflect a new, omnivorous cultural interest in a wide range of foods, "from high-brow classics to low-brow culinary treasures."[26] We just tend not to recognize the work involved in bringing all this food to restaurant tables—and most of us, unless we work in restaurants, don't realize that huge populations of workers of color are denied opportunities to advance and can't earn a living wage in restaurants. We tend not to realize that diversity is not the same as equity—that simply seeing a lot of restaurant workers from different backgrounds doesn't mean that restaurant workers have equal opportunities to advance to jobs that will allow them to support themselves and their families.

Let me be clear: I'm talking about extending opportunities to workers of color who *know* the menu, *know* the cuisine, and *really* care about the work they're doing to bring food to the table. In the same way, opportunities should be extended to white workers who have the skills, loyalty, and dedication to do the job—not just "the right look."

As consumers, we can support equal opportunity policies in a number of ways; I've discussed in other chapters many of the steps consumers can take to promote equality, and I will go into further detail in chapter 7, "Recipes for Change." Here, however, I want to emphasize the power we have as consumers when we ask questions in restaurants.

I frequently eat out with friends and acquaintances who ask servers questions like, "Is the arugula organic?" or "Is the burger grass-fed beef?" or "Are the strawberries locally grown?" These kinds of questions have compelled restaurateurs across the United States to rethink their menus, but we can help create more equitable restaurants and put a stop to segregation and discriminatory labor practices by asking another set of questions: "Do you have promotion and training opportunities in your restaurant? How diverse is your waitstaff?" Most managers value feedback from their customers. You can make an enormous difference by simply letting managers know that a diverse waitstaff is as important to you as the quality of your meal. As long as restaurateurs strive to be popular and profitable, they will listen when we tell them what we want and what we value in our dining experience.

6

Women Waiting on Equality

There's usually catcalls, whistles, "Hey mami, come over here."
I keep walking, [and when I] come back, it's the same thing. After
working there for almost two years, it gets tiring. They told me not to
get too emotional about it. [The manager] says it's perfectly normal
in society to see a woman and call after her, to touch her.

— Host, Woman, Two Years in the Industry, Miami

Women get less than preferential treatment across the board...
whether you're management, whether you're a hostess, whether
you're a waitress...whether you're a bartender....That less-than-
preferential treatment is from the client, that's from the management,
that's from the owners, that's from the bussers, that's from
the porters who are cleaning...across the board,
women get less.

— Bartender, Man, New York City

Beginning in 2006, the *New York Post* published several articles docu-
menting sexual harassment in restaurant kitchens in the United States.
I remember the scandalous headlines: "Tomatoes in the Kitchen," "Un-
just Desserts," "Dirty Dishes," "Ramsay Has a Little Side Dish," and
"Bar's Lurid 'Sex Dorm,'" to name a few. One woman chef described
how a sous chef had once followed her into a locker room to watch her
change clothes; she'd had to push him out. A woman pastry chef described how her former boss, an executive chef at Manhattan's Oak

Room, had nicknamed her "whore" and forced her to smear egg on her chest; when she protested or tried to leave his kitchen, he threatened to ruin her career.

At the time it seemed to me that these exceptional cases of sexual harassment and gender inequity coincided with the rise in celebrity chef reality TV shows. American television viewers were practically celebrating chefs like Gordon Ramsay, who starred in *Hell's Kitchen* and *Kitchen Nightmares,* for being loud-mouthed, sexist jerks. Ramsay boasted to journalists, "I told one woman in Los Angeles to get her boobs off my hot plate." Reflecting on his behavior on *Hell's Kitchen,* Ramsay said, "I know I give [people] verbal [abuse], but I don't hit them physically." Every time Ramsay opened his mouth he seemed to promote the ridiculous idea that being a great, "cool" chef meant aggressively harassing and demeaning other people in the kitchen, especially women.

Not surprisingly, dozens of women started coming to ROC's offices to report exactly the kind of abuses they'd read about in the papers. One woman told me that when she'd asked her manager for a promotion from server to bartender, he'd asked her what she'd be willing to *do* for a promotion. Several woman servers reported being forced to flash their managers before they punched in to work. Others described how aggressive men, mostly executive chefs, threw dishes, screamed racial epithets, and encouraged fights among workers. Since most of the men executive chefs ran hostile, testosterone-driven kitchens, women in the kitchen were constantly being ghettoized, pushed into pastry positions where they earned less money and had no opportunity for advancement in the restaurant. Few women could survive in "a man's kitchen."

Adding to women's frustration was the issue of unequal pay. The median weekly wage for women servers in the restaurant industry is $387; the median weekly wage for men servers is $423.[1] This wage gap is particularly troublesome for single mothers, who struggle to pay for child care. Women of color are at the greatest disadvantage. ROC surveys found a $4.50 an hour wage gap between women of color and other workers in the restaurant industry; this is largely because women of color work mostly in lower-paying segments of the industry, particularly fast food.[2]

So although the majority of restaurant workers in the United States are women, the majority of restaurant managers, chefs, and owners are men, and when women do make it into management positions, they earn less than their men counterparts. Why?

The answer, it seems, is just because.

Pushed into Pastry and Salad Prep Jobs

I met Alicia, a former pastry chef, around the height of the Gordon Ramsay scandal.

Alicia is a tall, light-skinned African American woman with a warm smile. She has the ability to build deep friendships with people from various backgrounds, even those who appear to be different from her in every way. People notice that she laughs a lot. She's open-minded, but also very principled. Most of all, she loves to cook.

Alicia was born in Baton Rouge, Louisiana. Her parents were Louisiana Creole. They met in college and got married. Her dad was an Air Force engineer, and so Alicia and her brother were military kids, moving from base to base every two years. They lived on bases in Louisiana, Arizona, Oklahoma, and other places in between.

Alicia fell in love with cooking at an early age. "At five or six I got an EasyBake Oven for Christmas," she says. "I'd make Kool-Aid. I'd have tea parties with my friends. I'd make cakes. My dad cooks, so I grew up cooking with my dad."

When Alicia was getting ready to go to college, it seemed natural to her that she'd go to culinary school. Her family had settled in Oklahoma, where her father had a contract at the nation's top military pilot training school. However, her father, who had taught her how to cook, was vehemently opposed to her becoming a chef. "My mom was a political science major in college. My dad had a master's degree in engineering," says Alicia. "So they didn't want me to go to culinary school. I was the smartest kid in the family. Coming from a middle-class African American family, they were saying, 'Why would you want to be a cook or a maid?' They said, 'If you choose that we won't help you out in school.' I couldn't apply for financial aid for culinary school without my parents, so I went to college with no idea what I'd do in life."

Alicia went to Northwestern Oklahoma State University and became a history major, but after graduation she was lost. If she wasn't going to be a chef, she had no idea what she would do. Her cousin in New Jersey invited her to spend some time with him while she figured it out. She moved to New Jersey and worked for a while as a babysitter, but soon her father called her and asked her to come back home; her mother had been diagnosed with multiple sclerosis, and her sister needed help. "My younger sister was at home, getting ready to go to college," says Alicia. "She was interested in going to school, but no one could help her with the application process. So I decided to move home, work, pay off my bills, and help my sister apply to schools."

As time went on, Alicia's father became more open to her following her own path. A few of Alicia's friends had moved to Philadelphia to work in various nonprofit organizations, and so after a year of being at home in Oklahoma, Alicia followed her friends to Philadelphia with her father's blessing. Philadelphia was the largest city in which Alicia had ever lived, and it was growing. New restaurants were opening left and right, and local chefs were gaining notoriety. "Philly" was becoming a real "foodie" town.

"Moving to Philly and figuring out who I am as a person, I had an epiphany," says Alicia. "I always wanted to go to culinary school. I did other stuff to please my parents. I thought, 'What the hell am I doing?' I always wanted to work in a restaurant. So I applied with no restaurant experience to culinary school and got in."

Alicia threw her heart and soul into the school and graduated with flying colors. One of her professors, who was genuinely impressed with her talent, became her mentor. He got her a cooking internship at one of the city's most famous new establishments, and so she became one of the thousands of culinary students who work in America's restaurant kitchens for free. Like a residency for medical students, the internship experience for new cooks is grueling. Alicia's internship was a crash course in kitchen politics. Everyone knew this restaurant had the potential to become something big, and everyone was trying to prove themselves. "It was a really hostile kitchen," says Alicia. "It was physically hostile. I remember seeing two sous chefs getting into a physical fight. The kitchen was in the basement, so they went up to the alley above and started pushing each other. It was just so fiercely competitive. The cooks would ruin each other's prepped foods, even change the temperature on ovens when someone else was cooking something. If one cook was trying to do a special, another cook would use up something that person needed to prep the menu item. The chef would then have to run out and buy what was needed."

There were about 20 cooks and chefs in the kitchen, 3 of whom were women. One was Alicia's boss, the pastry chef, who kept to herself and counseled Alicia to do the same. The other two were immigrant women who prepared the salads and also kept to themselves; they didn't speak much English. Alicia noted a similar arrangement in every kitchen she saw in Philadelphia: women were pretty much relegated to pastry and salad positions, jobs that were considered "easier," and they were paid less for their work. "Never have I seen women on the line," says Alicia, referring to the main cooking assembly line, which includes the butchering, grill, fry, sauté, and other stations. Line workers in her restaurant earned more money and had the opportunity to advance to sous chef and executive chef positions. Alicia almost never saw a woman sous or executive chef.

"The men thought we were cutesy, the cute girls back there making cookies," says Alicia. "They didn't think women were knowledgeable about steaks and wines."

The way that the men looked down on Alicia's boss and other women in the kitchen was also apparent. "They would call us 'little girls,'" says Alicia. "Once the executive sous chef called a managers meeting but left my boss out. When my boss asked why she wasn't invited, he said, 'You're a bunch of girls doing desserts.'"

Alicia knew her boss was frustrated. There were daily humiliations. "I remember seeing the sous chef grab my boss physically to move her out of the way," says Alicia. "He would always call her a little girl." The restaurant also seemed unwilling to acknowledge her boss's contributions to the menu or the kitchen, and when she finally quit, the restaurant kept her recipes without giving her any credit.

Alicia finished the internship gracefully and landed her first job in a restaurant in a downtown Philadelphia hotel. It was a totally different world. The kitchen was calmer and far less competitive. The hotel had a human resources department that actually listened to workers' concerns and was proactive in resolving complaints. She saw the same kind of segregation by gender—of the 25 cooks and chefs in the kitchen, all 3 women worked in pastry and salad—but the decent pay and good working atmosphere created a lot of loyalty among the staff, most of whom expected to be there for a long time.

Alicia, too, would have stayed a long time—but her mentor from culinary school called and told her about a great opportunity for a higher-paying pastry position in one of the city's finest fine-dining restaurants.

Sex and Power in "A Man's Kitchen"

The new restaurant met Alicia's every expectation. The kitchen was fast-paced, intense, and putting out amazing food. As pastry sous chef, Alicia was given tremendous freedom to be creative with the desserts. "I created ice cream flavors," says Alicia, "so I'd go to a special market and order a weird chocolate from Nigeria." Her direct supervisor, the executive pastry chef, encouraged her to be creative and supported her professional advancement in the industry.

Once again, however, she'd entered a segregated kitchen. The kitchen had 18 cooks and chefs, 2 of whom were women—Alicia, working pastry, and another woman in salad. The restaurant did have an ethnically diverse staff, but the lower the position, the darker the skin. The waitstaff was composed of all white workers, mostly men. The bussers were almost entirely Latino. The lower-level cooks, dishwashers, and cleaners were black. There was one waiter of color, a light-skinned young man who was half African American and half white. Whenever a darker-skinned person of color would apply for a waitstaff position, the light-skinned waiter would run to the back of the house to chat with Alicia, one of the only other black workers in the restaurant. "They're never going to hire her," he would joke. "After all, they already have me. I'm the token for the restaurant. The position is filled!" He was right—none of the black applicants ever got hired. He remained the only African American man on the dining floor.

Alicia figured that the restaurant would argue that no qualified people of color had applied to the restaurant for server positions, but she knew the real reason people of color didn't apply. "I remember telling one person from the hotel to apply at my restaurant," says Alicia. "She was black and had natural hair. She looked at me and said, 'Alicia, would they ever hire me in the front of the house at that restaurant?' I thought about it and told her, 'No I'm sorry. You're right. You'd never get hired.'" It wasn't just that most of the servers were white and that Alicia's friend was a dark-skinned black woman. It was that a woman had to look a certain way—skinny, about 5'7", with long, straight hair. The difference in pay was tremendous. Alicia's friend made about $35,000 as a server in the hotel. Some of the servers in Alicia's restaurant earned about double that amount. Even among those lucky servers in Alicia's restaurant, however, men earned significantly more in tips than women.

The fine-dining restaurant was part of a "rising star" restaurant company, with eight establishments and expanding in Philadelphia. Sometimes management called meetings for all the sous chefs and chefs in the company. Only 3 of 37 managers were people of color, and Alicia was the only woman of color in the entire crew. "We would have manager meetings, and some of the other chefs would joke around with me," says Alicia. "They'd be singing, 'One of these things is not like the other, one of these things is not the same'—that song from *Sesame Street*."

Still, Alicia was enjoying her experience. She got along well with almost everyone in the kitchen, especially the other cooks. She got to know the guys sautéing fish and making steaks. "There were no women on the line," says Alicia. "But I made it there. I got closer to the line guys, and they thought it would be great for me to learn the grill. So for a few nights in a row they taught me to work the grill. But when the executive chef found out, he said, 'I like women working pastry. I don't need you on the line.'"

The problem was that the line was the only way to move up in the restaurant. Pastry jobs quickly dead-ended. Executive pastry chefs rarely became executive chefs, and almost all the executive pastry chefs Alicia knew were men. So women were not only relegated to the lowest-paying positions in the kitchen; they also couldn't move up. Plus, there was the pay differential. As pastry sous chef, Alicia was a salaried employee, but her earnings boiled down to $13.80 an hour. A salad prep cook—the only other kitchen position regularly offered to women—could make only $8.50 or $9.00 an hour. A cook on the line, however, could make $16.00 or $17.00 an hour.

To make matters worse, the executive chef had a bad reputation with women. "When I first started, the restaurant was one of the top restaurants in Philly, and his ego was as big as he was," says Alicia. "Humungous. Before the executive chef got there, there had been quite a few women in the kitchen, but I heard that they all left after dealing with him. He was a big flirt. He would cross personal boundaries with me all the time, even though he was married. I used to live about a 35-minute train ride away from the restaurant, and one day I forgot my chef pants at home. There was no one there whose pants would fit me, so I had to wear my shorts. I was working, and I felt this finger running all the way up the back of my leg and thigh. I turned around and said, 'Chef!' and he said, 'Really nice legs.' I went out to the alley to tell the other guys, and then they told me about all the hostesses the chef had been sleeping with. Months later I found out that even my friend, a hostess, was sleeping with him. He picked who got the best hours and who got promotions based on who slept with him."

One evening, on another smoking break in the alley, Alicia's friend Michelle, a server, said that she'd been forced to train a skinny, tall, blonde woman, who had been working in the restaurant for only a month and had no previous experience in a fine-dining restaurant. Management took Michelle's two highest-paying shifts—Friday and Saturday evenings—and gave them to this new woman, despite her lack of experience. Everyone knew that the chef was sleeping with this new woman. Michelle was upset but not surprised. "You know who makes the schedule," she said.

The chef slept with at least five different employees during the time that Alicia worked at the restaurant. Alicia thought the chef's wife knew what was going on. "For a while his wife was always calling and stopping in," she says. "Why would she show up at 8:00 p.m. in the middle of the kitchen rush? He would take her out front, introduce her to VIP people. Normally he'd be flirting up front. His wife was very wealthy, old money, an heiress."

At first Alicia couldn't understand why her friends would agree to sleep with this man. The more Alicia observed the chef's behavior, however, the better she understood the power dynamic between him and women workers in the restaurant. "He flew my friend and her sister to Paris, and bought her all this jewelry," says Alicia. "She was a hostess, a 21-year-old college student. He was 38." The chef's impact on their work was also clear: hostesses and servers, like Michelle, whom the chef didn't favor, were cut from the best shifts and got the worst schedules.

Alicia continued to enjoy working in the restaurant, despite everything. She loved her work preparing delicious desserts, and she enjoyed the camaraderie with some of her more supportive coworkers. She believed it was a terrific opportunity. Plus, her direct supervisor, the executive pastry chef, Fred, was always wonderful, supportive, and nurturing. "He gave me a copy of *Indulge,* a cookbook by Claire Clark, the pastry chef for the world-famous restaurant French Laundry," says Alicia. "He said that Clark, as the only woman chef in a restaurant, reminded him of me." In the introduction to her book, Clark writes about the difficulties of being a woman chef in a kitchen dominated by white men chefs; she remarks that a woman chef couldn't show emotion or cry in this environment because that would leave her vulnerable to ridicule and condescension. Fred gave Alicia the book because he thought that Clark's struggles were similar to hers.

Fred eventually received a promotion and became the executive pastry chef for three of the company's restaurants. After getting promoted, he was rarely in the restaurant, and Alicia started doing the work of the executive pastry chef without a promotion or raise.

Alicia found that she was far more uncomfortable working under the executive chef without Fred around to support her. Fred had always served as a buffer, and now the executive chef was free to say and do to Alicia all the inappropriate things he often did to other women in the restaurant. Despite her friendships with many of the other cooks, Alicia felt tense a lot of the time and had less and less patience for the chef's antics. "I had my own problems with temper," says Alicia. "My temper could go from 0 to 60 in 10 seconds flat."

At one point the chef attempted to replace Fred with Alicia. In a back-stabbing move, he called Alicia into his office and asked if she would like to take Fred's job as executive pastry chef. He offered her a raise from her $38,000 salary as sous chef to $45,000 as executive pastry chef. Fred earned $60,000. "I said no," says Alicia. "I knew I would have been digging myself into a hole. I would have worked 70 to 80 hours per week for $45,000. At that time I was already working 55 hours per week at $38,000. But mainly, it was about loyalty. They were going to fire Fred. My first loyalty was to Fred, always."

After Alicia turned down the job, the situation in the kitchen became unbearable. "I told Fred, 'I'm giving you my two weeks' notice because I can't deal with it anymore.' He said, 'No, you're only doing this out of anger. Give me two weeks, and we'll talk again.' He also said he'd come by my restaurant a lot more. So I stayed there for his sake."

Fred indeed began spending more time in Alicia's restaurant, but this meant that Alicia had to help him produce pastries for the other restaurants he supervised. She was now producing pastries for three restaurants and getting burned out. When the restaurant company opened up yet another location, she thought she might have a shot at the executive pastry chef position—and at a salary that genuinely compensated her for her skills and experience. She also thought the job would enable her to escape the unethical, abusive executive chef.

"Everyone said I had good chance," says Alicia. "It wasn't even as good a restaurant as where I was working. It was more casual. It offered lunch service. But then I found out that the executive chef at my restaurant was also the opening chef at the new restaurant. He pulled me aside and told me, 'You're not qualified for the pastry chef position.'" Alicia didn't bother mentioning to him that he'd offered her the same position months before, when he apparently wasn't worried about her qualifications. He hired a less experienced white person for the position. When he asked Alicia to train this new chef, she quit.

What's Driving Gender Inequality in Restaurants?

Alicia took a break from the kitchen. She worked at a nonprofit organization for a year, writing grants and helping out on various projects, but she missed restaurants. "I missed the people," she says. "In the back of the house, there were people with everyday problems. I loved how redeeming the work could be. I remember there was this prep cook, an older black man, in one restaurant where I worked. He was a hardworking, honest guy. He became the kitchen manager, keeping track of safety standards, ordering cleaning supplies, keeping things organized for when the health inspector walked through. There was another guy, John, who had been in jail, but he ended up becoming a sous chef. There was definitely a glass ceiling they hit, but they always had the potential to do something bigger and better."

Alicia also missed the freedom to experiment with desserts, but it was hard to even get a foot in the door of a successful restaurant. After Fred had burned out as executive pastry chef, he'd become a pastry instructor at a local culinary school. He'd called Alicia one day and told her that 75 percent of his students were African American women. He said he felt for them because he knew how difficult it would be for them to get jobs in restaurants—and then how hard it would be for those who did get jobs, like Alicia, to cope with the politics.

Alicia thought about her own classmates from culinary school. Thanks to her mentor, she'd been the only black woman in her class to become a sous chef in a fine-dining restaurant. Most of the black women with whom she'd gone to school had become cake makers in local supermarkets. These women had paid close to $10,000 for culinary school. Now they earned about $12 an hour, and they actually had it good: most women of color resorted to fast food. The only other students who became chefs in nice restaurants were white men.

Alicia worked in a number of other restaurants before finding ROC-Philadelphia online. She e-mailed me to ask if she could volunteer with the organization, explaining that she wanted to change the industry she loved. I had plans to be in Philadelphia for ROC-Philadelphia's founding meeting, so I invited Alicia to meet me at a local coffee shop. It was a short meeting. Alicia and I talked about the goals of ROC and how she could become a member and help us conduct surveys. I was deeply impressed by Alicia's intelligence and candor.

Alicia conducted hundreds of surveys as a new member of ROC-Philly, and after a few months we hired her as a co-coordinator. She organized job-training classes, recruited dozens of new members, and when Philadelphia's mayor refused to sign a paid sick-leave ordinance, Alicia testified about her experience baking a cake for the mayor in a fine-dining restaurant when workers around her in the kitchen had severe colds. She also created a women's committee that gave woman restaurant workers a place in which to acknowledge the discrimination and harassment they faced on the job, and take action against it.

Both in her own experiences and in listening to the experiences of the workers she surveyed, Alicia observed what ROC research verifies: women in the restaurant industry earn less than men for four reasons.

First, although women make up 48 percent of all nontipped workers, they make up 66 percent of tipped workers, who, under federal law, must be paid only the lower minimum wage of $2.13. The restaurant industry is thus one of the only sectors of the U.S. economy in which lower wages for women are not simply a matter of employer practice; they are also a matter of law.

Second, women are concentrated in lower-level segments of the industry—meaning, they're not well represented in fine-dining restaurants. Women make up 72 percent of all servers nationwide—the largest group of tipped workers—and have three times the poverty rate of all other workers in the United States, partly because they tend to work in casual rather than fine-dining restaurants. Approximately 20 percent of the restaurant industry's jobs provide a livable wage, and almost all of those jobs are found in fine-dining restaurants. Women restaurant workers, especially women of color, are more likely to find employment in casual, family-style restaurants, diners, or fast-food chains.[3]

The third reason women in the restaurant industry earn less than men is that they typically have lower-level positions even when they make it to fine-dining restaurants (see fig. 5). Women in the kitchens of fine-dining restaurants are more likely to hold lower-paying pastry or salad positions.

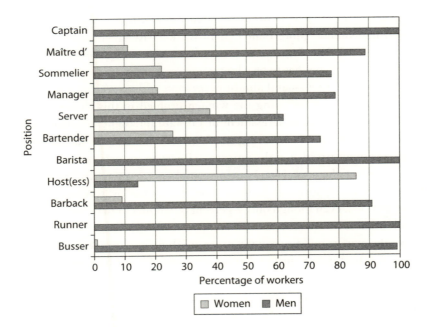

Figure 5. Gender in front of the house positions, New York, 2007. Adapted from Restaurant Opportunities Center of New York and the New York City Restaurant Industry Coalition, *Waiting on Equality: The Role and Impact of Gender in the New York City Restaurant Industry*, technical report (New York: Restaurant Opportunities Center of New York, 2010), fig. 1; http://rocunited.org/blog/waiting-on-equality-the-role-and-impact-of-gender-in-the-new-york-city-restaurant-industry-2/. *Source:* Restaurant Opportunities Center of New York Canvassing Data.

Consider that there are six times as many head chefs who are men as those who are women in the United States.[4] Cooking has traditionally been seen as a woman's role in the home, but when it comes to the highest-paying cooking positions in the United States, men reign supreme.

Finally, women make less than men even when they work in the same positions. Waitresses earn 85¢ to every $1 that waiters earn—a difference of almost $70 per week.[5] That difference often translates into the ability to pay for child care, transportation, or even rent.

Sexual Harassment in the Industry

On top of earning less, women have to deal with competitive, aggressive restaurant environments dominated by men that often encourage sexual harassment. More than 1 in 10 workers ROC surveyed nationwide reported that they or a coworker had experienced sexual harassment.[6] That number has to be a low estimate. Almost every woman who is a member of ROC—and almost every woman I've ever met who is a restaurant worker, including the women profiled in this chapter—can tell a story about sexual harassment in a restaurant. Some may not call it sexual harassment or even recognize it as such, because it's such a common, insidious practice in the industry. However, it's pervasive. In 2011, 37 percent of the sexual harassment complaints received by the Equal Employment Opportunity Commission were filed by women restaurant workers, even though only 7 percent of women in the United States work in restaurants.[7] One server with five years' experience told me, "A lot of the owners will fire you if you say anything back to them. Or if you don't flirt back when they're flirting with you. They'll find an easy way to fire you."[8]

One of ROC's members in Los Angeles, Donna, told me one of the worst stories I've ever heard. She worked in a Creole restaurant in Los Angeles for four years, during which time the owner harassed her constantly. Although he was in his seventies and she was 21, he constantly pressured her to have sex with him. He made comments about her breasts and vagina daily, and then he demoted her when she refused his advances.

Most women don't have to deal with daily comments about their body parts, but even benign comments can create tension for women on the job.

Yelena at a ROC-Chicago event. Courtesy of Sekou Luke.

I learned this from Yelena, another ROC leader in Philadelphia. In her mid-twenties, Yelena is a petite, slender young Russian immigrant with blonde, shoulder-length hair. She has sharp features and dark brown eyes.

Yelena was born in a ski resort town in the foothills of the Caucasus Mountains in southern Russia. As a teenager, she often went on hiking trips in the mountains with her classmates, sometimes camping along mountain trails for up to a week. She was surrounded by a vibrant tourism industry— hotels, restaurants, shopping complexes, skating rinks—and dreamed about one day owning her own hotel, restaurant, or even her own complex.

Yelena's parents wanted her to become a doctor, but she wasn't interested in medicine. "I was against it," she says. "I was really good in accounting and math, and I liked visiting other countries. I was interested in tourism.

I had grown up in a hotel and resort area. I wanted to have my own hotel and restaurant, a huge complex with everything in it." Keeping her dream in mind, Yelena worked hard to graduate from high school and attend a university to major in management and economics. "I ended up getting a degree in hospitality and tourism management," she says. "I also got an interpreting degree in the business field. I was working the whole time. In college I was a dealer in the casino. I'd be studying during the day and working at night. I also worked in a retail store, and at the Crystal Palace Hotel Bar and Restaurant. I was the front desk person, the manager of the hotel."

One summer during college, Yelena's girlfriend invited her to go on a trip to the United States. Yelena wanted to go, but her father was opposed. "I asked and asked, and eventually he let me go," says Yelena. "I came to the United States with a work and travel visa for three months."

Yelena landed in Chicago. She loved it. The big buildings, the L train, the mix of people—all were so different from what she had known in southern Russia. Yelena fell in love with the United States—and with an American. She started a romance that summer, knowing she'd come back to Chicago one day.

When Yelena returned to Russia, she completed her degrees and tried to imagine herself starting a career, but her memories of the United States—and her American boyfriend—kept urging her to return to Chicago. Against her parents' wishes, Yelena quit her graduate program, packed her bags, and joined a friend heading to the United States.

At first, it was all love and romance. Yelena moved in with her boyfriend, and they lived off of his income. "I read books every day to learn English, from 9:00 to 5:00 p.m.," says Yelena. "My boyfriend would ask me to write an essay for him based on the books I'd read, and he'd correct it. He'd send me questions, and I'd have to answer them. It was hard for a couple of months. But my English got so much better."

Unfortunately, the relationship was not meant to be. Yelena moved out of her boyfriend's apartment and moved in with a friend. She started looking for a job. Her visa was about to expire, and she wasn't having much luck finding work. She was about to give up and move back to Russia when she saw a posting on Craigslist: a new restaurant was opening and looking for servers. Since she didn't know of a school or training program for waiters and waitresses, she went on YouTube and watched servers demonstrate their craft—how they took orders, anticipated customers' needs, ran food to the table, cleared the table. She practiced in front of the computer repeatedly, and then went to the restaurant to apply.

The restaurant was an Irish pub. When Yelena arrived, workers were running around preparing the place for inspection and the opening. Yelena inquired about a waitressing position, and a manager told her she could "audition"—like an actress—that same day. An hour later, Yelena found herself standing in front of four managers who were men. "They asked me to stand up, wearing the uniform, and show them how I would come up to a table, how I would sell something to the table," she says. She knew her looks and body were on parade. "One of the managers told me, 'Looks good. I wish all my girls looked as good as you do.' They hired so many girls based on looks," says Yelena.

She was offered a job.

Yelena went into training for two weeks while the restaurant waited for its liquor license, and she served tables on opening night, but it didn't take her long to notice that something was wrong. All of the servers and bartenders in the pub were women, all the managers and workers in the back of the house were men, and the general manager frequently made strange, inappropriate comments. "The general manager had been taking advantage of everyone, sexually harassing us at work, every day," says Yelena. "No one could say anything against him. They all respected him. I would ignore it." His behavior got worse as the days passed. "If a woman let him, he would kiss her, grab her, say, 'I can tell what kind of underwear you're wearing,'" says Yelena. "He would kiss a woman's ear, make dirty comments all the time. Every day, he'd grab you, hold you, dance with you—come behind you and stick his tongue in your ear. He would kiss bartenders on the mouth, with his tongue, in front of everybody." He crossed the dining floor in the middle of lunch or dinner service to grab a server's butt or sneak up behind her, and over time he got bolder. "Women dreaded having to pick up their paychecks," says Yelena. "Before handing a check to a woman, the general manager would say, 'Where's my kiss?' and then expect a full kiss on the mouth before handing over the check.

The general manager's behavior sometimes seemed to be an extension of customer behavior in the pub. Drunken men at the bar would often comment to the servers and bartenders. "I heard Irish people don't wear any underwear," one man said. "Maybe you should sit in my lap so I can find out." One time a customer ran up behind Yelena and grabbed her around the waist. She was terrified.

The general manager had a preference for black women. He hired several of them and kissed them on the mouth. Many complained about it, but most were too worried about losing their job to do anything about it. Those who wouldn't put up with it quit after being grabbed or inappropriately touched.

Since cell phones were not allowed during dinner service, Yelena sometimes stuffed her phone into her bra. One time the general manager playfully asked, "Where's your phone?" He grabbed her breast pretending to look for it. Yelena was horrified, but she didn't say anything. She remained reserved and aloof around him, refusing to smile or play his games. After that, he seemed determined to punish her for not responding to his advances. He gave her the worst shifts and sections of the restaurant, where she was sure to earn less in tips than her coworkers. Other servers tolerated his antics to receive better shifts and tips, but Yelena remained unwilling to participate in any kind of flirtation. She suffered as a result.

One evening Yelena had a customer who stayed at his table for a very long time and got drunk. Although Yelena left the check for him, he never pulled out cash or a credit card. She mentioned the situation to the general manager, and he ignored her, saying, "Just grab his credit card." Yelena moved on to attend to other customers but kept an eye on the uncooperative customer, who moved to the bar to drink more. He belligerently stumbled around the restaurant, finally ending up at the hostess stand. The general manager, who was often just as drunk and high, got annoyed with the customer and kicked him out of the restaurant. Yelena did not notice until after the customer had left. She told the general manager that the guy had never paid. The general manger replied, "I'm sorry, but I told you to grab his card." It was the first customer walkout the new restaurant had experienced, but the general manager forced Yelena to pay the bill, over $100. She complained to other managers and the owner, all of whom said, "Don't worry. We'll take care of it." However, no one ever helped. It seemed as though the general manager was untouchable.

Another day during lunch the general manager came up behind one of the servers on the dining floor and grabbed her behind. A man customer was watching. When she went to take the customer's order, he told her he'd seen what had happened, and that she shouldn't put up with it. He said he was a lawyer, and that she should sue the restaurant for sexual harassment.

She was hesitant, for fear of losing her job, but later other coworkers heard about the incident and encouraged each other to go ahead and sue.

Yelena didn't join her coworkers in their lawsuit, but she'd had enough of the general manager's behavior and started looking for a new job. She contacted a friend who had left the pub to work in a fine-dining restaurant. The friend encouraged her to apply for a job in her restaurant; Yelena interviewed for a position and was hired. She made a lot more money in the new establishment, and the atmosphere was a lot better. Managers did not grope the servers. She felt happy, although she was less trusting and had a far more clear-eyed view of how women fared in restaurants in the United States. This, she thought, was the way of the industry: in fine-dining restaurants, where the tips were better, servers tended to be mostly men or a mixture of men and women; in more casual restaurants and pubs, where the tips were lower, the servers were mostly women. Sexual harassment happened in all kinds of restaurants, but the pub environment certainly allowed a general manager to get away with "auditioning" and hiring all women that looked a certain way, regardless of their service experience or ability.

Breaking through the Glass Ceiling

Why should diners care that women like Alicia and Yelena rarely get the same positions, pay, or treatment as men in the restaurant industry? One simple answer is that this kind of inequity ensures that the majority of restaurant workers nationwide continue to live in poverty. Recall that the majority of restaurant workers in the United States are women. More than 1 million of these women are mothers, often single mothers,[9] who must support themselves and their children on $8 an hour—a wage that leaves a family of three below the federal poverty line.[10]

Of course, there are stories of women who've made it to the top in the restaurant business, and many women have not experienced sexual harassment on the job. In fact, most of the responsible restaurant employers ROC partners with around the country are woman chefs and restaurateurs, like Diep (see chapter 2), who worked as servers, bartenders, and chefs before going on to open their own restaurants.

Shardha Young is another pioneering woman in the industry. She worked her way up from hostess to general manager of a profitable restaurant in New York City. When my ROC cofounder, Mamdouh, first came

Shardha Young and Fekkak Mamdouh at an early ROC planning retreat.
Courtesy of Restaurant Opportunities Center of New York

up with the idea for starting a worker-owned restaurant, we organized
a group of ROC members to start developing the concept and a business
plan. Shardha joined this group.

A young mom from Guyana, Shardha has dark brown skin, short black
hair, and a full, curvy figure. She grew up under the foot of British colonialism. When the British colonized Guyana in the late nineteenth and
early twentieth centuries, they brought thousands of indentured laborers

from India to work in the nation's growing sugarcane fields. These Indian laborers, including Shardha's relatives, lived in Guyana for generations but kept many of their Indian customs and traditions alive in their cooking and holidays.

"I grew up in a small village called Herstelling," says Shardha. "I went to school in a village a ways away from Herstelling. I walked to school every day, about a half-hour walk from home. I'd come home for lunch, go back to school, and then walk home again in the afternoon. I grew up with nine siblings, seven girls and three boys. With me, that made ten kids. My mom and dad worked on the sugar plantation. My mother worked in a cane-cutting gang, called the weeding gang. She and other women would clean the roots of the sugarcane with machetes, preparing the cane to be cut by men at harvesttime. My father drove a tractor, transporting the cane to the factory."

From a young age, Shardha heard about her great-aunt, who stood up for working women's rights under British rule. "She was my mom's mom's sister," says Shardha. "She worked for the estate, on one of the weeding gangs. At that time the overseers were British. My great-aunt and other women were protesting the cutting of hours and wages; my great-aunt stood up for her rights. She said, 'We are the workers. We are the ones doing all the hard work. You are riding on our backs. You should not do that.' She stood up on a bridge going into the fields, and she said, 'I'm not moving. I'm going to stay here until our demands are met.' The British ordered the tractor operator to drive over her, and that's how she died." Shardha heard about her great-aunt from her great-grandfather. "My cousins and I used to spend vacations with my great-grandparents on the plantation, in a different village in Guyana," says Shardha. "She was their child. My great-grandfather would tell us stories about her. She lived not too far away, so we used to go visit the house where she used to live. She was really pretty. A few years ago, the government of Guyana made a bust of her, as a martyr for the nation. Her bust is right next to the bust of the late president of Guyana. They have them in an area where people go and commemorate her."

When Shardha was 16 and in high school, she started going into the city of Georgetown after school to take accounting classes. "All of my siblings went to high school," she says. "None of them went to the university. Because of the level of jobs that my family had, they couldn't afford to send anyone to the university. But three of my siblings went to commercial schools and started working in offices. So I took accounting classes as an extra thing beyond high school. At that age, 16 or 17, if I had accounting skills, I could get a job in a law office, typing, doing basic office work." Shardha met a man who came regularly to the building where her accounting classes took place. "He worked for the government doing telecommunications," says Shardha. "He was working at different offices, checking their telephones. He came to check the telephones in the building, so I kept seeing him often and having conversations with him."

It was only a matter of time before their friendship became a romance. "I told my parents I was seeing this guy," says Shardha. "My mom said to invite him over so they could meet him. When my parents saw he was mixed race, black and white, they said, 'He cannot come here again.' They didn't want to hear about it; he wasn't Indian. But I didn't listen to my parents. I continued seeing him. I ended up having a relationship with him, and I got pregnant. We eloped. I waited until I was 18, and then we got married."

Shardha, her new husband, and her newborn son spent a few years living with her husband's relatives and parents, until her husband's career started to take off. "After my son turned two years old, we moved out on our own," says Shardha. "My husband was a technician in telecommunications. He used to go to courses in Miami to study, to be an engineer. He moved on from the company, opened his own business in Georgetown, Guyana. We were not very wealthy, but we were having a very good life. We had people working for us. My husband had 50 or 60 employees working for him, and I had people working for me, in my house, in my yard. I never worked there. I became a housewife, taking my son to school, taking him to swimming lessons, catechism classes."

Shardha reunited with her estranged parents, who were thrilled to be a part of their grandson's life. Shardha and her family were living an upper-middle-class life compared to other Guyanese. "We were traveling," she says. "We went on vacations to Canada, the United States, most of the islands in the Caribbean."

Everything changed with globalization and the entry of the United States into the Guyanese market. "An American company bought the Guyanese telecommunications firm, and the American company never renewed my husband's contract," says Shardha. "He went for two years without a contract. He would take side jobs with private companies, the United Nations Development Programme, but we quickly realized that because of lifestyle we were living, we weren't able to support ourselves. The money wasn't as much as what we were getting with the old contract."

Around this time Shardha told her husband she wanted to move to the United States. "The crime rate was very high in Guyana," she says. "I was afraid. By this time we had a second son, and a daughter."

They were also spiraling into poverty. "I said to my husband at one point, 'Before we go down too far, I want to go to the U.S. with my kids.' He wasn't in agreement to come to the United States," says Shardha. "He knew the way we'd have to live. I said I'd take a chance."

Shardha and the kids immigrated to the United States first. It was 1999. They moved in with relatives in Jamaica, Queens, and Shardha, like most new immigrants, found her first job in a restaurant. "It was a West Indian restaurant in Queens," says Shardha. "One of my husband's friends used to eat there all the time. He asked the management whether I could apply, and they said yes." After interviewing and getting the job, Shardha was told she'd be paid $75 "shift pay" for every eight hours of work. She'd mostly be in charge of taking orders over the phone, delivering those orders to the kitchen, and sometimes serving guests at their tables.

Shardha was excited about her first job in the United States, but she didn't know how she would afford child care. "My daughter, Lee, was just 2 years old, my younger son was in second grade, and my oldest son was 14 and in high school," she says. "So I had to wait until my oldest son came home from school before I could to go work at the restaurant. I'd wait for him outside the apartment building so that the minute I saw him I could run to the restaurant." Some days her son had after-school activities, which meant that she couldn't go to work. "There was a woman in the building who offered to watch the kids while I was at work, but she charged $60 a night," says Shardha. "I'd earn $75 and pay $60 in child care for eight hours of work. It wasn't worth it." Nevertheless, if the restaurant called and said they really needed her, Shardha had no choice but to work. "It was so frustrating," she says. "I remember I used to cry about it, not knowing what to do with the kids. I didn't have anybody to help me." At one point Shardha called a neighbor, who was also from Guyana, and begged her to babysit Lee. The neighbor was reluctant to get involved, and Lee was even less happy about the situation. Lee cried most of the time Shardha was away. "She wasn't used to strangers watching her," says Shardha. "Back home in Guyana we had a live-in nanny who would watch her."

Despite her difficulties, Shardha knew she was doing better than many other mothers in the immigrant community. Her husband eventually came to New York and was usually able to watch the children in the evenings. Another woman who worked with Shardha in the West Indian restaurant was a single mom. "I don't know how she managed it," says Shardha. "She told me she used to have her mother pick up her kids from school and watch them for a few hours, but that didn't always work out. She worked seven days a week; I don't know if she ever saw her kids."

After working a few months in the West Indian restaurant, Shardha moved on to slightly better-paying jobs. "First, I got a job with an agency that would send me to be a companion to an elderly person," says Shardha. "I was making $10 an hour." Then a friend told her about an opportunity to earn even more money as a secretary in an office near the World Trade Center.

Meanwhile, Shardha's husband was working odd jobs in telecommunications. Together they struggled to make ends meet, but Shardha had expected a struggle and wanted to stay in the United States. "I knew what I was getting into," she says. "I knew I wouldn't have the lifestyle I was accustomed to in Guyana. I knew it was something I'd have to adjust to. But I could also see the exchange rate of money—I was earning a lot here. With two jobs, I'd make $600 to $800 per week, and my husband used to make $23 an hour. I saw that there was a way for us to move up." They lived in a two-bedroom apartment and juggled child-care responsibilities. "We had to decide who would work on what day because we didn't have a babysitter," says Shardha. "My job wasn't every day, so my husband started going to work when I had a day off, or he would work at night if I came home in the afternoon."

On September 11, 2001, everything changed. "Both of us lost our jobs. 9/11 came, and I didn't know what to do," says Shardha. "September, October, November, went by—all the money we had saved was spent. No one was working." In December, Shardha went searching for help. She saw a flyer about ROC at a local job-placement agency. "When I saw the flyer saying Restaurant Opportunities Center, I thought there might be an opportunity for me," she says. "I called the number, and Mamdouh answered the phone. I told him about my situation, and he said, 'Why don't you come in? We'll let you know what we're doing.'"

I was actually the first person to meet Shardha when she came to ROC. "I came for an orientation," says Shardha, "and I heard about a group of people who wanted to open their own restaurant, a cooperative. I had always been interested in cooking. I had also wanted to work in a restaurant again because I had worked in one before. So I was interested. I thought, This is a great opportunity for me to get together with these folks. I tried to sign up to join the cooperative, but I was told I couldn't get in because it was already full. My name ended up being first on the waiting list."

Shardha started visiting ROC regularly. She watched plans for the cooperative develop, and meanwhile picked up odd jobs to make ends meet. "I started to do cleaning," she says. "I would go to people's apartments and clean, and do babysitting, just to make ends meet. My husband was also doing different day jobs, not working full-time. We weren't making the money we were making before. We would struggle and struggle. My husband would get a job for a few months, and we'd clear our debts, but then he wouldn't work, and we'd spend again. This had been going on for a while. At some point Mamdouh said to go to Catholic Charities—they were helping people who had lost their jobs after 9/11. I went, and they agreed to pay all my bills for one year. So then I was at ROC all the time, in classes, in meetings."

Shardha continued to hope for a position at the soon-to-be-opening worker-owned restaurant. Since the restaurant was a cooperative, everything had to be decided democratically. We held a contest to decide on the name for the restaurant. The workers chose COLORS to reflect their diversity. We had spent three years struggling to raise funds and find management that understood our mission and knew how to run a restaurant. Still, workers like Shardha never gave up hope. "I got pregnant in 2003, got a cleaning job, had a baby. Shortly after that I got a babysitting job," she says. "In the meantime, I was told if there was an opening at COLORS, I would be next. So I never let go of that. I stayed on. When COLORS was about to open, I was told I would be training as a hostess. So I quit the babysitting job and moved to COLORS as a hostess."

Shardha had her fourth child, a baby boy named Alex, just before COLORS opened. By this time Lee was in school and Shardha's older sons could babysit in the evenings, but there was still no one to watch Alex on school days. The managers at COLORS ultimately agreed to give Shardha only evening shifts. "I knew it made the other workers upset," says Shardha, "that I alone was always given the night shifts. But they didn't have kids, and they couldn't understand." At one point Shardha asked the general manager if she could bring Alex to work with her; this was the only way that she could take on a daytime shift. The general manager agreed, and fortunately the arrangement worked out all right for everyone. Alex cooed and gurgled in his stroller while Shardha answered phone calls and booked reservations. "When he fell asleep, I'd put him in the coat-check room," says Shardha.

During this period, Shardha was also moving up the ranks at COLORS, demonstrating her leadership ability. She watched as six general managers came and left the restaurant, each with his or her own style, none really able to make COLORS successful. "Every time someone left," she says, "I had to clean up their mess. Then someone else would come."

COLORS struggled like every other new restaurant, perhaps more so because it did not have a profit-motivated investor to help it survive those early years. Shardha stayed through the restaurant's serious financial difficulties and long, slow periods of little or no business. We searched tirelessly for managers who understood the importance of our mission—treating workers with dignity and respect—and could run a successful business. Unfortunately, most managers had spent a lifetime learning from an industry that didn't appreciate the cooperative model, and they failed to adapt. Shardha watched each of the general managers and learned which business practices succeeded and which ones failed. She was the one who kept the restaurant going during each transition. She moved up to assistant manager, then to events manager, and eventually she became the general manager. She took accounting classes on the side and learned how to do everything in the restaurant—from the cooking, serving, bartending, and parties to the bookkeeping, hiring and firing, and management of the bank account.

In 2007, we turned COLORS into a school during the day to help our growing membership of low-wage workers advance to living-wage jobs in the industry. The COLORS Hospitality & Opportunities for Workers Institute (CHOW) continues to offer special "Career Ladders" classes for women so that more women like Shardha can advance to higher positions in restaurants. In 2011, we opened a second COLORS restaurant in Detroit, and we're planning to open more restaurants in other cities. We currently train more than 1,000 workers each year to advance to living-wage jobs in the industry.

Under Shardha's leadership, COLORS finally became profitable, bringing in more revenue per week than the restaurant brought in under all the previous managers. "The thing that kept me there all along is that I go into COLORS every day knowing it's a worker-owned cooperative," says Shardha. "I always had hope because of that. I also think that, being an immigrant woman, I wouldn't have had the opportunities that I have here anywhere else. I wouldn't be able to be a manager, not possible. Maybe I could get a floor manager position, a hostess position. That's one of the things that always stays in the back of my mind.

"Being here all these years, I've been there; I've seen different people with different approaches. At one point we all agreed to give ourselves a pay cut, but we stayed on. Another thing that kept me here is that I don't have anyone yelling and screaming at me. We're all immigrants, people of color. I've felt security here. We're people from different backgrounds, but we're all immigrants. I've also stayed here because I've gotten to know so much more than what I knew before—knowing my rights as an immigrant, as a woman, as a restaurant worker. You learn all of these things. I decided, 'You know what? This is where I can apply myself. Show other people that any woman in my position can also be where I am today. It's not that you have to have a master's or a bachelor's or an MBA. I'm not saying that's not useful, but I think that sometimes people with those degrees take advantage of other people. They think you're a stupid woman. You're not educated like they are. They think that way about you."

Toward Equity for Women in the Restaurant Industry

Most of us can agree that reality TV cooking shows sensationalize events behind the kitchen door. Most famous chefs aren't as grandiose and provocative as Gordon Ramsay, and most aspiring cooks aren't brutalized and degraded in a cooking competition. Still, the attitudes on TV reflect *something* in our culture, and stories of women restaurant workers reveal that while we have twenty-first-century restaurants—complete with trendy organic menus and contemporary flair—we still have sixties-era labor practices that should outrage our mothers and grandmothers, who rallied for equal pay and the right to vote.

So what can you, as a consumer, do to support industry-wide change? First, you can choose to support restaurants that allow working women to move up the ladder, and you can avoid restaurants known to discriminate against and underpay women employees. If you see that ROC has launched a public campaign against discrimination in a restaurant, you can bet that the restaurant is mistreating its women workers. Don't eat there.

In addition, you can support legislation that mandates change across the board. In New York City and Detroit, ROC has initiated legislative campaigns to revoke liquor licenses from businesses that have been caught discriminating against women and permitting sexual harassment. We've also launched legislative campaigns to provide incentives for restaurants that have equitable promotion policies that allow all workers, regardless of their background and gender, to move up the ladder.

At the federal level, you can support women in the industry by demanding an increase in the ridiculously low tipped minimum wage of $2.13. If we increased the tipped minimum wage from $2.13 to $5.08 (70 percent of the federal minimum wage for nontipped workers), we would not only raise wages immediately for almost 1 million women and raise the wage floor for another 4 million women, but we would also reduce the pay gap between men and women by almost one-fifth.[11]

Every one of us can take small steps to make an enormous impact. Every time you eat out and every time you vote you can advocate for women and fight for equitable labor practices in the restaurants that women count on to support themselves and their families.

RECIPES FOR CHANGE

As a lifelong restaurant worker and single mother, I had all but
abandoned hope that this industry could ever improve. Employers
have really succeeded in making workers feel a sense of inevitability.
However, when I found ROC my entire world changed. I suddenly realized
that I was not alone and that if we worked together we could transform
the industry. I went through the front of the house, bartending, and
even a photography class, and now I have a good job where I can support
my son. I went from being a minimum-wage earner to a leader at ROC
Chicago, from invisible worker to powerful woman. But more
important, I now have a sense of my worth in the industry and
in life, and a deeper political understanding that it is up to us
to make the restaurant industry a better place for all of us.

—BARTENDER, WOMAN, 10 YEARS IN THE INDUSTRY, CHICAGO

There is so much to celebrate about restaurants in the United States. We
have the most diverse array of cuisines you'll ever find in one place. Kimchi
taco trucks. Vegan barbecue. Israeli falafels. Turkish kebabs. Ethiopian
stews. Russian blini with red caviar. Puerto Rican empanadas. We have restaurateurs like Diep who strive daily to bring the best, most sustainable food
to the table. We have a growing food movement that increasingly embraces
sustainability along the food chain—from the workers who pick the strawberries to the pastry chefs who put them on delicious gourmet fruit tarts. Ten
million workers from all walks of life—different races, religions, ages, and
cultural backgrounds—bring their unique flavors to our dining experience.

There's also a clear path to making the restaurant industry better for everyone. Every worker profiled in this book is involved in this growing movement for change. My aim is *not* to paint these workers as perfect heroes or victims, but to show how their lives directly affect ours every time we eat out. I hope their stories can inspire you, as they've inspired me, to take small steps to improve your dining experience *and* help extend opportunities and a living wage to workers in the second-largest private-sector industry in the United States. As I say throughout this book, the quality of your food depends on the health and well-being of the people preparing, cooking, and serving it. Restaurant workers can't survive on $2.13 an hour, and they need health benefits, such as paid sick leave, if we want them to bring us germ-free meals.

Here's another way of looking at this movement: while most of us resumed "eating out as usual" after 9/11, a small group of restaurant workers, who were fundamentally changed by their loss at Windows on the World, got together and devoted themselves to improving the intolerable working conditions described in this book. Now, twelve years after 9/11, they're coming to us, the restaurant-goers, and saying, "Here's how our lives affect your food, and here's what you can do to make a difference."

Over the last twelve years ROC has grown from a small, determined group of low-wage restaurant workers in New York City to a national organization with more than 10,000 members in around 20 states nationwide. We've won 11 campaigns against exploitation in high-profile restaurant companies, obtaining more than $6 million in stolen tips and wages, as well as policy changes to improve the lives of thousands of workers. We've educated and organized responsible employers to promote a different way of doing business in the industry. We've opened worker-owned restaurants called COLORS in New York City and Detroit. We've trained more than 2,500 low-wage workers, largely immigrants and workers of color, to advance to living-wage jobs in the industry, and we've conducted all of the research described in this book, influencing policy along the way at the local, state, and federal levels.

My colleague Mamdouh, a former Windows worker and 9/11 survivor, was one of the first people to start ROC on this path. He has become my confidant, adviser, and best friend. Sekou Siby, who became ROC's first official member, is another key figure in this movement. Many look to

Siby for leadership, and to me he epitomizes the remarkable diversity and audacity of people in the restaurant industry.

One Windows Worker—the Road to 9/11

Siby is an African immigrant, French teacher, chef, 9/11 survivor, and one of the wisest people I know. Standing over six feet tall, he is lean and dark-skinned. He has a crew cut and a clean-shaven face, and he wears glasses. If you didn't know him, you'd probably be intimidated by him. He has a loud, commanding voice, and he stares at you intently. Everyone knows him for his voice—it's the voice of a preacher or storyteller. It fills the room. Siby also laughs loudly—sometimes right at the moment you think he's angry or upset. We call him "Siby," his last name, because the Windows workers mostly called each other by last name, as if to tease each other about how their schoolteachers back home addressed them.

I think of Siby as a special case because he has brilliantly overcome the challenges that most immigrants experience—low wages, discrimination, and the struggle to be heard in a foreign country—plus the loss of his co-workers, his workplace, and his job security on 9/11. Siby's livelihood, worldview, and even his feelings about himself changed when the Twin Towers fell. After 9/11, he struggled with enormous grief and feelings of guilt. What I find so moving about Siby, however, is that while he could have disappeared from the scene after losing his job at Windows on the World, he instead felt compelled to reconnect with his coworkers and do something to help them. That decision changed his life. Over the last eleven years Siby has gone from being a low-wage immigrant worker to becoming the executive director of ROC-New York. He has completely changed his circumstances because he chose, in a moment of distress, to do something courageous, to step up and become a leader in an organization that had limited resources and didn't seem at the time like a "safe" or promising career move. Siby basically gave up whatever job security he'd found after 9/11 to traverse the sidewalks of the Manhattan and survey restaurant workers. Only a certain type of person would do such a thing.

Siby immigrated to New York City from the capital of Ivory Coast, Abidjan. A bustling, metropolitan city, Abidjan is known to many as the center of everything cosmopolitan in West Africa. Siby's family did not partake in the glitz and glamour of the metropolis. They were immigrants from Mali, and although Siby was born in Abidjan, he and his family were never officially treated as citizens of Ivory Coast. Since birth Siby has been an immigrant wherever he has lived. "My entire life I never had the sense that I am in my country," says Siby. "I don't have one."

Siby was the sixth of fourteen children. Both his parents were entrepreneurs. His father sold fabric for men's clothing and used the income to raise fourteen children. Siby's mother sold ice in the marketplace and sometimes made popsicles to sell to children. "As kids we'd be helping my mom with the ice," says Siby. "She'd say, 'You have to help me sell, put the ice in the container.' I remember walking with my bike several hours trying to sell the ice."

Siby's parents never set foot in a school, but they were determined to make sure their children received as much education as possible. "My older brothers and sisters all got college degrees, so my younger siblings and I couldn't stop at high school or we'd be seen as dumb," says Siby. "It was motivation. We thought, 'He did it, we can do it.' We didn't compare ourselves to our parents. We compared ourselves to our older brothers and sisters." Siby's third-eldest brother, Mustafa, completed his graduate education and was offered two different scholarships—one from the United Nations—to attend a PhD program in the United States, but his father refused to let him go. His father was afraid that he was getting too old to support the family, and needed Mustafa to stay in the country. Mustafa became a high school principal instead.

For his part, Siby's goal was to become a doctor. He loved science. He received good grades in high school, but a bureaucratic error prevented him from going to college. A government commission annually posted a list of the students who would be permitted to attend the country's public universities. Siby's name never appeared on the list. "I went to the minister of education to complain, but nothing happened," says Siby. "They said they wouldn't reconvene the committee that made the decision, even though I had the best grades in math and physics. People with lesser grades got into medical school."

Siby was desperate to go to college. He asked his sister, a state employee, for help. She made him a fake identification card so he could pose as a state worker and enroll in the local university's continuing education program for state employees. The program was for working adults; classes took place at night. Siby completed a three-year degree in four years and then followed his brothers into education. He became a French teacher at a private high school. "Teaching was my best experience with any kind of work," says Siby. "I really enjoyed it. It felt very natural to me. I did it for four years, but the salary wasn't good. It was a time of austerity, with the IMF putting pressure on the country. There was a salary freeze and a hiring freeze. The government was not hiring any more teachers, and the public school system was getting bad. The salary they offered me at the private school was one-third of the government teachers' salary. But there was no way to get a good job at that time."

The owner of the private school had an authoritarian, nontransparent management style, and although he promised the teachers that they'd be paid every month, he stopped paying them after the second month of school. Several of the teachers told Siby that they were owed more than three months of back pay. "I called all the teachers together, and we agreed that we'd stop working if we didn't get paid," says Siby. "On the day of the strike, two-thirds of the teachers went to work. One-third sat in the teacher's room. They were just too scared. They told me, 'We support you, but we need to take care of our family.' The next month we weren't paid again, so I got more people to strike. After that we were paid regularly."

Siby and the private school's owner maintained a strained relationship after the strikes. The owner didn't like that Siby had the audacity to organize teachers if they didn't get paid, but he also couldn't get rid of one of the best teachers in his school. After three years, he called Siby into his office and asked him to become the school's headmaster. Siby thought it over. Of course, a promotion would have been great, but he felt as though the owner was trying to disorganize the teachers by taking away their leader. "I said, 'I love teaching, but I don't want to be in a position where everything depends on me at this school,'" says Siby. "I had an uneasy feeling in the country, because we were immigrants from Mali. I could have everything in the country, but I never felt like I belonged. I always felt like the 'other.'"

Siby started the process of applying for a tourist visa to go to the United States. Immigrants from Africa had to prove that they had enough money and were financially stable enough to travel—that they weren't trying to move to the United States permanently for work. Siby asked his family and friends to lend him enough money to show the U.S. government that he had a significant sum in his bank account, an incentive to return to Ivory Coast, and he got the visa.

Of course, Siby didn't know anyone in the United States, so he didn't know where he could go or what he could do once he arrived in New York City. He told family members that he was nervous about not having any contacts, and so before he departed his younger brother asked a coworker for help; the coworker had a brother, Karim, in the Bronx. In typical immigrant networking fashion, Siby ended up connecting with Karim, who was also an immigrant from Ivory Coast. When Siby arrived at Karim's apartment in the Bronx, he had no idea that Karim would become not only his closest friend in the United States, but also a very important person in his life.

Siby set out to find a job once he settled in the Bronx. Karim was a food service worker at the Museum of Natural History in Manhattan, but Siby didn't know enough English to have a job like that. "I went looking for a job, and I saw other African guys making supermarket deliveries," says Siby. "I asked about a job at one of the supermarkets, but it was August, and they weren't making too many deliveries, so they said come back in September. The first week in September I went back, and I ended up working in a Midtown supermarket. I worked there for two years, but I never had an hourly wage. I lived almost entirely off of tips. We got $1 per delivery, and sometimes, when we dropped food off at corporate cafeterias, we didn't get any tips at all. I made $220 per week, based on making 220 deliveries, and only about half of the money came from tips. The bottom line was that however hard the situation was in the United States, I was still better able to help my family while working here than I could have back home."

Siby sent home a few hundred dollars every month.

After nearly a year of struggle, Siby and Karim got lucky—a huge opportunity landed in their laps. Karim had been working with a chef at the Museum of Natural History who was hired at Windows on the World, the restaurant at the top of the World Trade Center. The chef took Karim with him, and when Windows got extremely busy, he asked Karim if he knew anyone who could work a prep cook job. Karim suggested Siby. Siby had a work permit by that time, and he'd learned to speak English fairly well, so he got the job as a prep cook in the world's highest restaurant.

Siby didn't know how to cook anything other than the African meals he cooked for himself, but he was a quick learner. "It was only when I got to Windows on the World that I learned how to cook," says Siby. "I just needed to be smart about it. The first three months I was doing a lot of prep work, looking at recipes, mainly in the orders station. If I didn't know something

Siby with a fellow worker in the kitchen of Windows on the World.
Courtesy of Restaurant Opportunities Center of New York.

well, I would write it down, ask the chef. The chef would say, 'The quantity's not correct, change this portion, add this thing.'" Many of the line cooks, a step above Siby, were Latino and somewhat competitive about moving up the ranks, so Siby was careful not to step on their toes. "I got a good knowledge of all the recipes without the knowledge of my coworkers," he says. "I spent six months with them without telling them I knew Spanish. I wanted them to teach me, and I didn't want them to feel threatened. So I spent a lot of time just listening to them. They would take the ingredients from [the station] in front of me, and I wrote everything down."

After six months Siby could handle cooking for an entire party, but he couldn't get a promotion to reflect the higher-level work he'd started doing. Windows on the World was one of the few unionized restaurants in the nation, and Siby was well acquainted with his union rights from his organizing experiences back home, so he took his concerns to the union representative. "I said, 'When there is a party, I order the food, do the prep work, do the cooking, do the service. But I'm still called a prep cook. It's not right,'" says Siby. "I also spoke to the chef about it. He said, 'It's too quick. It has been six months, and you think you know everything.'" Although the chef initially refused Siby's request for a promotion, he reconsidered it when the head prep cook resigned. Siby was promoted over the other cooks who had worked at Windows for several years. He also got a raise.

Siby started doing the work of a true chef. He designed menus, conducted menu tastings, ordered menu ingredients, ran banquet events, and taught his coworkers how to cook. He also became friendlier with his coworkers and joined them for soccer. "We would start work at six in morning, and by two or three in the afternoon we'd be done," says Siby. "I'd go out with all the Mexican line cooks and pastry guys. We'd get in two or three cars and head out to Corona Park in Queens to play soccer until eight or nine at night. I was the only one who'd have to head back to the Bronx after that."

One day a cook-in-training, Moises Rivas, asked Siby if he could swap shifts with him. Siby usually had Saturdays and Sundays off, but Moises needed a Sunday off and wanted to know if Siby could work on Sunday and take off Tuesday. Siby agreed.

That switch saved his life.

Siby was at home that Tuesday morning when two planes hit the Twin Towers. His wife, who had followed him to the United States from Ivory Coast, was with him. She was eight months pregnant and was resting in bed with Siby when Karim's wife knocked on the door. "Have you seen the TV?" she asked. "Your building is burning. I keep trying to reach Karim, and I can't find him."

Siby turned on the television—every channel had the Twin Towers burning. "A plane had just hit the first building, and I was trying to call Karim, and I wasn't reaching him," says Siby. "I tried calling him, and the phone kept ringing."

When the second plane hit the other tower, the first building collapsed, and Karim's phone wouldn't even ring. "I started calling my friends, but the phone lines were down," says Siby. "A few people were getting through to me, asking if I was OK. I was trying to reach my family because I had sent a postcard of the Twin Towers to my mom, and I wrote on it that I worked there. I couldn't reach family, so I tried calling other friends. Finally, I said to my wife, 'Let's try to go out,' but the police had sealed the city completely, and we couldn't go anywhere. We couldn't go in the roads."

In the days following, Siby and family friends went to every hospital in New York City. "Someone said they saw Karim in New Jersey, and we got hope," says Siby. "Every day we said, 'Tomorrow we'll start another search,' and we'd gather the following morning and start to go to hospitals. There were no cars driving in Manhattan. We had to walk. We took some of Karim's pictures, made copies with our phone number, saying, 'If you see this person, please call us.' We went to different hospitals. But no one came to the hospitals—everyone was dead." It appeared that most people had died, and far fewer had been injured. After three weeks, Siby and Karim's wife called the community imam to organize a funeral, even though they didn't have a body. Many surviving kitchen workers from Windows showed up at Karim's funeral, but Siby wasn't there; he was in the hospital with his wife for the birth of his first daughter, Fanta.

"The Windows on the World chef went, everybody went," says Siby. "They were asking for me. They didn't know where I was. It was Fanta's birthday, October 3, in the afternoon."

What a Small Group of Workers Can Achieve

I started receiving phone calls from the Windows workers' union around the time of Karim's funeral. I was told that 250 displaced Windows workers needed support, but the tiny union couldn't provide it. The Windows workers were technically no longer members of the union because there was no restaurant—no restaurant, no union contract. I hesitated to get involved, not knowing exactly what was being asked of me, but upon meeting many of the surviving Windows workers I felt as though I needed to take on the challenge. These workers composed the most diverse group of people I had ever met in my life. The original owner of Windows on the World had wanted workers from every nation on earth—staff that could speak every tourist's language. These workers could barely communicate with each other, but they had worked together for several years, survived the trauma of 9/11, and emerged united. Inspired by them, I jumped in to help their cause.

I met Mamdouh on April 8, 2002. I met Siby on April 9. I remember watching Siby walk through the door. Mamdouh and I were arranging desks, setting up phone lines, and figuring out what exactly we'd be doing over the next several months. Siby appeared with his infant daughter, Fanta, in his arms. He wanted information about health care, since Windows workers no longer had benefits guaranteed through the union. I was relieved to have good news for him: the union was using money donated by people all over the world to provide surviving Windows workers with health insurance for up to one year.

What struck me first about Siby was his height. This tall African man had all kinds of questions for me. He could speak several languages, and since I was new to the incredible diversity of restaurant workers, I found his story fascinating. He also seemed like the quintessential Windows worker—a person of color and an immigrant who on 9/11 had lost not only the person who brought him to Windows on the World, but also his best friend in the United States.

Siby became the first official member of ROC and started coming to membership meetings and other activities. Although he didn't want a job at the Windows owner's new restaurant, he joined his former coworkers for the protest on the restaurant's opening night. He brought Fanta in a baby carrier. "I was really pissed at the restaurant management," says Siby. "They received all kinds of donations in our name but didn't pay us a dime." Siby was with us when we found out that our protest had been covered on the front page of the Metro section of the *New York Times,* and when the owner agreed to hire former Windows employees who wanted to work in the new restaurant.

Our victory brought hundreds of restaurant workers from all over New York City to ROC's doors, making our mission clear. Prior to the formation of ROC, there had never been an organization that gave voice to restaurant workers. However, after the victory in Midtown, workers came to us with startling stories of workplace injustice. Many hadn't been paid wages, tips, or overtime. Some had been injured on the job and then fired. We also heard outrageous stories about racial discrimination and sexual harassment. Our contacts at the state and federal departments of labor later told us that they received more complaints about legal violations from workers in the restaurant industry than from workers in any other private-sector industry.

While more and more people were coming through our doors, Siby kind of withdrew. He got a job as a taxi driver and stopped coming to our meetings. He was grieving and wanted space. "I didn't want to get too close to anyone," he says. "I had just lost so many people close to me."

After about a year, one of our members called him. The African and Haitian workers were organizing a special remembrance event for the African and Haitian Windows workers who died on 9/11. "I got a phone call from a Haitian guy," says Siby. "He wanted to organize something for the Africans and Haitians from Windows. I thought, OK, I haven't seen those guys for a long time. Let me go and see what is going on." Siby showed up at the event and saw Mamdouh, who encouraged him to take a job at ROC, still a fledgling organization. Mamdouh knew that Siby was a natural leader, but Siby wasn't immediately interested in the offer. "I was hesitant to organize because I had become more cynical about people," says Siby. "They agree with you today and change their mind to-morrow." He also felt as though people took advantage of organizers and didn't appreciate their breadth of knowledge and commitment to public education. "You go to school and pay for the things you learn from orga-nizers at ROC—people don't realize it," says Siby. "Compare this work to teaching. People I taught would say, 'I really want to thank you; you opened my eyes.' In organizing, people don't admit that. They just think you're getting paid to help them."

Although Siby had reservations about organizing, his wife encouraged him to take the job. She worried about the danger of driving a cab at all hours of the night; she didn't want anything to happen to him. So Siby agreed to start working with us.

During his first year at ROC, Siby's job was to do outreach to restaurant workers. We especially needed him to help us conduct surveys on wages and working conditions. The surveys he conducted in New York City were the first of thousands conducted by ROC members around the country, eventually giving us the data presented in this book. Siby went to Midtown Manhattan, the East Village, anywhere with a high concentration of restaurants, and followed workers as they left their late-night shifts. He did outreach during the freezing-cold winters and hot sticky summers. "As a tall African man trying to approach workers, especially late at night—many would run in the opposite direction when I tried to approach them," says Siby. Nevertheless, he managed to collect over 1,000 surveys in two different research projects. He also brought hundreds of restaurant workers to ROC.

I could almost write a second book on Siby's contributions. He has shown how one person can make an enormous impact in a social justice movement, and his experiences also reflect the importance of building unity across racial lines and other barriers to confront institutional injustice.

One of the first major campaigns Siby helped ROC lead was against a fancy Midtown restaurant that refused to pay its workers overtime—Floriberto's restaurant (see chapter 1). It was 2004. The restaurant belonged to a high-profile restaurant company and didn't feel threatened by immigrants and other low-wage restaurant workers. In that campaign, Siby organized workers from the restaurant and led efforts to build support among consumers across the country. Some consumers wrote to the restaurant from as far away as Atlanta to say that although they used to eat at the restaurant, they would not eat there on their next trip to New York unless the company did the right thing. The restaurant's company listened and promised the workers not only what they were owed but also significant policy changes at the restaurant. The company's lawyer later said that the campaign had helped the restaurant company institute policies that it really should have instituted long before.

In 2005, Siby helped recruit members for ROC's worker-led policy committee, which was fighting for an increase in the New York state minimum wage. A state senator had been blocking legislation that would raise the state's minimum wage, but since this senator didn't want to appear "anti-immigrant" in an election season, he capitulated and moved the bill forward. "This was a great experience because usually I was running a campaign that involved 20 or 30 people," says Siby. "Policy is a different kind of work. When you're campaigning for policy change you're doing something that could impact a wider group, hundreds of thousands of people."

In 2006, Siby helped open COLORS Restaurant, the largest worker-owned restaurant in North America. "In this case I was helping people understand what a cooperative is," says Siby. "Typical businesses have an all-powerful general manager, but a cooperative is something different. In a cooperative you're developing people's leadership skills. You need the employees to understand that they aren't in a typical business. So I was educating the new COLORS employees in why ROC is creating a cooperative restaurant. We also wanted them to still be organizers and be involved in policy work. That way they'd be taking action not just as workers but as partial business owners, and they could have a lot more of an impact in the community. So keeping everyone at COLORS involved in ROC was a big part of what I was doing."

In 2007, Siby played a key role in our campaign against discrimination in New York City's only four-star restaurant (see chapter 5). In that campaign, ROC organizers told a group of Latino bussers that they needed to build unity among other workers of color in their restaurant, particularly among the Bangladeshi bussers and runners. Their managers would find it difficult to "divide and conquer" if workers were united. The Latino workers, however, did not know how to reach out to their Bangladeshi coworkers, and when several ROC organizers tried to assist in opening lines of communication, the Bangladeshi workers wouldn't listen because they were terrified of losing their jobs. Siby finally broke through the communication barrier. He asked Mohamed Quddus, a Bangladeshi ROC leader, to join him in doing outreach. "We met a Bengali guy on our first night of outreach together," says Siby. "I'd tried to talk to him before, but when I did it with Quddus, it was different—turned out they knew each other. We followed him home to Queens and continued talking to him in a café until late in the night when we finally convinced him to join the campaign." When the other Bangladeshi workers followed suit and joined ROC's effort, we were able to push the restaurant to establish a new promotions policy and give raises to all the bussers and runners.

Siby was exhausted but full of hope after the night he spent with Quddus and the Bangladeshi worker. "I shut off my phone because I wanted to rest," he says. "But my family started calling me from the Ivory Coast, and I didn't know it. They couldn't reach me. Finally, someone knocked at the door and said there was bad news and that I should call my family. It was night in New York and morning in the Ivory Coast. That same night I lost my younger brother, my buddy. He was the only person I would call back home. It was my first successful night as an organizer, and the night I lost my brother." Siby couldn't go home for the funeral because his immigration status in the United States was still pending. He was devastated.

In 2008, Siby and Rekha Eanni, another former restaurant worker, took over as codirectors of ROC-New York, allowing Mamdouh and me to launch the national organization, ROC United. So, in the process of empowering thousands of restaurant workers across the country, Siby empowered himself in a country that doesn't exactly roll out a red carpet to welcome new African immigrants.

"What keeps me going is my desire to teach, my desire to help," says Siby. "My background back home was in teaching, training, and educating people. I've always supported others. That's my reputation in life. Coming to ROC, things weren't different. Getting people together, running committees—all that really fit in with my inner motivation. I've always been there for other people, always loved helping people get from Plan A to Plan B and developing people as leaders."

I think Siby has continued to be a successful leader in part because he is an immigrant and former restaurant worker who really struggled himself. He understands the challenges of being a low-wage worker of color in the restaurant industry, and he knows the pain of not being able to see family and the fear of being fired or deported. His success can also be attributed to his calm intelligence and humanity. He has a gift for quietly analyzing people and situations. Siby doesn't say much, but when he does speak, his words and commanding voice are memorable, often profound.

I think all of us can appreciate that Siby went from being the guy who delivers your groceries and drives your cab to executive director of a successful organization. He demonstrated that someone from his circumstances can get involved and do extraordinary things.

Siby represents the potential of workers across the restaurant industry.

How You Can Help

If people like Siby, Nikki, Claudia, Alicia, Oscar, and Shardha can bring about substantial change in the restaurant industry as part of a small but growing group of low-wage workers, imagine the power consumers could wield if they demanded more from restaurants.

When Mamdouh, Siby, and I speak at food and labor events around the country, people inevitably ask us how they as consumers can help restaurant workers rise above the poverty line and improve the working conditions that directly affect our food system. In response, we have created the *ROC National Diners' Guide* to make it easier for consumers to support restaurants that treat workers well, and demand more from restaurants that have not adopted responsible, sustainable labor practices. You can find this guide online at www.rocunited.org/dinersguide. Every year ROC will publish an updated *National Diners' Guide* that grades restaurants nationwide on employee wages, benefits, and equal opportunity promotion policies. In addition, you will find on our website a pledge you can sign to join an online consumer community that promotes the *National Diners' Guide* and adds new information to it. You can also get a smartphone "app" that lets you know the grades local restaurants have received in the guide. Your pledge lets restaurants know that you—the consumer—care about a restaurant's ranking, that you support responsible employers, and that you want to move other restaurants to improve their practices and get a better ranking. Your pledge also lets legislators know that a tipped minimum wage of $2.13 an hour is unacceptable, that paid sick days are crucial to everyone's health, and that new promotion policies are needed to end segregation by race and gender in the industry.

At the organizational level, ROC has been using a tri-pronged model to improve it for all its stakeholders—workers, employers, and consumers. First, we fight against exploitation in high-profile restaurant companies to send a signal to the whole industry. Second, we promote the "high road" to profitability by partnering with responsible employers and running our own worker-owned restaurants, which put our principles into practice and give us a space to train workers so that they may advance to living-wage jobs. Third, we conduct worker-led research and advocate for policy changes to lift standards industry-wide. We're showing the restaurant industry the negative consequences of irresponsible business practices and the benefits of responsible, sustainable practices. Simultaneously, we're creating uniform policies, such as an increase in the tipped minimum wage, to make it easier for all employers to lift standards across the board.

You can support our efforts on the ground, every time you eat out, by taking each of the following steps. The *ROC National Diners' Guide* will make the process even easier, pointing you in the direction of responsible restaurants. So be sure to get a copy and share it with others.

1. Adopt a definition of "sustainable food" that includes sustainable labor practices

This is actually very simple, a matter of talking to your friends and family about what eating sustainable food really means to you. You can tell the people in your life that it's not enough to care about food being organic, locally grown, slow, cage-free, and grass-fed. While we're obsessing about things like omega-3s, corn syrup, deep-fried shrimp, and farm-raised salmon, we absolutely must consider the health and sustainability of the workforce preparing, cooking, and serving our meals.

2. Talk to the workers when you eat in a restaurant

This is the very best way to find out how a restaurant is really doing. The *ROC National Diners' Guide* certainly doesn't have data on all our nation's restaurants, so we need you to engage with workers when you go out to eat in your neighborhood. Ask your servers, bussers, and food runners about their wages and tips and find out how their managers treat them when they're sick.

Here's Siby's advice: "Always try to know from the workers if they will be getting all of their tips. If I'm giving a $20 tip, I want to know from the worker whether he's getting that $20. And if you realize that a restaurant is doing well by its workers, tell your friends and tell the management that you will keep supporting the restaurant. You want to be able to say, 'I came to this restaurant, I spoke to the workers, I spoke to the management—they treat their workers really well.' We need people to be engaged."

In addition, you can encourage workers to join ROC and speak up for themselves on the job.

3. Engage restaurant managers in a conversation about labor practices

Always be ready to engage management in a conversation about how they think workers should be treated. Restaurants can't exist without customers; managers know this, and so they're interested in what customers have to say about food, service, and the overall dining experience. The *ROC National Diners' Guide* can help you start a conversation, but you can talk to management about what you observe in a restaurant regardless of whether you have the guide. Ask about training and promotion opportunities for lower-level workers, and praise great bussers and runners so that managers will consider promoting them.

4. Help raise the federal minimum wage for tipped workers! Tell policymakers and restaurant managers that you think $2.13 is unacceptable

Raising the federal minimum wage for tipped workers has been a top priority for ROC. Chapter 4, "$2.13—The Tipping Point," describes the dysfunctional and incredibly complex minimum-wage system that permits and even encourages employers to pay their workers $2.13 an hour. To put this in perspective, $2.13 is about one-third of the minimum wage paid to all other workers, and since the tipped minimum wage has been frozen at $2.13 for the last two decades, restaurant workers earn the lowest median wages in the United States, even with tips included. Some restaurant conglomerates claim that increasing the tipped minimum wage would force restaurateurs out of business, but we know this is untrue. Seven states (Alaska, California, Minnesota, Montana, Nevada, Oregon, and Washington) do not have a lower minimum wage for tipped workers, and all of these states have growing restaurant industries.

5. Vote for paid sick days for restaurant workers. And tell restaurant managers you consider workers' health when choosing where to eat

We need your support to win paid sick days and other health benefits for restaurant workers—and all other workers in the United States. Over the last several years we've lobbied for paid sick days at the local, state, and federal levels, and in some cities we've been successful. Chapter 3, "Serving While Sick," discusses paid sick days that passed into law in San Francisco and Washington, D.C., and cites a recent study indicating that workers experienced positive health outcomes after these laws went into effect. In fact, employers in these cities have become supportive of the legislation because it has had a positive impact in their workplaces.

So let your policymaker know—in an e-mail, on a postcard, or on a paper plate—that you want a living wage *and* health benefits for the workers who handle our food. If all consumers speak out, several million workers will be able to move out of poverty, and we won't have to worry about sick workers serving our meals. After all, who wants an organic strawberry that someone has sneezed on because taking a day off work is too expensive?

6. Picket with your wallet—don't eat in restaurants segregated by race and gender

We continue to wage campaigns against discrimination in high-profile restaurant companies to inform the industry that there will be negative consequences for segregation and discrimination based on race and gender. I'll never forget how the public responded when one of our campaigns was featured in an article on the front page of the *New York Times* Dining section (see chapter 5). The article sparked tremendous public dialogue and a vigorous debate about the restaurant industry. ROC received both threatening letters from restaurant companies and an outpouring of gratitude from workers who said they could not believe that this issue, though highly visible, was finally being acknowledged.

I realize that we can't move all workers of color into the 20 percent of restaurant jobs that provide a living wage—so while ROC is fighting to end discriminatory labor practices, we are simultaneously working to make all jobs good jobs. This is an enormous challenge—lifting all boats while ensuring they have equal opportunity to sail.

You can support this effort by joining ROC campaigns! Join us on the picket line or make a phone call to a discriminatory restaurant company. Or, just don't eat in restaurants that you know refuse to promote from within.

7. Join our campaign to support workers all along the food chain

In January 2008, ROC helped launch the Food Chain Workers Alliance, a coalition of worker-run organizations along the food chain. The Alliance includes farmworkers, meat- and poultry-processing workers, food retail and distribution workers, supermarket workers, restaurant workers, and more. Together we are developing standards by which we can recognize and promote responsible business practices throughout the food chain. At the same time, we are campaigning against exploitative labor practices in the food system and creating consequences for employers who exploit their workers.

"We need people to look at the entire picture," says Siby. "Right now they say, 'I got great food. The chef cooks really well. There's great service.' They don't really question how they get all that, and the people involved. They don't wonder about the farmers, the people who transport the food to restaurants, and the people who cook the food. They don't ask if those people are getting a good share in this. They just consider whether they had a good experience. People want organic and locally grown—but do you want to eat food that is handled by somebody who is being paid slavery wages? That's a question everyone should ask."

To get involved, you can contact us at info@rocunited.org.

For my part, I have become much more observant when eating out. I watch the workers, how they are treated and how happy or unhappy they look. I notice the race and gender of workers in different positions throughout the restaurant, and I always peek behind the kitchen door.

And I continue to love restaurants. Like most Americans, I eat out regularly. I still go to restaurants to celebrate the happiest moments in life—birthdays, anniversaries, and reunions with people I love. My view of restaurants has changed as I've learned about industry-wide exploitation, discrimination, and even nasty consumer-safety issues, but I truly believe that these institutional problems can be tackled. Learning about these problems has only strengthened my resolve to demand an even better dining experience—one in which I can eat with peace of mind, knowing that the people who prepare, cook, and serve my food are well paid, healthy, and treated with dignity and respect.

I hope you'll feel the same after reading this book.

Next time you eat out take the *ROC National Diners' Guide* with you. Tell the restaurant management you care about what the guide says, and where the restaurant stands in terms of wages and benefits like paid sick days. Write to your legislator—or better yet, join us in meeting with her—and tell her that you really can't stomach a federal minimum wage of $2.13 and that you don't approve of the fact that your cook, server, and busser are all serving food while sick because they don't have paid sick leave. Ask restaurateurs about their promotion policies and the opportunities they provide for workers in the kitchen to advance up the ladder in the restaurant.

Your dining experience will never be the same. It will only get better.

Appendix

A Note on Sources and Data

Industry Studies, Surveys, and Reports

This book includes data from comprehensive restaurant industry studies, each titled *Behind the Kitchen Door,* conducted by the Restaurant Opportunities Center (ROC) in eight locations, and from an additional 500 worker surveys and 20 employer interviews focused on the health-care needs of restaurant workers. Information was also drawn from ROC's 2009 reports *Burned: High Risks and Low Benefits for Workers in the New York City Restaurant Industry* and *The Great Service Divide: Occupational Segregation and Inequality in New York City's Thriving Restaurant Industry,* its 2010 reports *Waiting on Equality: The Role and Impact of Gender in the New York City Restaurant Industry* and *Serving While Sick: High Risks and Low Benefits for the Nation's Restaurant Workforce, and Their Impact on the Consumer,* and its 2012 report *Tipped over the Edge: Gender Inequality in the Nation's Restaurant Industry.*

The *Behind the Kitchen Door* studies were conceived of and designed by the Restaurant Opportunities Center and Restaurant Industry Coalitions in Chicago, Los Angeles, Maine, Miami, New Orleans, New York, southeast Michigan, and Washington, D.C., from 2005 to the present. In each location, the Restaurant Industry Coalition working with the local ROC affiliate consists of academics, policy analysts, worker advocates, worker organizers, unions, and others and includes participation from restaurant workers and restaurant industry employers. This book includes summary data from the *Behind the Kitchen Door* studies from those eight locations, with pooled survey data weighted for position, industry segment, and local workforce size. In each locality, *Behind the Kitchen Door* is one of the most comprehensive research analyses of the restaurant industry conducted in that region's history.

Each of the eight *Behind the Kitchen Door* studies presents and analyzes data from more than 500 worker surveys, approximately 30 one-hour interviews with restaurant workers, and 30 one-hour interviews with restaurant employers in each region. Together the eight reports make use of 4,323 worker surveys—the largest national survey sample of restaurant workers ever conducted—and more than 240 employer interviews and 240 worker interviews. The surveys contained questions regarding job hazards, wages and benefits, working conditions, injuries, abuse, wage theft, and other employment law violations. Great care was taken to match the survey sample in each city with the ethnic and gender demographics of the local restaurant industry as found in the U.S. Census Bureau's American Community Survey (ACS). In each locality, the results of the survey research were supplemented by analysis of industry and government data as well as a review of existing academic literature.

The research for *Burned* was conducted between August 2005 and July 2009 with primary funding from the National Institute for Occupational Safety and Health. The Restaurant Opportunities Center of New York (ROC-NY) spearheaded a local Health and Safety Task Force to study the occupational safety and health of New York City restaurant workers. The Health and Safety Task Force includes the Queens College Center for the Biology of Natural Systems, the Mount Sinai School of Medicine, the New York Committee for Occupational Safety and Health, the NYU Center for the Study of Asian American Health, and Make the Road New York. Our study analyzed data from 502 surveys of restaurant workers, 10 focus groups with workers of different ethnicities, and 35 one-hour employer interviews. The survey sample was strictly matched to race proportions of New York City restaurant workers in the 2000 census.

The two reports *The Great Service Divide* and *Waiting on Equality,* conducted by the Restaurant Opportunities Center of New York, focused on race and gender discrimination in the New York City restaurant industry. *The Great Service Divide* was largely based on a matched pairs audit testing study, in which ROC sent equally credentialed pairs of white testers and testers of color to apply for server positions in 138 Manhattan fine-dining restaurants. The data were coupled with demographic canvassing, in which 15 research assistants were sent to observe workers' demographics in the "front of the house" at 45 Manhattan fine-dining restaurants. Canvassers tabulated the number of white people and people of color and male and female workers they observed in various front of the house positions. *Waiting on Equality* added to this set of original data with seven focus groups conducted with different subsets of women in the industry, including young women ages 18–25 and women working in the kitchen.

Serving While Sick, published in 2010, was ROC's first report to draw on the combined 4,323 *Behind the Kitchen Door* surveys, analyzing health and safety issues for restaurant workers nationwide. *Serving While Sick* also draws on an additional 500 worker surveys and 20 employer interviews focused on the health-care needs of restaurant workers.

Finally, *Tipped over the Edge* was published in February 2012 by ROC and a coalition of 12 national women's organizations. The report draws on data from the U.S. Department of Labor, Bureau of Labor Statistics, and from the Current Population Survey (CPS), as well as from numerous secondary sources compiled and analyzed by the 13 organizations that coauthored the report: the Restaurant Opportunities Centers United, Family Values @ Work, the Institute for Women's Policy Research, the HERvotes coalition, MomsRising, the Black Women's Roundtable of the National Coalition on Black Civic Participation, the National Council for Research on Women, the National Partnership for Women & Families, the National Women's Law Center, the National Organization for Women, Wider Opportunities for Women, the Women of Color Policy Network at NYU Wagner, and 9to5, the National Association of Working Women. The report also draws on original data from the national *Behind the Kitchen Door* survey and interview sample sets. In addition, the report includes information from Wider Opportunities for Women's Basic Economic Security Tables™ Index (BEST) to measure the basic needs and assets workers require for economic security throughout a lifetime and across generations.

The *Behind the Kitchen Door* Survey Sample

As mentioned above, this book draws from several data sets. The largest data set is derived from 4,323 surveys of restaurant workers conducted between 2003 and 2010 by staff, members, and volunteers from Restaurant Opportunities Center affiliates in Chicago, Detroit, Los Angeles, Maine, Miami, New Orleans, New York City, and Washington, D.C. The surveys were conducted face to face with workers inside restaurants and in the vicinity of restaurants during breaks and at the end of shifts.

Since there is no government data on individual restaurant workers in the United States, it would have been nearly impossible to get a random sample of workers in the restaurant industry. Thus, ROC conducted convenience sample surveys but used stratification to ensure that our sample was as representative as possible of the city's restaurant industry. We used U.S. Bureau of Labor Statistics industry data to identify the size of key restaurant industry segments, and U.S. Census data to identify the size of key demographic groups (race, gender, age, and county of residence). Our sampling methodology has advantages and limitations, like all methodologies. Although we could not determine a random sample of restaurant workers for our surveys, our method of tracking down workers as they left restaurants helped us include populations of workers typically underrepresented in the U.S. Census. In addition, our in-person surveys enabled us to obtain high response rates on specific questions.

After fielding the surveys, we weighted the data as a final step to ensure representativeness. Using data from the Bureau of Labor Statistics, we weighted our sample to match the distribution of "back of the house" and "front of the house" staff in "full-service" establishments and "limited-services" eating places in the nation's restaurant industry. Finally, after pooling all of the local data into one national data set, we weighted each city's sample by the relative size of its restaurant industry to ensure that restaurant workers in different-sized markets were represented appropriately.

Notes

1. The Hands on Your Plate

1. Those employed in the restaurant industry number 10.09 million (10,090,650), of which 9,376,900 are workers in food services and drinking places. The rest are food service and preparation workers in industries that include limited- or full-service restaurants: amusement parks and arcades (31,940); gambling industries (28,100); other amusement and recreation industries (206,540); performing arts, spectator sports, and related industries (25,040); traveler accommodations (418,460); and RV parks and recreational camps (3,580). U.S. Bureau of Labor Statistics, *May 2010 National Industry-Specific Occupational Employment and Wage Estimates,* Occupational Employment Statistics (Washington, D.C.: U.S. Department of Labor, Bureau of Labor Statistics, May 2011), http://www.bls.gov/oes/2010/may/naics3_722000.htm. For information on low-paying occupations in the restaurant industry, see U.S. Bureau of Labor Statistics, *2010 National Cross-Industry Estimates Sorted by Median Hourly Wage for All Standard Occupational Classifications,* Occupational Employment Statistics, http://bls.gov/pub/special.requests/oes/oesm10nat.zip.

2. Restaurant Opportunities Centers United, *National Survey Data, 2011.*

3. Rajesh D. Nayak and Paul K. Sonn, *Restoring the Minimum Wage for America's Tipped Workers,* technical report (New York: National Employment Law Project, 2009), 5.

4. Restaurant Opportunities Centers United, *National Survey Data, 2011.*

5. Ibid.

6. Hayden Stewart, Noel Blisard, and Dean Jollife, *Let's Eat Out: Americans Weigh Taste, Convenience, and Nutrition,* Economic Information Bulletin 19 (Washington, D.C.: U.S. Department of Agriculture, October 2006), http://www.ers.usda.gov/publications/eib19/eib19.pdf.

7. Ibid.

8. Restaurant Opportunities Centers United, *National Survey Data, 2011.*

2. *Real* Sustainability, Please!

1. "About Us," Slow Food International, www.slowfood.com (accessed January 30, 2012).

2. Josh Viertel, telephone interview by author, July 30, 2011.

3. Josee Johnston and Shyon Baumann, *Foodies: Democracy and Distinction in the Gourmet Foodscape* (New York: Routledge, 2009), 132; David Kamp, *The United States of Arugula: How We Became a Gourmet Nation* (New York: Broadway Books, 2006), 124.

4. Jennifer Lawinski, "For Restaurants, Going Green Can Pay Off Quickly," *Nation's Restaurant News,* October 20, 2010, http://www.nrn.com/article/restaurants-going-green-can-pay-quickly.

5. See *Food, Inc.,* Magnolia Pictures, 2008.

6. "Our Philosophy," Slow Food International, www.slowfood.com (accessed June 28, 2012).

7. Jeffrey H. Birnbaum, "Washington's Power 25: Which Pressure Groups Are Best at Manipulating the Laws We Live By?" *Fortune,* December 8, 1997, http://money.cnn.com/magazines/fortune/fortune_archive/1997/12/08/234927/index.htm; Associated Press, "Restaurant Group Spent $613,000 in 1Q Lobbying," *Yahoo News,* June 30, 2011, http://news.yahoo.com/restaurant-group-spent-613–000–1q-lobbying-210006255.html.

8. Janet Novack, "The Minimum Wage: It's All Local," *Forbes,* November 1, 2006, http://www.forbes.com/2006/11/01/minimum-wage-debate-biz-wash-cz_jn_1101beltway.html.

3. Serving While Sick

1. U.S. Centers for Disease Control and Prevention, *Estimates of Foodborne Disease* (Atlanta: U.S. Centers for Disease Control and Prevention, 2011), http://www.cdc.gov/foodborneburden.

2. Restaurant Opportunities Centers United, *Serving While Sick: High Risks and Low Benefits for the Nation's Restaurant Workforce, and Their Impact on the Consumer,* technical report (New York: Restaurant Workers Opportunities Centers United, 2010).

3. Restaurant Opportunities Centers United, *National Survey Data, 2011.*

4. U.S. Bureau of Labor Statistics, *Workplace Injuries and Illnesses—2008,* Table 4: Number of Cases and Incidence Rate of Nonfatal Occupational Injuries and Illnesses for Industries with 100,000 or More Cases, 2008 (Washington, D.C.: U.S. Bureau of Labor Statistics, 2009).

5. Restaurant Opportunities Centers United, *National Survey Data, 2011.*

6. Ibid.

7. Ibid.

8. U.S. Bureau of Labor Statistics, *May 2010 National Cross-Industry Estimates, Food Preparation and Serving Related Occupations,* Occupational Employment Statistics, http://www.bls.gov/oes/current/oes_nat.htm#35–0000.

9. Restaurant Opportunities Centers United, *National Survey Data, 2011.*

10. PR Newswire, "New Research Report Shows Nearly 50 Percent of Restaurants Are Women-Owned," *Reuters,* February 11, 2011, http://www.reuters.com/article/2011/02/11/id US219071+11-Feb-2011+PRN20110211.

11. Restaurant Opportunities Center of Michigan, Restaurant Opportunities Centers United, and Southeast Michigan Restaurant Industry Coalition, *Behind the Kitchen Door: Inequality and Opportunity in Metro Detroit's Growing Restaurant Industry,* technical report (New York: Restaurant Opportunities Center of Michigan, 2010), 16.

12. Restaurant Opportunities Centers United, *Serving While Sick,* 15.

13. Ibid., 16.

14. Kathryn Baer, "D.C. Carrotmob Promotes Paid Sick Leave," *Change.org,* November 10, 2010, http://news.change.org/stories/dc-carrotmob-promotes-paid-sick-leave.

15. Spencer Woodman, "ROC vs. the NRA," *The Nation,* May 12, 2010.

16. San Francisco Department of Public Health, Communicable Disease Control & Prevention Section, *Annual Report of Communicable Diseases in San Francisco, 2006* (San Francisco: San Francisco Department of Public Health, 2008), http://www.sfcdcp.org/document.html?id=210; *Annual Report of Communicable Diseases in San Francisco, 2007* (San Francisco: San Francisco Department of Public Health, 2008), http://www.sfdph.org/dph/files/reports/StudiesData/CommDiseasesSFAnnlRpt122008.pdf; *Annual Report of Communicable Diseases in San Francisco, 2008* (San Francisco: San Francisco Department of Public Health, 2010), http://www.sfdph.org/dph/files/reports/StudiesData/CommDiseases SFAnnlRpt01201042008.pdf.

4. $2.13—The Tipping Point

1. Rajesh D. Nayak and Paul K. Sonn, *Restoring the Minimum Wage for America's Tipped Workers,* technical report (New York: National Employment Law Project, 2009), 6.

2. Ibid., 7.

3. Restaurant Opportunities Centers United, *National Survey Data, 2011.*

4. U.S. Bureau of Labor Statistics, *2010 National Cross-Industry Estimates Sorted by Median Hourly Wage for All Standard Occupational Classifications,* Occupational Employment Statistics, http://bls.gov/pub/special.requests/oes/oesm10nat.zip.

5. http://aspe.hhs.gov/poverty/12fedreg.shtml; *Federal Register,* vol. 76, no. 13, January 20, 2011, pp. 36737–38. Hereafter, unless otherwise stated, "poverty line" or "poverty wage" refers to the income below which a family of four falls into poverty as defined by 2011 HHS Poverty Guidelines. A poverty wage of $10.75 assumes full-time, year-round work.

6. U.S. Bureau of Labor Statistics, *Quarterly Census of Employment and Wages,* www.bls.gov/cew (accessed January 20, 2011).

7. Restaurant Opportunities Centers United, *National Survey Data, 2011.*

8. Restaurant Opportunities Center of Michigan, Restaurant Opportunities Centers United, and Southeast Michigan Restaurant Industry Coalition, *Behind the Kitchen Door: Inequality and Opportunity in Metro Detroit's Growing Restaurant Industry,* technical report (New York: Restaurant Opportunities Center of Michigan, 2010), 20.

9. Restaurant Opportunities Centers United, *Calculations of Current Population Survey (CPS),* March 2010.

10. Restaurant Opportunities Centers United, *National Survey Data,* 2011; Economic Policy Institute, "Basic Family Budget Calculator," http://www.epi.org/resources/budget/calculator-intro-methodology.

11. National Low Income Housing Coalition, *Out of Reach 2012: America's Forgotten Housing Crisis,* technical report (Washington, D.C.: National Low Income Housing Coalition, 2012), 3.

12. Restaurant Opportunities Centers United, *National Survey Data, 2011.*

13. Sabrina Tavernese, "Middle-Class Areas Shrink as Income Gap Grows, New Report Finds," *New York Times,* November 15, 2011, http://www.nytimes.com/2011/11/16/us/middle-class-areas-shrink-as-income-gap-grows-report-finds.html.

14. U.S. Bureau of Labor Statistics, "Occupational Employment and Wages—May 2010," news release (Washington, D.C.: U.S. Bureau of Labor Statistics, May 2011), www.bls.gov/news.release/pdf/ocwage.pdf.

5. Race in the Kitchen

1. "Darden Is the World's Largest Full-Service Restaurant Company," Darden, http://www.darden.com (accessed May 30, 2012).

2. Ibid.

3. Sasha Chavkin, "Business Lobbyists Earned Defeat of Minimum Wage Bill," New York World, May 22, 2012, http://www.thenewyorkworld.com/2012/05/22/business-lobbyists-earned-defeat-of-minimum-wage-bill.

4. Darden, "Key Consumer Challenges and Restaurant Trends for 2011," February 2, 2011, http://www.beefusa.org/CMDocs/BeefUSA/resources/CC2011-Trends-and-Trendsetters-Darden.pdf; "Darden Restaurants Inc. DRI," Morningstar, Inc., http://insiders.morningstar.com/trading/executive-profile.action?t=DRI&PersonId=PS00001QXJ&flag=Executive&insider=Clarence_Otis&region=USA&culture=en-us (accessed May 30, 2012).

5. Chavkin, "Defeat of Minimum Wage Bill."

6. Restaurant Opportunities Center United, *National Survey Data, 2011.*

7. Restaurant Opportunities Center of Michigan, Restaurant Opportunities Centers United, and Southeast Michigan Restaurant Industry Coalition, *Behind the Kitchen Door: Inequality and Opportunity in Metro Detroit's Growing Restaurant Industry,* technical report (New York: Restaurant Opportunities Center of Michigan, 2010), 44.

8. Restaurant Opportunities Centers United, *National Survey Data, 2011.*

9. Restaurant Opportunities Center of Michigan, Restaurant Opportunities Centers United, and Southeast Michigan Restaurant Industry Coalition, *Behind the Kitchen Door,* 43.

10. Restaurant Opportunities Center of Miami, *Behind the Kitchen Door: The Social Impact of Inequality in Miami's Growing Restaurant Industry,* technical report (New York: Restaurant Opportunities Center of Miami, 2011), 39.

11. Restaurant Opportunities Centers United, *National Survey Data, 2011.*

12. Ibid.

13. U.S. Census Bureau, *Household Income for States: 2008 and 2009,* American Community Survey Briefs (Washington, D.C.: U.S. Census Bureau, 2010), http://www.census.gov/prod/2010pubs/acsbr09–2.pdf; Census Scope, *Segregation: Neighborhood Exposure by Race* (Ann Arbor, Mich.: Social Science Data Analysis Network, University of Michigan, n.d.), http://www.censusscope.org/us/m8840/chart_exposure.html.

14. U.S. Census Bureau, *Household Income for States: 2008 and 2009.* See also Census Scope, *Segregation: Neighborhood Exposure by Race.*

15. Restaurant Opportunities Center of Washington, D.C., Restaurant Opportunities Centers United, and Washington, D.C., Restaurant Industry Coalition, *Behind the Kitchen Door: Inequality & Opportunity in Washington, D.C.'s Thriving Restaurant Industry,* technical report (New York: Restaurant Opportunities Center of Washington, D.C., 2011), 41.

16. Restaurant Opportunities Center of Michigan, Restaurant Opportunities Centers United, and Southeast Michigan Restaurant Industry Coalition, *Behind the Kitchen Door,* 44.

17. Census Scope, *Segregation: Dissimilarity Indices* (Ann Arbor, Mich.: Social Science Data Analysis Network, University of Michigan, 2009), http://www.censusscope.org/us/rank_dissimilarity_white_black.html; Dante Chinni, "Along Detroit's Eight Mile Road, a Stark Racial Split," *Christian Science Monitor,* November 15, 2002, http://www.csmonitor.com/2002/1115/p01s02-ussc.html.

18. Restaurant Opportunities Center of Michigan, Restaurant Opportunities Centers United, and Southeast Michigan Restaurant Industry Coalition, *Behind the Kitchen Door.*

19. Restaurant Opportunities Centers United, "Total Commute Time Regression Table," *National Survey Data, 2011.*

20. Ibid.

21. Restaurant Opportunities Centers United, *National Survey Data, 2011.*

22. Restaurant Opportunities Center of Michigan, Restaurant Opportunities Centers United, and Southeast Michigan Restaurant Industry Coalition, *Behind the Kitchen Door,* 40.

23. Restaurant Opportunities Center of New Orleans, Restaurant Opportunities Centers United, and New Orleans Restaurant Industry Coalition, *Behind the Kitchen Door: Inequality,*

Instability, and Opportunity in the Greater New Orleans Restaurant Industry, technical report (New York: Restaurant Opportunities Center of New Orleans, 2010), 42.

24. Restaurant Opportunities Center of New York and the New York City Restaurant Industry Coalition, *The Great Service Divide: Occupational Segregation and Inequality in New York City's Thriving Restaurant Industry,* technical report (New York: Restaurant Opportunities Center of New York, 2009), 24.

25. Ibid., 29.

26. Kate Cairns, Josee Johnston, and Shyon Baumann, "Caring about Food: Doing Gender in the Foodie Kitchen," *Gender and Society* 24 (2010): 593.

6. Women Waiting on Equality

1. U.S. Census Bureau, *Median Weekly Earnings of Full-Time Wage and Salary Workers by Detailed Occupation and Sex, 2010* (Washington, D.C.: U.S. Bureau of Labor Statistics, June 2011), ftp://ftp.bls.gov/pub/special.requests/lf/aat39.txt.

2. Restaurant Opportunities Centers United, *Tipped over the Edge: Gender Inequity in the Nation's Restaurant Industry,* technical report (New York: Restaurant Opportunities Centers United, 2012), 19.

3. Restaurant Opportunities Centers United, *National Survey Data, 2011.*

4. U.S. Census Bureau, *Median Weekly Earnings, 2010.*

5. Ibid.

6. Restaurant Opportunities Centers United, *National Survey Data, 2011.*

7. See Eve Tahmincioglu, "Sexual Claims Common in Pressure Cooker Restaurant World," *The Bottom Line* (blog), November 1, 2011, http://bottomline.msnbc.msn.com/_news/2011/11/01/8565198-sexual-claims-common-in-pressure-cooker-restaurant-world (accessed January 2012), for a review of data from the Equal Employment Opportunity Commission.

8. Restaurant Opportunities Center of Michigan, Restaurant Opportunities Centers United, and Southeast Michigan Restaurant Industry Coalition, *Behind the Kitchen Door: Inequality and Opportunity in Metro Detroit's Growing Restaurant Industry,* technical report (New York: Restaurant Opportunities Center of Michigan, 2010), 51.

9. Restaurant Opportunities Centers United, *Tipped over the Edge.*

10. National Women's Law Center, "Minimum Wage: Does the State Have a Minimum Wage That Allows a Family of Three to Reach the Federal Poverty Threshold?" http://hrc.nwlc.org/policy-indicators/minimum-wage.

11. An increase in the subminimum wage to $5.08 would give immediate relief to nearly 837,200 workers and their families, 630,000 of whom are female tipped workers, and many of whom live below the poverty line, while also raising the wage floor for over 10 million restaurant workers and 5 million women. Raising the subminimum wage to $5.08 would also decrease the gender wage-equity gap within the occupation by a fifth. When taking into consideration that full-time year-round female servers are paid $17,000 annually and that their male counterparts are paid $25,000, raising the minimum wage for tipped workers earning $2.13 would reduce the gender wage-equity gap from 68 percent to 74 percent. Because women are paid so much less and because they represent a larger share of the workers, the increase would benefit women much more than men and help to close the gender wage gap.

SELECTED BIBLIOGRAPHY

Associated Press. "Restaurant Group Spent $613,000 in 1Q Lobbying." *Yahoo News,* June 30, 2011. http://news.yahoo.com/restaurant-group-spent-613-000–1q-lobbying-210006255.html.

Barr, Ann, and Paul Levy. *The Official Foodie Handbook: Be Modern—Worship Food.* New York: Timbre Books, 1984.

Birnbaum, Jeffrey H. "Washington's Power 25: Which Pressure Groups Are Best at Manipulating the Laws We Live By?" *Fortune,* December 8, 1997. http://money.cnn.com/magazines/fortune/fortune_archive/1997/12/08/234927/index.htm.

Bourdain, Anthony. *Typhoid Mary: An Urban Historical.* New York: Bloomsbury, 2001.

Cairns, Kate, Josee Johnston, and Shyon Baumann. "Caring about Food: Doing Gender in the Foodie Kitchen." *Gender and Society* 24 (2010): 591–615.

Census Scope. *Segregation: Dissimilarity Indices.* Ann Arbor, Mich.: Social Science Data Analysis Network, University of Michigan, 2009. http://www.censusscope.org/us/rank_dissimilarity_white_black.html.

——. *Segregation: Neighborhood Exposure by Race.* Ann Arbor, Mich.: Social Science Data Analysis Network, University of Michigan, n.d. http://www.censusscope.org/us/m8840/chart_exposure.html.

Chinni, Dante. "Along Detroit's Eight Mile Road, a Stark Racial Split." *Christian Science Monitor,* November 15, 2002, http://www.csmonitor.com/2002/1115/p01s02-ussc.html.

Compdata Surveys. "2010 Voluntary Turnover" and "2010 Total Turnover." Compdata Surveys. http://www.compensationforce.com/2011/03/2010-turnover-rates-by-industry.html.

Connecticut Department of Public Health. *Working Safely In Restaurants.* Hartford, Conn.: Connecticut Department of Public Health, Environmental Health Section, Environmental & Occupational Health Assessment Program, 2007. http://www.ct.gov/dph/lib/dph/environmental_health/eoha/pdf/restaurant_safety.pdf.

Economic Policy Institute. "Basic Family Budget Calculator." http://www.epi.org/resources/budget/calculator-intro-methodology.

Johnston, Josee, and Shyon Baumann. *Foodies: Democracy and Distinction in the Gourmet Foodscape.* New York: Routledge, 2010.

Kamp, David. *The United States of Arugula: How We Became a Gourmet Nation.* New York: Broadway Books, 2006.

Kant, Ashima, and Barry Graubard. "Eating Out in America, 1987–2000: Trends and Nutritional Correlates." *Preventive Medicine* 38 (2004): 243–49.

Lawinski, Jennifer. "For Restaurants, Going Green Can Pay Off Quickly." *Nation's Restaurant News,* October 20, 2010. http://www.nrn.com/article/restaurants-going-green-can-pay-quickly.

Levinstein, Harvey. *Paradox of Plenty: A Social History of Eating in Modern America.* Berkeley and Los Angeles: University of California Press, 2003 [1993].

National Low Income Housing Coalition. *Out of Reach: Renters in the Great Recession, the Crisis Continues.* Technical report. Washington, D.C.: National Low Income Housing Coalition, 2010.

Nayak, Rajesh D., and Paul K. Sonn. *Restoring the Minimum Wage for America's Tipped Workers.* Technical report. New York: National Employment Law Project, 2009.

Novack, Janet. "The Minimum Wage: It's All Local." *Forbes,* November 1, 2006. http://www.forbes.com/2006/11/01/minimum-wage-debate-biz-wash-cz_jn_1101beltway.html.

Open Secrets.org: Center for Responsive Politics. "National Restaurant Association." http://www.opensecrets.org/orgs/summary.php?id=D000000150.

———. "PACS: National Restaurant Association." http://www.opensecrets.org/pacs/lookup2.php?strID=C00003764&cycle=2012.

Prewitt, Milford. "Hand Injuries on the Rise among Restaurant Workers." *Nation's Restaurant News,* November 21, 2005. http://findarticles.com/p/articles/mi_m3190/is_47_39/ai_n15923107.

PR Newswire. "New Research Report Shows Nearly 50 Percent of Restaurants Are Women-Owned." *Reuters,* February 11, 2011. http://www.reuters.com/article/2011/02/11/idUS219071+11-Feb-2011+PRN20110211.

Puglisi, Dave. "Knives and Cutting: What Dangers Are Lurking in Your Workplace?" *EHS Today: The Magazine for Environment, Health, and Safety Leaders,* May 1, 2009. http://ehstoday.com/safety/news/knives-dangers-workplace-3993.

Restaurant Opportunities Center of Los Angeles, Restaurant Opportunities Centers United, and the Los Angeles Restaurant Industry Coalition. *Behind the Kitchen Door: Inequality and Opportunity in Los Angeles, the Nation's Largest Restaurant Industry.* Technical report. New York: Restaurant Opportunities Center of Los Angeles, 2011.

Restaurant Opportunities Center of Maine, Restaurant Opportunities Centers United, and the Maine Restaurant Industry Coalition. *Behind the Kitchen Door: Low Road Jobs, High Road Opportunities in Maine's Growing Restaurant Industry.* Technical report. New York: Restaurant Opportunities Center of Maine, 2010.

Restaurant Opportunities Center of Michigan, Restaurant Opportunities Centers United, and Southeast Michigan Restaurant Industry Coalition. *Behind the Kitchen Door: Inequality and Opportunity in Metro Detroit's Growing Restaurant Industry.* Technical report. New York: Restaurant Opportunities Center of Michigan, 2010.

Restaurant Opportunities Center of New Orleans, Restaurant Opportunities Centers United, and New Orleans Restaurant Industry Coalition. *Behind the Kitchen Door: Inequality, Instability, and Opportunity in the Greater New Orleans Restaurant Industry.* Technical report. New York: Restaurant Opportunities Center of New Orleans, 2010.

Restaurant Opportunities Center of New York and the New York City Restaurant Industry Coalition. *The Great Service Divide: Occupational Segregation and Inequality in New York City's Thriving Restaurant Industry.* Technical report. New York: Restaurant Opportunities Center of New York, 2009.

——. *Waiting on Equality: The Role and Impact of Gender in the New York City Restaurant Industry.* Technical report. New York: Restaurant Opportunities Center of New York, 2010.

Restaurant Opportunities Center of New York, Restaurant Opportunities Centers United, New York City Restaurant Health and Safety Taskforce, and New York City Restaurant Industry Coalition. *Burned: High Risks and Low Benefits for Workers in the New York City Restaurant Industry.* Technical report. New York: Restaurant Opportunities Center of New York, 2009.

Restaurant Opportunities Center of Washington, D.C., Restaurant Opportunities Centers United, and Washington, D.C., Restaurant Industry Coalition. *Behind the Kitchen Door: Inequality & Opportunity in Washington, D.C.'s Thriving Restaurant Industry.* Technical report. New York: Restaurant Opportunities Center of Washington, D.C., 2011.

Restaurant Opportunities Centers United. *Behind the Kitchen Door: A Multisite Study of the Restaurant Industry.* Technical report. New York: Restaurant Opportunities Centers United, 2011.

——. *Serving While Sick: High Risks and Low Benefits for the Nation's Restaurant Workforce, and Their Impact on the Consumer.* Technical report. New York: Restaurant Opportunities Centers United, 2010.

——. *Tipped over the Edge: Gender Inequality in the Nation's Restaurant Industry.* Technical report. New York: Restaurant Opportunities Centers United, 2012.

San Francisco Department of Public Health, Communicable Disease Control & Prevention Section. *Annual Report of Communicable Diseases in San Francisco, 2006.* San Francisco: San Francisco Department of Public Health, 2008. http://www.sfcdcp.org/document.html?id=210.

——. *Annual Report of Communicable Diseases in San Francisco, 2007.* San Francisco: San Francisco Department of Public Health, 2008. http://www.sfdph.org/dph/files/reports/StudiesData/CommDiseasesSFAnnlRpt122008.pdf.

——. *Annual Report of Communicable Diseases in San Francisco, 2008.* San Francisco: San Francisco Department of Public Health, 2010. http://www.sfdph.org/dph/files/reports/StudiesData/CommDiseasesSFAnnlRpt01201042008.pdf.

Slow Food International. "About Us." www.slowfood.com.

——. "Our Philosophy." www.slowfood.com.

Stewart, Hayden, Noel Blisard, and Dean Jollife. *Let's Eat Out: Americans Weigh Taste, Convenience, and Nutrition.* Economic Information Bulletin 19. Washington, D.C.: U.S. Department of Agriculture, October 2006. http://www.ers.usda.gov/publications/eib19/eib19.pdf.

Sumner, Steven, Laura Green Brown, Roberta Frick, Carmily Stone, L. Rand Carpenter, et al. "Factors Associated with Food Workers Working While Experiencing Vomiting and Diarrhea." *Journal of Food Protection* 74:2 (2011): 215–20.

U.S. Bureau of Labor Statistics. *May 2009 National Industry-Specific Occupational Employment and Wage Estimates.* Occupational Employment Statistics. Washington, D.C.: U.S. Bureau of Labor Statistics, May 2010. http://www.bls.gov/oes/2009/may/naics3_722000.htm.

——. *Median Weekly Earnings of Full-Time Wage and Salary Workers by Detailed Occupation and Sex 2010.* Washington, D.C.: U.S. Bureau of Labor Statistics, June 2011. ftp://ftp.bls.gov/pub/special.requests/lf/aat39.txt.

——. "Occupational Employment and Wages—May 2010." News release. Washington, D.C.: U.S. Bureau of Labor Statistics, May 2011. www.bls.gov/news.release/pdf/ocwage.pdf.

——. *Occupational Employment Statistics Query System/Food Service and Drinking Places (NAICS Code 722000)/Food Preparation and Serving Related Occupations (350000).* Washington, D.C.: U.S. Bureau of Labor Statistics, May 2010. http://data.bls.gov/oes/datatype.do.

——. *Quarterly Census of Employment and Wages.* Washington, D.C.: U.S. Bureau of Labor Statistics, 2011.

——. *Workplace Injuries and Illnesses—2008,* Table 4: Number of Cases and Incidence Rate of Nonfatal Occupational Injuries and Illnesses for Industries with 100,000 or More Cases, 2008. Washington, D.C.: U.S. Bureau of Labor Statistics, 2009.

U.S. Bureau of Labor Statistics and U.S. Census Bureau. *Current Population Survey.* Washington, D.C.: U.S. Bureau of Labor Statistics and U.S. Census Bureau, March 2010.

U.S. Census Bureau. *American Community Survey Public Use Microdata Sample, 2005.*

——. *Household Income for States: 2008 and 2009.* American Community Survey Briefs. Washington, D.C.: U.S. Census Bureau, 2010. http://www.census.gov/prod/2010pubs/acsbr09–2.pdf.

——. *Median Weekly Earnings of Full-Time Wage and Salary Workers by Detailed Occupation and Sex, 2010.* Washington, D.C.: U.S. Bureau of Labor Statistics, June 2011. ftp://ftp.bls.gov/pub/special.requests/lf/aat39.txt.

——. *Poverty Thresholds for 2010 by Size of Family and Number of Related Children under 18 Years.* Washington, D.C.: U.S. Census Bureau, 2011. http://www.census.gov/hhes/www/poverty/data/threshld/thresh10.xls.

U.S. Centers for Disease Control and Prevention. *Estimates of Foodborne Disease.* Atlanta: U.S. Centers for Disease Control and Prevention, 2011. http://www.cdc. gov/foodborneburden.

———. *Norovirus Activity—United States, 2006–2007.* Atlanta: U.S. Centers for Disease Control and Prevention, August 2007. http://www.cdc.gov/mmwr/preview/ mmwrhtml/mm5633a2.htm.

———. "Norovirus Outbreak Associated with Ill Food-Service Workers—Michigan." *Centers for Disease Control and Prevention Morbidity and Mortality Weekly Report* (January–February 2006). http://jama.ama-assn.org/content/299/2/164.

U.S. Department of Health and Human Services. "HHS Secretary Kathleen Sebelious, Sesame Workshop, and the Ad Council Launch National Campaign to Protect Families from the H1N1 Virus and Stay Healthy." News release, May 22, 2009. http://www.hhs.gov/news/press/2009pres/05/20090522a.html.

U.S. Department of Health and Human Services, Office of the Assistant Secretary for Planning and Evaluation. *2011 HHS Poverty Guidelines.* Washington, D.C.: U.S. Department of Health and Human Services, 2011. http://aspe.hhs.gov/poverty/11poverty. shtml.

U.S. Department of Homeland Security. "Press Briefing on Swine Influenza with Department of Homeland Security, Centers for Disease Control and Prevention, and White House." News release, April 26, 2009. http://www.dhs.gov/ynews/releases/ pr_1240773850207.shtm.

U.S. Occupational Safety and Health Administration. "OSHA Enforcement." http:// www.osha.gov/dep/index.html.

———. "OSHA Publications." http://www.osha.gov/pls/publications/publication.html.

U.S. Occupational Safety and Health Administration, Safety Pays Program. *Estimated Costs of Occupational Injuries and Illnesses and Estimated Impact on a Company's Profitability Worksheet.* Washington, D.C.: U.S. Occupational Safety and Health Administration, April, 2010. http://www.osha.gov/dcsp/smallbusiness//safetypays/ estimator.html.

Wagner, Matthew, and Jason Baker. "A New World of Choices." *Occupational Health and Safety,* June 1, 2006. http://ohsonline.com/articles/2006/06/a-new-world-of-choices.aspx.

Zenk, Shannon, Amy Schulz, Barbara Israel, Sherman James, Shuming Bao, and Mark Wilson. "Neighborhood Racial Composition, Neighborhood Poverty, and the Spatial Accessibility of Supermarkets in Metropolitan Detroit." *American Journal of Public Health* 95 (April 2005): 660–67.